SQL Easy

Kalman Toth

SQL Easy

Copyright © 2012 by Kalman Toth

Trademark Notices

Warning and Disclaimer

SQL Easy

Contents at a Glance

About the Author

Kalman Toth started working with relational database technology in 1990. Kalman was a C/C++ developer but has always been fascinated by SQL. In his C job spare moments he studied a Transact-SQL manual three times from start to end "dry", without any server access. One day, his boss at a commodity brokerage firm in Greenwich, Connecticut, had to leave early and gave Kalman his SQL Server login and password to complete a small SQL task. Kalman completed the task, a very exciting moment of his life. His boss was satisfied with the execution of the SQL task and a few days later Kalman's dream came true: he got his very own SQL Server login. Kalman loves SQL because the same friendly, yet powerful commands can process 2 records, 2 million records, or 200 million records with the same ease. Since then, his relational database career has included database design, database development, database administration, OLAP architecture and Business Intelligence development. Applications for these included enterprise-level general ledger & financial accounting, bond funds auditing, international stock market feeds processing, broker-dealer firm risk management, derivative instruments analytics, consumer ecommerce database management for online dating, personal finance, physical fitness, diet and health. Kalman has a Master of Arts in Physics and a Master of Philosophy in Computing Science, both from Columbia University. He also holds Microsoft certifications in database administration, development and Business Intelligence. Currently, he is a full-time writer & lecturer. His MSDN forum participation in the Transact-SQL and SQL Server Tools was rewarded with the "Microsoft Community Contributor Award". He is moderator on the Transact-SQL and Database Design forums. His dream SQL career took him across the United States and Canada, as well as South America and Europe. Kalman also credits SQL for being part of the World Trade Center history. At one time, he worked for Deloitte & Touche on the 96th floor of World Trade Center North. On September 11, 2001, he was an RDBMS consultant at Citibank on 111 Wall Street, just half a mile from where nearly 3,000 victims were buried under steel. He narrowly escaped the collapse of the second tower that fateful Tuesday morning and was only able to return to his relational database development job 10 days after. Kalman's current interest is Artificial Intelligence. He is convinced that machine intelligence will not only replace human intelligence but surpass it a million times over in the near future. His hobby includes flying gliders and vintage fighter planes. Accessibility: @dbdesign1 at Twitter (http://twitter.com/dbdesign1); http://twitter.com/sqlusa; http://www.sqlusa.com/contact2005/

V

CONTENTS

This page is intentionally left blank.

INTRODUCTION

Developers across the world are facing database issues daily. While they are immersed in procedural languages with loops , RDBMS forces them to think in terms of sets without loops. It takes transition. It takes training. It takes experience. Developers are exposed also to Excel worksheets or spreadsheets as they were called in the not so distant past. So if you know worksheets how hard databases can be? After all worksheets look pretty much like database tables? The big difference is connections among well-designed tables. A database is a set of connected tables which represent entities in the real world. A database can be 100 connected tables or 3000. The connection is very simple: row A in table Alpha has affiliated data with row B in table Beta. But even with 200 tables and 300 connections (FOREIGN KEY references), it takes a good amount of time to familiarize to the point of acceptable working knowledge.

"The Cemetery of Computer Languages" is expanding. You can see tombstones like PL/1, Forth, Ada, Pascal, LISP, RPG, APL, SNOBOL, JOVIAL, Algol and the list goes on. For some, the future is in question: PowerBuilder, ColdFusion, FORTRAN & COBOL. SQL on the other hand running strong after 3 decades of glorious existence. What is the difference? The basic difference is that SQL can handle large datasets in a consistent manner based on mathematical foundations. You can throw together a computer language easy: assignment statements, looping, if-then conditional, 300 library functions, and voila! Here is the new language: Mars/1, named after the red planet to be fashionable with NASA's new Mars robot. But can Mars/1 JOIN a table of 1 million rows with a table of 10 million rows in a second? The success of SQL language is so compelling that other technologies are tagged onto it like XML/XQuery which deals with semi-structured information objects.

In SQL you are thinking at a high level. In C# or Java, you are dealing with details, lots of them. That is the big difference. Why is so much of the book dedicated to database design? Why not plunge into SQL coding and sooner or later the developer will get a hang of the design? Because high level thinking requires thinking at the database design level. A farmer has 6 mules, how do we model it in the database? We design the Farmer and FarmAnimal tables, then connect them with FarmerID FOREIGN KEY in FarmAnimal referencing the FarmerID PRIMARY KEY in the Farmer table. What is the big deal about it, looks so simple? In fact, how about just calling the tables Table1 & Table2 to be more generic? Ouch... meaningful naming is the very basis of good database design. Relational database design is truly simple for simple well-understood models. The challenge starts in modeling complex objects such as financial derivative instruments, airplane passenger scheduling or social network website. When you need to add 5 new tables to a 1000 tables database and hook them in (define FOREIGN KEY references) correctly, it is a huge challenge. To begin with, some of the 5 new tables may already be redundant, but you don't know that until you understand what the 1000 tables are really storing. Frequently, learning the application area is the biggest challenge for a developer when starting a new job.

The SQL language is simple to program and read even if when touching 10 tables. Complexities are abound though. The very first one: does the SQL statement touch the right data set? 999 records and 1000 or 998? T-SQL statements are turned into Transact-SQL scripts, stored procedures, user-defined functions and triggers, server-side database objects. They can be 5 statements or 1000 statements long programs. The style of Transact-SQL programming is different from the style in procedural programming languages. There are no arrays, only tables or table variables. Typically there is no looping, only set-based operations. Error control is different. Testing & debugging is relatively simple in Transact-SQL due to the interactive environment and the magic of selecting & executing a part without recompiling the whole.

WHO THIS BOOK IS FOR

Developers, programmers and systems analysts who are new to relational database technology. Also developers, designers and administrators, who know some SQL programming and database design, wish to expand their RDBMS design & development technology horizons. Familiarity with other computer language is assumed. The book has lots of queries, lots of T-SQL scripts, plenty to learn. The best way to learn it is to type in the query in your own SQL Server copy and test it, examine it, change it. Wouldn't it be easier just to copy & paste it? It would but the learning value would diminish. You need to feel the SQL language in your fingers. SQL queries must "pour" out from your fingers into the keyboard. Why is that so important? After everything can be found on the web and just copy & paste? Well not exactly. If you want to be an expert, it has to be in your head not on the web. Second, when your supervisor is looking over your shoulder, "Charlie, can you tell me what is the total revenue for March?", you have to be able to type in the query without SQL forum search and provide the results to your superior promptly.

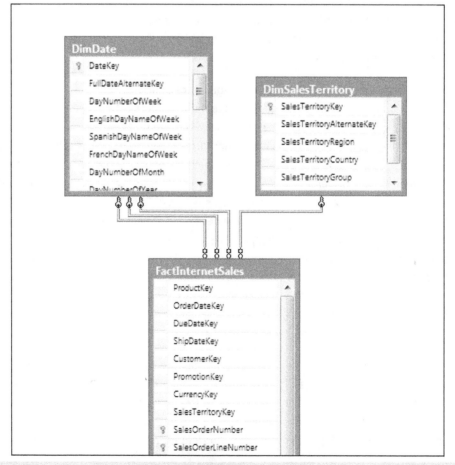

ABOUT THIS BOOK

Beginning relational database design and beginning Transact-SQL programming. It is not a reference manual, rather learn by examples: there are over 1,100 SELECT queries in the book. Instead of imaginary tables, the book uses the SQL Server sample databases for explanations and examples: pubs (PRIMARY KEYs 9, FOREIGN KEYs 10), Northwind (PRIMARY KEYs 13, FOREIGN KEYs 13) and the AdventureWorks family. Among them: AdventureWorks, AdventureWorks2008, AdventureWorks2012 (PRIMARY KEYS 71, FOREIGN KEYs 90), & AdventureWorksDW2012 (PRIMARY KEYs 27, FOREIGN KEYs 44). The book introduces relational database design concepts, then reinforces them again and again, not to bore the reader, rather indoctrinate with relational database design principles. Light weight SQL starts at the beginning of the book, because working with database metadata (not the content of the database, rather data which describes the database) is essential for understanding database design. By the time the reader gets to T-SQL programming, already knows basic SQL programming from the database design section of the book. The book was designed to be readable in any environment, even on the beach laptop around or no laptop in sight at all. All queries are followed by results row count and /or full/partial results listing in tabular (grid) format. For full benefits though, the reader should try out the T-SQL queries and scripts as he progresses from page to page, topic to topic. Example for SQL Server 2012 T-SQL query and results presentation.

```
SELECT          V.Name                                AS Vendor,
                FORMAT(SUM(POH.TotalDue), 'c', 'en-US')   AS [Total Purchase],
                FORMAT(AVG(POH.TotalDue), 'c', 'en-US')   AS [Average Purchase]
FROM AdventureWorks.Purchasing.Vendor AS V
   INNER JOIN AdventureWorks.Purchasing.PurchaseOrderHeader AS POH
      ON V.VendorID = POH.VendorID
GROUP BY V.Name  ORDER BY Vendor;
-- (79 row(s) affected) - Partial results.
```

Vendor	Total Purchase	Average Purchase
Advanced Bicycles	$28,502.09	$558.86
Allenson Cycles	$498,589.59	$9,776.27
American Bicycles and Wheels	$9,641.01	$189.04
American Bikes	$1,149,489.84	$22,539.02

CONVENTIONS USED IN THIS BOOK

The Transact-SQL queries and scripts (sequence of statements) are shaded.

The number of resulting rows is displayed as a comment line: -- (79 row(s) affected) .

The results of the queries is usually displayed in grid format.

Less frequently the results are enclosed in comment markers: /*...... */ .

When a query is a trivial variation of a previous query, no result is displayed.

While the intention of the book is database design & database development, SQL Server installation and some database administration tasks are included.

"Apparatus Intelligentia

vincet

Humanum Intelligentia"

Dedicated to

Dan Bricklin and Bob Frankston

The Inventors of VisiCalc

The first computer spreadsheet program in 1979 running on an Apple II

This page is intentionally left blank.

CHAPTER 1: SQL Server Sample & System Databases

AdventureWorks Series of OLTP Databases

AdventureWorks sample On Line Transaction Processing (OLTP) database has been introduced with SQL Server 2005 to replace the previous sample database Northwind, a fictional gourmet food items distributor. The intent of the AdventureWorks sample database is to support the business operations of AdventureWorks Cycles, a fictitious mountain, touring and road bike manufacturer. The company sells through dealer network and online on the web. In addition to bikes, it sells frames and parts as well as accessories such as helmets, biking clothes and water bottles. The AdventureWorks2012 database image of Touring-1000 Blue, 50 bike in Production.ProductPhoto table.

T-SQL query to generate the list of tables of AdventureWorks2012 in 5 columns. The core query is simple. Presenting the results in 5 columns instead of 1 column adds a bit of complexity.

```
;WITH cteTableList AS (        SELECT CONCAT(SCHEMA_NAME(schema_id), '.', name)              AS TableName,
  (( ROW_NUMBER() OVER( ORDER BY CONCAT(SCHEMA_NAME(schema_id),'.', name)) ) % 5)     AS Remainder,
  (( ROW_NUMBER() OVER( ORDER BY CONCAT(SCHEMA_NAME(schema_id),'.', name)) - 1 )/ 5)  AS Quotient
                        FROM AdventureWorks2012.sys.tables),
CTE AS (SELECT TableName, CASE WHEN Remainder=0 THEN 5 ELSE Remainder END AS Remainder, Quotient
        FROM cteTableList)
SELECT    MAX(CASE WHEN Remainder = 1 THEN TableName END),
          MAX(CASE WHEN Remainder = 2 THEN TableName END),
          MAX(CASE WHEN Remainder = 3 THEN TableName END),
          MAX(CASE WHEN Remainder = 4 THEN TableName END),
          MAX(CASE WHEN Remainder = 5 THEN TableName END)
FROM  CTE GROUP  BY Quotient ORDER  BY Quotient;
GO
```

CHAPTER 1: SQL Server Sample & System Databases

The query result set in grid format: tables in AdventureWorks2012

dbo.AWBuildVersion	dbo.DatabaseLog	dbo.ErrorLog	HumanResources.Department	HumanResources.Employee
HumanResources.EmployeeDepartmentHistory	HumanResources.EmployeePayHistory	HumanResources.JobCandidate	HumanResources.Shift	Person.Address
Person.AddressType	Person.BusinessEntity	Person.BusinessEntityAddress	Person.BusinessEntityContact	Person.ContactType
Person.CountryRegion	Person.EmailAddress	Person.Password	Person.Person	Person.PersonPhone
Person.PhoneNumberType	Person.StateProvince	Production.BillOfMaterials	Production.Culture	Production.Document
Production.Illustration	Production.Location	Production.Product	Production.ProductCategory	Production.ProductCostHistory
Production.ProductDescription	Production.ProductDocument	Production.ProductInventory	Production.ProductListPriceHistory	Production.ProductModel
Production.ProductModelIllustration	Production.ProductModelProductDescriptionCulture	Production.ProductPhoto	Production.ProductProductPhoto	Production.ProductReview
Production.ProductSubcategory	Production.ScrapReason	Production.TransactionHistory	Production.TransactionHistoryArchive	Production.UnitMeasure
Production.WorkOrder	Production.WorkOrderRouting	Purchasing.ProductVendor	Purchasing.PurchaseOrderDetail	Purchasing.PurchaseOrderHeader
Purchasing.ShipMethod	Purchasing.Vendor	Sales.CountryRegionCurrency	Sales.CreditCard	Sales.Currency
Sales.CurrencyRate	Sales.Customer	Sales.PersonCreditCard	Sales.SalesOrderDetail	Sales.SalesOrderHeader
Sales.SalesOrderHeaderSalesReason	Sales.SalesPerson	Sales.SalesPersonQuotaHistory	Sales.SalesReason	Sales.SalesTaxRate
Sales.SalesTerritory	Sales.SalesTerritoryHistory	Sales.ShoppingCartItem	Sales.SpecialOffer	Sales.SpecialOfferProduct
Sales.Store	NULL	NULL	NULL	NULL

CHAPTER 1: SQL Server Sample & System Databases

Diagram of Person.Person & Related Tables

Database diagram displays the Person.Person and related tables. PRIMARY KEYs are marked
with a gold (in color display) key. The "oo-------->" line is interpreted as many-to-one
relationship. For example a person (one) can have one or more (many) credit cards. The "oo"
side is the table with **FOREIGN KEY** referencing the gold key side table with the **PRIMARY KEY**.

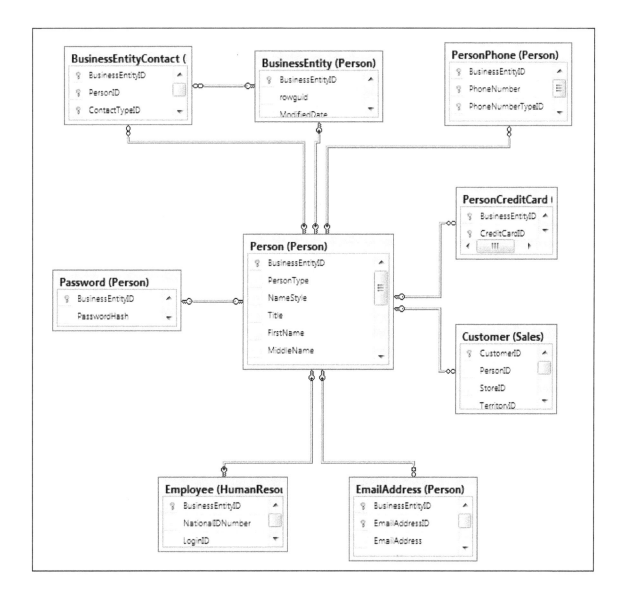

Diagram of Sales.SalesOrderHeader and Related Tables

Database diagram displays Sales.SalesOrderHeader and all tables related with **FOREIGN KEY** constraints. The SalesOrderHeader table stores the general information about each order. Line items, e.g. 5 Helmets at $30 each, are stored in the SalesOrderDetail table.

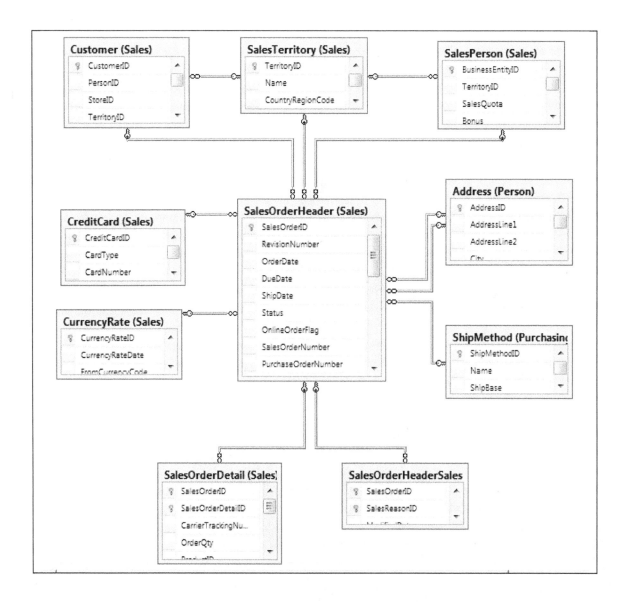

SELECT Query Basics

We have to use "light-weight" SQL (Structured Query Language) in the database design lessons. The reason is that rather difficult to discuss any database related topic without demonstration T-SQL scripts, in fact it would not make sense. **Relational database** and the **SQL language** are "married" to each other forever and ever.

The Simplest SELECT Statement

The simplest SELECT statement is "SELECT * FROM TableNameX" as demonstrated following. The "*" means wildcard inclusion of all columns in the table. Since there is no any other clause in the SELECT statement, it means also to retrieve all rows in the **table in no particular order**. Small tables which were populated in order are usually retrieved in order even though there is no ORDER BY clause. But this behaviour is purely coincidental. **Only ORDER BY clause can guarantee a sorted output.**

SELECT * FROM AdventureWorks2012.HumanResources.Department;
-- (16 row(s) affected)

DepartmentID	Name	GroupName	ModifiedDate
1	Engineering	Research and Development	2002-06-01 00:00:00.000
2	Tool Design	Research and Development	2002-06-01 00:00:00.000
3	Sales	Sales and Marketing	2002-06-01 00:00:00.000
4	Marketing	Sales and Marketing	2002-06-01 00:00:00.000
5	Purchasing	Inventory Management	2002-06-01 00:00:00.000
6	Research and Development	Research and Development	2002-06-01 00:00:00.000
7	Production	Manufacturing	2002-06-01 00:00:00.000
8	Production Control	Manufacturing	2002-06-01 00:00:00.000
9	Human Resources	Executive General and Administration	2002-06-01 00:00:00.000
10	Finance	Executive General and Administration	2002-06-01 00:00:00.000
11	Information Services	Executive General and Administration	2002-06-01 00:00:00.000
12	Document Control	Quality Assurance	2002-06-01 00:00:00.000
13	Quality Assurance	Quality Assurance	2002-06-01 00:00:00.000
14	Facilities and Maintenance	Executive General and Administration	2002-06-01 00:00:00.000
15	Shipping and Receiving	Inventory Management	2002-06-01 00:00:00.000
16	Executive	Executive General and Administration	2002-06-01 00:00:00.000

When tables are JOINed, SELECT * returns all the columns with all the data in the participant tables.

SELECT TOP 3 * FROM Sales.SalesOrderHeader H
          INNER JOIN Sales.SalesOrderDetail D
             ON H.SalesOrderID = D.SalesOrderID;
-- 121,317 rows in the JOIN

CHAPTER 1: SQL Server Sample & System Databases

Query Result Set In Text Format

If no grid format available, text format can be used. While it works, it is a challenge to read it, but computer geeks are used to this kind of data dump.

```
/* SalesOrderID RevisionNumber OrderDate        DueDate         ShipDate        Status
OnlineOrderFlag SalesOrderNumber        PurchaseOrderNumber     AccountNumber CustomerID
SalesPersonID TerritoryID BillToAddressID ShipToAddressID ShipMethodID CreditCardID
CreditCardApprovalCode CurrencyRateID SubTotal        TaxAmt          Freight         TotalDue
Comment                                                          rowguid
ModifiedDate        SalesOrderID SalesOrderDetailID CarrierTrackingNumber   OrderQty ProductID
SpecialOfferID UnitPrice        UnitPriceDiscount   LineTotal        rowguid          ModifiedDate
----------- -------------- ------------------ --------------------- --------------------- ------ --------------- --------------------
------ -------------- --------------- --------------------- ----------- ----------
- -------------------- ------------ ----------------- ------------------ --------------------- ------------- -------------- ------------
-------------------------------------------------------------- -------------------
---------- -------------------- ---------------------- ------------------ --------------------- ----------- ----------- -------------- ---------
-------- -------------------- ------------ ------------------ ------------------ --------------------- --------------------

43735    3       2005-07-10 00:00:00.000 2005-07-22 00:00:00.000 2005-07-17 00:00:00.000 5    1
SO43735         NULL            10-4030-016522 16522    NULL    9       25384       25384
1      6526    1034619Vi33896      119     3578.27         286.2616        89.4568
3953.9884       NULL                                                            98F80245-
C398-4562-BDAF-EA3E9A0DDFAC 2005-07-17 00:00:00.000 43735    391     NULL            1
749    1       3578.27         0.00    3578.270000             74838EF7-FDEB-4EB3-8978-
BA310FBA82E6 2005-07-10 00:00:00.000
43736    3       2005-07-10 00:00:00.000 2005-07-22 00:00:00.000 2005-07-17 00:00:00.000 5    1
SO43736         NULL            10-4030-011002 11002    NULL    9       20336       20336
1      1416    1135092Vi7270       119     3399.99         271.9992        84.9998
3756.989        NULL                                                            C14E29E7-
DB11-44EF-943E-143925A5A9AE 2005-07-17 00:00:00.000 43736    392     NULL            1
773    1       3399.99         0.00    3399.990000             3A0229FA-0A03-4126-
97CE-C3425968B670 2005-07-10 00:00:00.000
43737    3       2005-07-11 00:00:00.000 2005-07-23 00:00:00.000 2005-07-18 00:00:00.000 5    1
SO43737         NULL            10-4030-013261 13261    NULL    8       29772       29772
1      NULL    NULL            136     3578.27         286.2616        89.4568         3953.9884
NULL                                                            0B3E274D-E5A8-4E8C-A417-
0EAFABCFF162 2005-07-18 00:00:00.000 43737    393     NULL            1    750     1
3578.27         0.00    3578.270000             65AFCCE8-CA28-41C4-9A07-0265FB2DA5C8
2005-07-11 00:00:00.000                 (3 row(s) affected)  */
```

```sql
SELECT MatchingRows = COUNT(*) FROM AdventureWorks2012.Sales.SalesOrderHeader H
  INNER JOIN AdventureWorks2012.Sales.SalesOrderDetail D
      ON H.SalesOrderID = D.SalesOrderID;    -- INNER JOIN MatchingRows 121317
```

```sql
SELECT AllRowsInDetail = COUNT(*) FROM AdventureWorks2012.Sales.SalesOrderDetail
-- AllRowsInDetail 121317
```

CHAPTER 1: SQL Server Sample & System Databases

SELECT Query with WHERE Clause Predicate

Query to demonstrate how can we be selective with columns, furthermore, filter returned rows (WHERE clause) and sort them (ORDER BY clause).

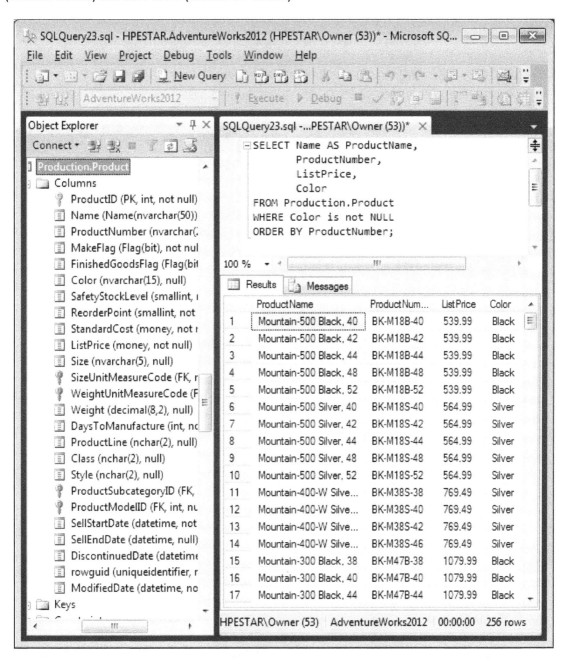

Aggregating Data with GROUP BY Query

The second basic query is GROUP BY aggregation which creates a **summary** of detail data. GROUP BY query can be used to preview, review, survey , assess, and analyze data at a high level.

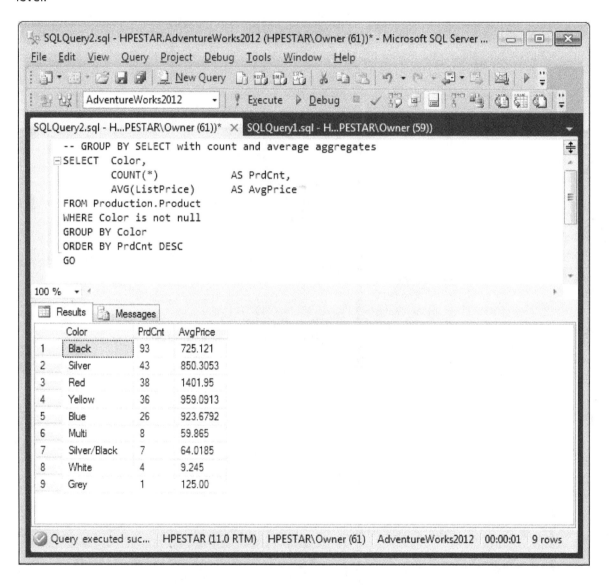

NOTE
GROUP BY aggregate queries can efficiently "fingerprint" (profile) data in tables, even millions of rows.
GROUP BY aggregates form the computational base of Business Intelligence.

GROUP BY Query with 2 Tables & ORDER BY for Sorting

JOINing two tables on matching KEYs, FOREIGN KEY to PRIMARY KEY, to combine the data contents in a consistent fashion.

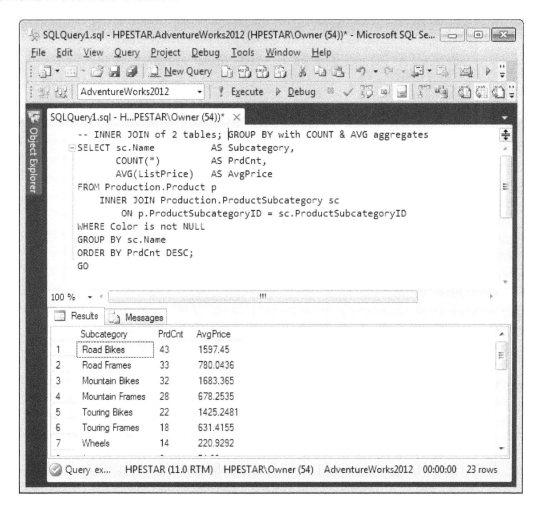

LEN(), DATALENGTH(), LTRIM() & RTRIM() Functions

The LEN() function counts characters without the trailing spaces. DATALENGTH() counts storage bytes including trailing spaces. LTRIM() trims leading spaces, RTRIM() trims trailing spaces.

```
DECLARE @W varchar(32)= CHAR(32)+'Denver'+CHAR(32);
DECLARE @UW nvarchar(32) = CHAR(32)+N'MEGŐRZÉSE'+CHAR(32);  -- UNICODE 2 bytes per character
SELECT Length=LEN(@W), DLength=DATALENGTH (@W);                               -- 7  8
SELECT Length=LEN(@UW), DLength=DATALENGTH (@UW);                             -- 10 22
SELECT Length=LEN(LTRIM(RTRIM(@W))), DLength=DATALENGTH (LTRIM(RTRIM(@W)));   -- 6  6
SELECT Length=LEN(LTRIM(RTRIM(@UW))), DLength=DATALENGTH (LTRIM(RTRIM(@UW))); -- 9  18
```

CHAPTER 1: SQL Server Sample & System Databases

Finding All Accessories in Production.Product Table

Query to list all accessories (a category) for sale.

USE AdventureWorks2012;

```
SELECT          UPPER(PC.Name) AS Category, PSC.Name              AS Subcategory,
                P.Name AS Product, FORMAT(ListPrice, 'c', 'en-US')  AS ListPrice,
                FORMAT(StandardCost, 'c', 'en-US')                AS StandardCost
FROM Production.Product AS P
   INNER JOIN Production.ProductSubcategory AS PSC
          ON PSC.ProductSubcategoryID = P.ProductSubcategoryID
   INNER JOIN Production.ProductCategory AS PC
          ON PC.ProductCategoryID = PSC.ProductCategoryID
WHERE PC.Name = 'Accessories'
ORDER BY Category, Subcategory, Product;        -- (29 row(s) affected) - Partial results.
```

Category	Subcategory	Product	ListPrice	StandardCost
ACCESSORIES	Bike Racks	Hitch Rack - 4-Bike	$120.00	$44.88
ACCESSORIES	Bike Stands	All-Purpose Bike Stand	$159.00	$59.47
ACCESSORIES	Bottles and Cages	Mountain Bottle Cage	$9.99	$3.74
ACCESSORIES	Bottles and Cages	Road Bottle Cage	$8.99	$3.36
ACCESSORIES	Bottles and Cages	Water Bottle - 30 oz.	$4.99	$1.87
ACCESSORIES	Cleaners	Bike Wash - Dissolver	$7.95	$2.97

Using Implicit or Explicit Conversion

Implicit conversion results in simpler code and may even be faster. However, if we really need a specific conversion, explicit conversion should be used. In the ShipDate datetime column example, the implicit & explicit conversions yield the same results.

```
SELECT SalesOrderID, OrderDate, ShipDate, CustomerID, SubTotal
FROM Sales.SalesOrderHeader
WHERE ShipDate = '2008-03-08';                          -- Implicit conversion to datetime

/*      WHERE Shipdate = CONVERT(DATETIME, '2008-03-08');   -- Explicit conversion
        WHERE Shipdate = CONVERT(DATE, '2008-03-08');       -- Explicit conversion */
-- (247 row(s) affected) - Partial results.
```

SalesOrderID	OrderDate	ShipDate	CustomerID	SubTotal
65089	2008-02-29 00:00:00.000	2008-03-08 00:00:00.000	30079	1466.01
65090	2008-02-29 00:00:00.000	2008-03-08 00:00:00.000	29812	98.774
65151	2008-03-01 00:00:00.000	2008-03-08 00:00:00.000	30072	76.20

How Can SQL Work without Looping?

Looping is implicit in the SQL language. The commands are set oriented and carried out for each member of the set be it 5 or 500 millions in an unordered manner.

SELECT * FROM AdventureWorks2012.Sales.SalesOrderDetail;   (121317 row(s) affected)

SQL Server database engine looped through internally on all rows in SalesOrderDetail table in an unordered way. In fact the database engine may have used some ordering for efficiency, but that behaviour is a blackbox as far as programming concerned. Implicit looping makes SQL statements so simple, yet immensely powerful for information access from low level to high level.

Single-Valued SQL Queries

Single-valued SQL queries are very important because **we can use them where ever the T-SQL syntax requires a single value just by enclosing the query in parenthesis**. The next T-SQL query returns a single value, a cell from the table which is the intersection of a row and a column.

SELECT ListPrice FROM AdventureWorks2012.Production.Product WHERE ProductID = 800;
-- (1 row(s) affected)

ListPrice
1120.49

The ">" comparison operator requires a single value on the right hand side so we plug in the single-valued query. The WHERE condition is evaluated for each row (implicit looping).

SELECT ProductID, Name AS ProductName, ListPrice
FROM AdventureWorks2012.Production.Product   -- 504 rows
WHERE ListPrice > 2 * (
                SELECT ListPrice FROM AdventureWorks2012.Production.Product
                WHERE ProductID = 800
)
ORDER BY ListPrice DESC, ProductName;   -- (35 row(s) affected) - Partial results.

ProductID	ProductName	ListPrice
750	Road-150 Red, 44	3578.27
751	Road-150 Red, 48	3578.27
752	Road-150 Red, 52	3578.27
753	Road-150 Red, 56	3578.27
749	Road-150 Red, 62	3578.27
771	Mountain-100 Silver, 38	3399.99

CHAPTER 1: SQL Server Sample & System Databases

Data Dictionary Description of Tables in the Sales Schema

It is not easy to understand a database with 70 tables, even harder with 2,000 tables. Documentation is very helpful, if not essential, for any database. SQL Server provides Data Dictionary facility for documenting tables and other objects in the database. Data which describes the design & structure of a database is called **metadata**. Here is the high level documentation of tables in the Sales schema using the fn_listextendedproperty system function.

```
SELECT
        CONCAT('Sales.', objname COLLATE DATABASE_DEFAULT)      AS TableName,
        value                                                   AS [Description]
FROM fn_listextendedproperty (NULL, 'schema', 'Sales', 'table', default, NULL, NULL)
ORDER BY TableName;
```

TableName	Description
Sales.ContactCreditCard	Cross-reference table mapping customers in the Contact table to their credit card information in the CreditCard table.
Sales.CountryRegionCurrency	Cross-reference table mapping ISO currency codes to a country or region.
Sales.CreditCard	Customer credit card information.
Sales.Currency	Lookup table containing standard ISO currencies.
Sales.CurrencyRate	Currency exchange rates.
Sales.Customer	Current customer information. Also see the Individual and Store tables.
Sales.CustomerAddress	Cross-reference table mapping customers to their address(es).
Sales.Individual	Demographic data about customers that purchase Adventure Works products online.
Sales.SalesOrderDetail	Individual products associated with a specific sales order. See SalesOrderHeader.
Sales.SalesOrderHeader	General sales order information.
Sales.SalesOrderHeaderSalesReason	Cross-reference table mapping sales orders to sales reason codes.
Sales.SalesPerson	Sales representative current information.
Sales.SalesPersonQuotaHistory	Sales performance tracking.
Sales.SalesReason	Lookup table of customer purchase reasons.
Sales.SalesTaxRate	Tax rate lookup table.
Sales.SalesTerritory	Sales territory lookup table.
Sales.SalesTerritoryHistory	Sales representative transfers to other sales territories.
Sales.ShoppingCartItem	Contains online customer orders until the order is submitted or cancelled.
Sales.SpecialOffer	Sale discounts lookup table.
Sales.SpecialOfferProduct	Cross-reference table mapping products to special offer discounts.
Sales.Store	Customers (resellers) of Adventure Works products.
Sales.StoreContact	Cross-reference table mapping stores and their employees.

NULL Values in Tables & Query Results

NULL means no value. If so why do we capitalize it? We don't have to. Somehow, it became a custom in the RDBMS industry, nobody knows anymore how it started. Since the U.S. default collation for server and databases are case insensitive, we can just use "null" as well. **NULL value is different from empty string ('') or 0 (zero) which can be tested by the "=" or "!=" operators.** If a database table does not have a value in a cell for whatever reason, it is marked (flagged) as NULL by the database engine. When a value is entered, the NULL marking goes away. **NULL values can be tested by "IS NULL" or "IS NOT NULL" operators, but not the "=" or "!=" operators.**

The likelihood is high that the color attribute is not applicable to items like tire tube, that is the reason that some cell values were left unassigned (null).

```
SELECT TOP 5   Name                         AS ProductName,
               ProductNumber,
               ListPrice,
               Color
FROM AdventureWorks2012.Production.Product
WHERE Color IS NULL  ORDER BY ProductName DESC;
```

ProductName	ProductNumber	ListPrice	Color
Water Bottle - 30 oz.	WB-H098	4.99	NULL
Touring Tire Tube	TT-T092	4.99	NULL
Touring Tire	TI-T723	28.99	NULL
Touring Rim	RM-T801	0.00	NULL
Touring End Caps	EC-T209	0.00	NULL

We can do random selection as well and get a mix of products with color and null value.

```
SELECT TOP 5   Name AS ProductName,
               ProductNumber,
               ListPrice,
               Color
FROM AdventureWorks2012.Production.Product  ORDER BY NEWID();    -- Random sort
```

ProductName	ProductNumber	ListPrice	Color
Touring-1000 Yellow, 46	BK-T79Y-46	2384.07	Yellow
HL Spindle/Axle	SD-9872	0.00	NULL
ML Mountain Tire	TI-M602	29.99	NULL
Road-650 Red, 60	BK-R50R-60	782.99	Red
Pinch Bolt	PB-6109	0.00	NULL

CHAPTER 1: SQL Server Sample & System Databases

NULL Values Generated by Queries

NULL values can be generated by queries as well. Typically, LEFT JOIN, RIGHT JOIN and some functions generate NULLs. The meaning of OUTER JOINs: include no-match rows from the left or right table in addition to the matching rows.

```
SELECT TOP 5
            PS.Name                        AS Category,
            P.Name                         AS ProductName,
            ProductNumber,
            ListPrice,
            Color
FROM AdventureWorks2012.Production.Product P
  RIGHT JOIN AdventureWorks2012.Production.ProductSubcategory PS
        ON    PS.ProductSubcategoryID = P.ProductSubcategoryID
              AND ListPrice >= 3500.0
ORDER BY newid();
GO
```

Category	ProductName	ProductNumber	ListPrice	Color
Road Bikes	Road-150 Red, 62	BK-R93R-62	3578.27	Red
Road Bikes	Road-150 Red, 52	BK-R93R-52	3578.27	Red
Bib-Shorts	NULL	NULL	NULL	NULL
Socks	NULL	NULL	NULL	NULL
Cranksets	NULL	NULL	NULL	NULL

Some system functions, like the brand new TRY_CONVERT(), can generate NULL values as well. If the PostalCode cannot be converted into an integer, TRY_CONVERT() returns NULL.

```
SELECT TOP 5   ConvertedZip = TRY_CONVERT(INT, PostalCode),
            AddressLine1,
            City,
            PostalCode
FROM Person.Address  ORDER by newid();
```

ConvertedZip	AddressLine1	City	PostalCode
91945	5979 El Pueblo	Lemon Grove	91945
NULL	7859 Green Valley Road	London	W1V 5RN
3220	6004 Peabody Road	Geelong	3220
NULL	6713 Eaker Way	Burnaby	V3J 6Z3
NULL	5153 Hackamore Lane	Shawnee	V8Z 4N5

The SOUNDEX() Function to Check Sound Alikes

The soundex() function is very interesting for testing different spelling of words such as names.

```
USE AdventureWorks2012;
GO

SELECT DISTINCT LastName
FROM Person.Person
WHERE soundex(LastName) = soundex('Steel');
GO
```

LastName
Seidel
Sotelo
Stahl
Steel
Steele

```
SELECT DISTINCT LastName
FROM Person.Person
WHERE soundex(LastName) = soundex('Brown');
```

LastName
Bourne
Brian
Brown
Browne
Bruno

```
SELECT DISTINCT FirstName FROM Person.Person
WHERE soundex(FirstName) = soundex('Mary');
```

FirstName
Mari
Maria
María
Mariah
Marie
Mario
Mary
Mary Lou
Mayra

Building an FK-PK Diagram in AdventureWorks2012

The **FOREIGN KEY - PRIMARY KEY** diagram of AdventureWorks2012 database with over 70 tables can be built just by adding the tables to the diagram. The FK-PK lines are automatically drawn. An FK-PK line represents a predefined referential constraint.

While all tables are important in a database, tables with the most connections play central roles, in a way analogous to the Sun with planets around it.

```
-- PRIMARY KEY tables with the most FOREIGN KEY references
SELECT          schema_name(schema_id)        AS SchemaName,
                o.name                         AS PKTable,
                count(*)                       AS FKCount
FROM sys.sysforeignkeys s    INNER JOIN sys.objects o    ON s.rkeyid = o.object_id
GROUP BY schema_id, o.name    HAVING count(*) >= 5    ORDER BY FKCount DESC;
```

SchemaName	PKTable	FKCount
Production	Product	14
Person	Person	7
HumanResources	Employee	6
Person	BusinessEntity	5
Sales	SalesTerritory	5

AdventureWorksDW2012 Data Warehouse Database

AdventureWorksDW series contain second hand data only since they are Data Warehouse databases. All data originates from other sources such as the AdventureWorks OLTP database & Excel worksheets. Tables in the data warehousing database are divided into two groups: dimension tables & fact tables.

Simple data warehouse query.

```
SELECT          D.CalendarYear AS [Year], C.SalesTerritoryCountry AS [Country],
                FORMAT(SUM(S.SalesAmount),'c0','en-US') AS TotalSales
FROM FactInternetSales AS S  INNER JOIN DimDate AS D ON S.OrderDateKey = D.DateKey
        INNER JOIN DimSalesTerritory AS C ON S.SalesTerritoryKey = C.SalesTerritoryKey
GROUP BY D.CalendarYear, C.SalesTerritoryCountry  ORDER BY Year DESC, SUM(S.SalesAmount) DESC;
```

Year	Country	TotalSales
2008	United States	$3,324,031
2008	Australia	$2,563,884
2008	United Kingdom	$1,210,286
2008	Germany	$1,076,891
2008	France	$922,179

CHAPTER 1: SQL Server Sample & System Databases

Diagram of a Star Schema in AdventureWorksDW2012

The high level star schema diagram in AdventureWorksDW2012 Data Warehouse database with FactResellerSales fact table and related dimension tables. The temporal dimension table DimDate plays a central role in Business Intelligence data analytics.

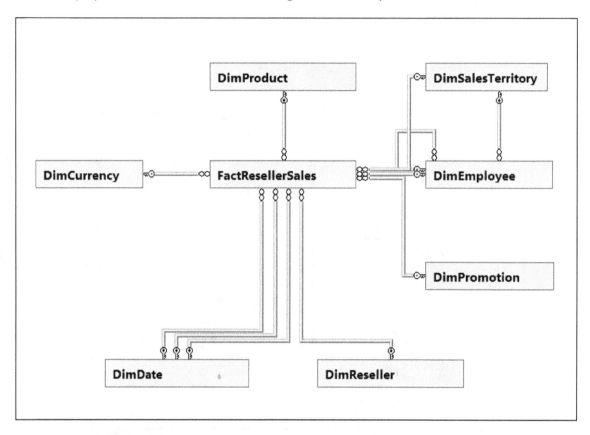

Distribution of **PRIMARY KEY - FOREIGN KEY** relationships can be generated from metadata (system views) for the entire Data Warehouse.

```
SELECT  schema_name(schema_id) AS SchemaName, o.name AS PKTable,  count(*) AS FKCount
FROM sys.sysforeignkeys s  INNER JOIN sys.objects o   ON s.rkeyid = o.object_id
GROUP BY schema_id, o.name  HAVING COUNT(*) > 2 ORDER BY FKCount DESC;
```

SchemaName	PKTable	FKCount
dbo	DimDate	12
dbo	DimCurrency	4
dbo	DimSalesTerritory	4
dbo	DimEmployee	3
dbo	DimProduct	3

AdventureWorks2008 Sample Database

There were substantial changes made from the prior version of the sample database. Among them demonstration use of the **hierarchyid** data type which has been introduced with SS 2008 to support sophisticated tree hierarchy processing. In addition employee, customer and dealer PRIMARY KEYs are pooled together and called BusinessEntityID.

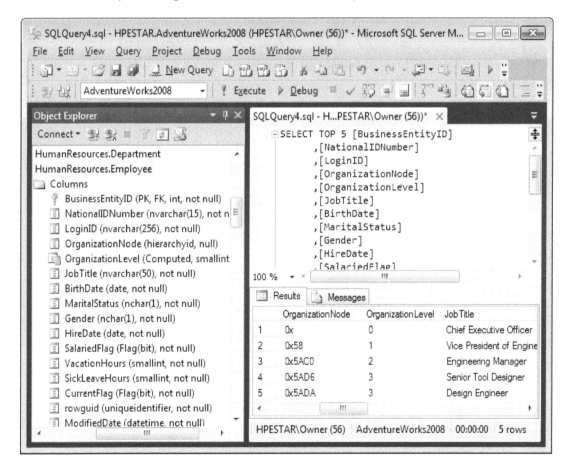

AdventureWorks2012 Sample Database

There were no apparent design changes made from the prior version of the sample database. A significant content change: dates were advanced 4 years. An OrderDate (Sales.SalesOrderHeader table) of 2004-02-01 in previous versions is now 2008-02-01.

The OrderDate statistics in the two sample databases.

```
SELECT [Year]          = YEAR(OrderDate),    OrderCount    = COUNT(*)
FROM AdventureWorks2008.Sales.SalesOrderHeader GROUP BY YEAR(OrderDate)
ORDER BY [Year];
```

Year	OrderCount
2001	1379
2002	3692
2003	12443
2004	13951

```
SELECT [Year]          = YEAR(OrderDate),    OrderCount    = COUNT(*)
FROM AdventureWorks2012.Sales.SalesOrderHeader GROUP BY YEAR(OrderDate)
ORDER BY [Year];
```

Year	OrderCount
2005	1379
2006	3692
2007	12443
2008	13951

Starting with SQL Server 2012, numeric figures, among others, can be formatted with the FORMAT function.

```
SELECT [Year]          = YEAR(OrderDate),
       OrderCount    = FORMAT(COUNT(*), '###,###')
FROM AdventureWorks2012.Sales.SalesOrderHeader
GROUP BY YEAR(OrderDate)  ORDER BY [Year];
```

Year	OrderCount
2005	1,379
2006	3,692
2007	12,443
2008	13,951

Production.Product and Related Tables

The Product table is the "center" of the database. The reason is that AdventureWorks Cycles is a product base company selling through dealers and directly to consumers through the internet. You may wonder why are we pushing **FOREIGN KEY - PRIMARY KEY** relationship so vehemently? Because there is nothing else to a database just **well-designed tables and their connections which are FK-PK constraints**.

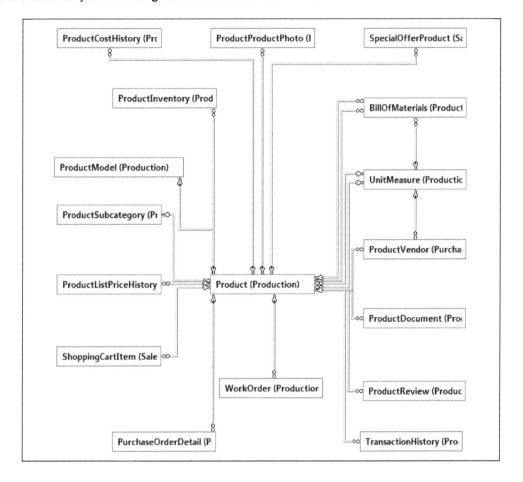

Simple OLTP query.

```
SELECT Color, WOCount=COUNT(*)  FROM Production.WorkOrder W
      INNER JOIN Production.Product P   ON W.ProductID = P.ProductID  WHERE Color != ''
GROUP BY Color ORDER BY WOCount DESC;
```

Color	WOCount
Black	18952
Silver	6620
Yellow	5231
Red	4764
Blue	2319

CHAPTER 1: SQL Server Sample & System Databases

Descriptions of Columns in Production.Product Table

Queries to list the description of table and columns from Extended Property (data dictionary).

```
USE AdventureWorks2012;
SELECT          objname AS TableName, value   AS [Description]
FROM fn_listextendedproperty( NULL, 'schema', 'Production', 'table', 'Product', NULL, NULL);
```

TableName	Description
Product	Products sold or used in the manfacturing of sold products.

```
SELECT          'Production.Product'          AS TableName,                    -- String literal
                objname                        AS ColumnName,
                value                          AS [Description]
FROM fn_listextendedproperty( NULL, 'schema', 'Production', 'table',
                              'Product', 'column', default);
```

TableName	ColumnName	Description
Production.Product	ProductID	Primary key for Product records.
Production.Product	Name	Name of the product.
Production.Product	ProductNumber	Unique product identification number.
Production.Product	MakeFlag	0 = Product is purchased, 1 = Product is manufactured in-house.
Production.Product	FinishedGoodsFlag	0 = Product is not a salable item. 1 = Product is salable.
Production.Product	Color	Product color.
Production.Product	SafetyStockLevel	Minimum inventory quantity.
Production.Product	ReorderPoint	Inventory level that triggers a purchase order or work order.
Production.Product	StandardCost	Standard cost of the product.
Production.Product	ListPrice	Selling price.
Production.Product	Size	Product size.
Production.Product	SizeUnitMeasureCode	Unit of measure for Size column.
Production.Product	WeightUnitMeasureCode	Unit of measure for Weight column.
Production.Product	Weight	Product weight.
Production.Product	DaysToManufacture	Number of days required to manufacture the product.
Production.Product	ProductLine	R = Road, M = Mountain, T = Touring, S = Standard
Production.Product	Class	H = High, M = Medium, L = Low
Production.Product	Style	W = Womens, M = Mens, U = Universal
Production.Product	ProductSubcategoryID	Product is a member of this product subcategory. Foreign key to ProductSubCategory.ProductSubCategoryID.
Production.Product	ProductModelID	Product is a member of this product model. Foreign key to ProductModel.ProductModelID.
Production.Product	SellStartDate	Date the product was available for sale.
Production.Product	SellEndDate	Date the product was no longer available for sale.
Production.Product	DiscontinuedDate	Date the product was discontinued.
Production.Product	rowguid	ROWGUIDCOL number uniquely identifying the record. Used to support a merge replication sample.
Production.Product	ModifiedDate	Date and time the record was last updated.

Mountain Bikes in Production.Product Table

Query to list all mountain bikes offered for sale by AdventureWorks Cycles with category, subcategory, list price and standard cost information.

```
USE AdventureWorks2012;
SELECT  UPPER(PC.Name) AS Category, PSC.Name AS Subcategory,
        P.Name AS Product, FORMAT(ListPrice, 'c', 'en-US') AS ListPrice,
        FORMAT(StandardCost, 'c', 'en-US') AS StandardCost
FROM Production.Product AS P
  INNER JOIN Production.ProductSubcategory AS PSC
          ON PSC.ProductSubcategoryID = P.ProductSubcategoryID
  INNER JOIN Production.ProductCategory AS PC
          ON PC.ProductCategoryID = PSC.ProductCategoryID
WHERE PSC.Name = 'Mountain Bikes'
ORDER BY Category, Subcategory, Product;
```

Category	Subcategory	Product	ListPrice	StandardCost
BIKES	Mountain Bikes	Mountain-100 Black, 38	$3,374.99	$1,898.09
BIKES	Mountain Bikes	Mountain-100 Black, 42	$3,374.99	$1,898.09
BIKES	Mountain Bikes	Mountain-100 Black, 44	$3,374.99	$1,898.09
BIKES	Mountain Bikes	Mountain-100 Black, 48	$3,374.99	$1,898.09
BIKES	Mountain Bikes	Mountain-100 Silver, 38	$3,399.99	$1,912.15
BIKES	Mountain Bikes	Mountain-100 Silver, 42	$3,399.99	$1,912.15
BIKES	Mountain Bikes	Mountain-100 Silver, 44	$3,399.99	$1,912.15
BIKES	Mountain Bikes	Mountain-100 Silver, 48	$3,399.99	$1,912.15
BIKES	Mountain Bikes	Mountain-200 Black, 38	$2,294.99	$1,251.98
BIKES	Mountain Bikes	Mountain-200 Black, 42	$2,294.99	$1,251.98
BIKES	Mountain Bikes	Mountain-200 Black, 46	$2,294.99	$1,251.98
BIKES	Mountain Bikes	Mountain-200 Silver, 38	$2,319.99	$1,265.62
BIKES	Mountain Bikes	Mountain-200 Silver, 42	$2,319.99	$1,265.62
BIKES	Mountain Bikes	Mountain-200 Silver, 46	$2,319.99	$1,265.62
BIKES	Mountain Bikes	Mountain-300 Black, 38	$1,079.99	$598.44
BIKES	Mountain Bikes	Mountain-300 Black, 40	$1,079.99	$598.44
BIKES	Mountain Bikes	Mountain-300 Black, 44	$1,079.99	$598.44
BIKES	Mountain Bikes	Mountain-300 Black, 48	$1,079.99	$598.44
BIKES	Mountain Bikes	Mountain-400-W Silver, 38	$769.49	$419.78
BIKES	Mountain Bikes	Mountain-400-W Silver, 40	$769.49	$419.78
BIKES	Mountain Bikes	Mountain-400-W Silver, 42	$769.49	$419.78
BIKES	Mountain Bikes	Mountain-400-W Silver, 46	$769.49	$419.78
BIKES	Mountain Bikes	Mountain-500 Black, 40	$539.99	$294.58
BIKES	Mountain Bikes	Mountain-500 Black, 42	$539.99	$294.58
BIKES	Mountain Bikes	Mountain-500 Black, 44	$539.99	$294.58
BIKES	Mountain Bikes	Mountain-500 Black, 48	$539.99	$294.58
BIKES	Mountain Bikes	Mountain-500 Black, 52	$539.99	$294.58
BIKES	Mountain Bikes	Mountain-500 Silver, 40	$564.99	$308.22
BIKES	Mountain Bikes	Mountain-500 Silver, 42	$564.99	$308.22
BIKES	Mountain Bikes	Mountain-500 Silver, 44	$564.99	$308.22
BIKES	Mountain Bikes	Mountain-500 Silver, 48	$564.99	$308.22
BIKES	Mountain Bikes	Mountain-500 Silver, 52	$564.99	$308.22

Prior SQL Server Sample Databases

There are two other sample databases used in the releases of SQL Server: **Northwind** and **pubs**. Northwind has been introduced with SQL Server 7.0 in 1998. That SQL Server version had very short lifetime, replaced with SQL Server 2000 in year 2000. The pubs sample database originates from the time Microsoft & Sybase worked jointly on the database server project around 1990. Despite the relative simplicity of pre-2005 sample databases, they were good enough to demonstrate basic RDBMS SQL queries.

Book sales summary GROUP BY aggregation query.

```
USE pubs;
SELECT pub_name            AS Publisher,
    au_lname               AS Author,
    title                  AS Title,
    SUM(qty)               AS SoldQty
FROM  authors
    INNER JOIN titleauthor
        ON authors.au_id = titleauthor.au_id
    INNER JOIN titles
        ON titles.title_id = titleauthor.title_id
    INNER JOIN publishers
        ON publishers.pub_id = titles.pub_id
    INNER JOIN sales
        ON sales.title_id = titles.title_id
GROUP  BY       pub_name,
                au_lname,
                title
ORDER BY Publisher, Author, Title;
-- (23 row(s) affected) - Partial results.
```

Publisher	Author	Title
Algodata Infosystems	Bennet	The Busy Executive's Database Guide
Algodata Infosystems	Carson	But Is It User Friendly?
Algodata Infosystems	Dull	Secrets of Silicon Valley
Algodata Infosystems	Green	The Busy Executive's Database Guide
Algodata Infosystems	Hunter	Secrets of Silicon Valley
Algodata Infosystems	MacFeather	Cooking with Computers: Surreptitious Balance Sheets
Algodata Infosystems	O'Leary	Cooking with Computers: Surreptitious Balance Sheets
Algodata Infosystems	Straight	Straight Talk About Computers
Binnet & Hardley	Blotchet-Halls	Fifty Years in Buckingham Palace Kitchens
Binnet & Hardley	DeFrance	The Gourmet Microwave

Northwind Sample Database

The Northwind database contains well-prepared sales data for a fictitious company called Northwind Traders, which imports & exports specialty gourmet foods & drinks from wholesale suppliers around the world. The company's sales offices are located in Seattle & London. Among gourmet food item products: Carnarvon Tigers, Teatime Chocolate Biscuits, Sir Rodney's Marmalade, Sir Rodney's Scones, Gustaf's Knäckebröd, Tunnbröd & Guaraná Fantástica.

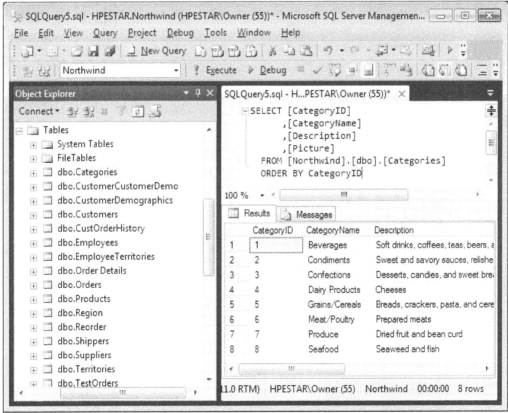

Diagram of Northwind Database

The basic diagram of Northwind database excluding a few ancillary tables. The Orders table is central since the business is wholesale distribution (reselling) of high-end food products.

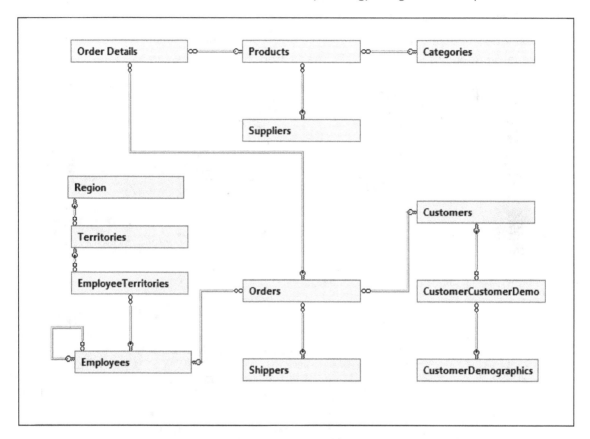

CHAPTER 1: SQL Server Sample & System Databases

pubs Sample Database

The pubs database is a very small and simple publishing database, yet it demonstrates the main features of database design such as PRIMARY KEYs, FOREIGN KEYs, and junction table reflecting many-to-many relationship. The main entities (tables) are: (book) titles, authors, titleauthor (junction table), publishers, sales & royalties.

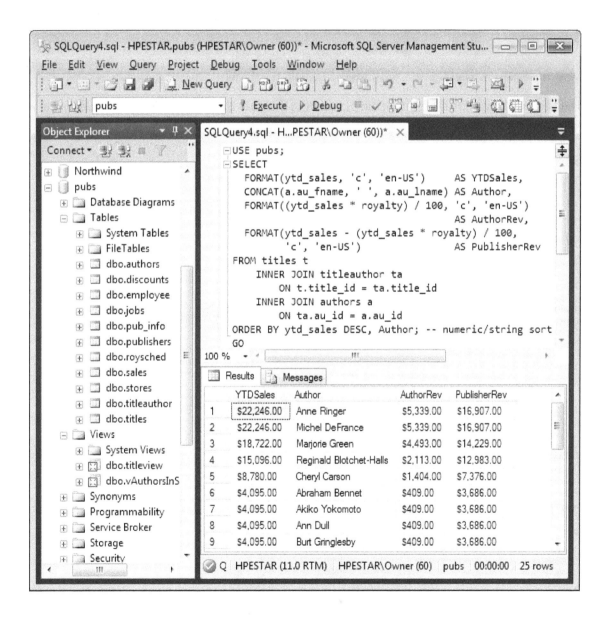

Book Titles in pubs Database

The titles table has the most interesting content in the pubs database as demonstrated by the following T-SQL query.

```
SELECT  TOP 4 title_id AS TitleID, title AS Title, type                          AS Type,
        pub_id AS PubID, FORMAT(price, 'c','en-US')                               AS Price,
        FORMAT(advance, 'c','en-US')                                             AS Advance,
        FORMAT(royalty/100.0, 'p') AS Royalty, FORMAT(ytd_sales, 'c', 'en-US')    AS YTDSales,
        Notes
FROM pubs.dbo.titles
ORDER BY title;
```

TitleID	Title	Type	PubID	Price	Advance	Royalty	YTDSales	Notes
PC1035	But Is It User Friendly?	popular_comp	1389	$22.95	$7,000.00	16.00 %	$8,780.00	A survey of software for the naive user, focusing on the 'friendliness' of each.
PS1372	Computer Phobic AND Non-Phobic Individuals: Behavior Variations	psychology	0877	$21.59	$7,000.00	10.00 %	$375.00	A must for the specialist, this book examines the difference between those who hate and fear computers and those who don't.
BU1111	Cooking with Computers: Surreptitious Balance Sheets	business	1389	$11.95	$5,000.00	10.00 %	$3,876.00	Helpful hints on how to use your electronic resources to the best advantage.
PS7777	Emotional Security: A New Algorithm	psychology	0736	$7.99	$4,000.00	10.00 %	$3,336.00	Protecting yourself and your loved ones from undue emotional stress in the modern world. Use of computer and nutritional aids emphasized.

Diagram of pubs Database

Since pubs is a small database, the diagram conveniently fits on a page.

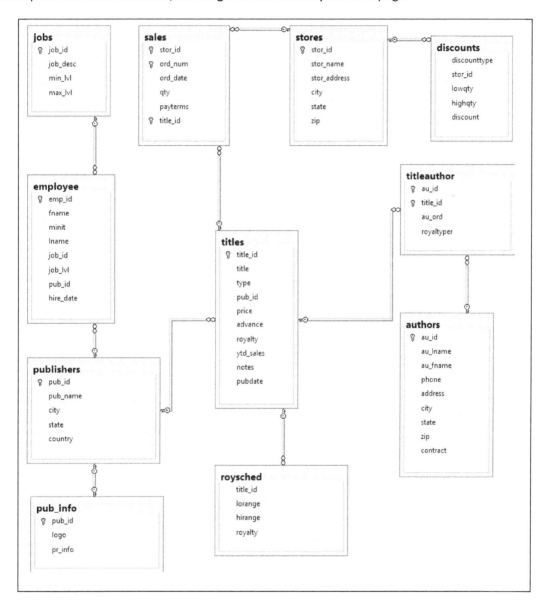

Simple JOIN on non-key columns.

USE pubs; SELECT p.*, a.* FROM authors AS a
INNER JOIN publishers AS p ON a.city = p.city ORDER BY p.city, a.au_lname;

pub_id	pub_name	city	state	country	au_id	au_lname	au_fname	phone	address	city	state	zip	contract
1389	Algodata Infosystems	Berkeley	CA	USA	409-56-7008	Bennet	Abraham	415 658-9932	6223 Bateman St.	Berkeley	CA	94705	1
1389	Algodata Infosystems	Berkeley	CA	USA	238-95-7766	Carson	Cheryl	415 548-7723	589 Darwin Ln.	Berkeley	CA	94705	1

CHAPTER 1: SQL Server Sample & System Databases

SQL Server System Databases

The master, model, tempdb and msdb are system databases for special database server operations purposes. SSMS Object Explorer drill-down listing of system databases.

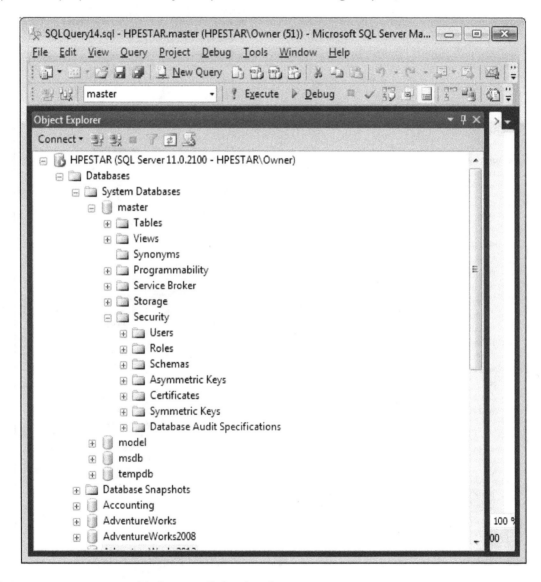

Query to create a new table in tempdb for development purposes.

```
SELECT * INTO tempdb.dbo.Product
FROM AdventureWorks2012.Production.Product
WHERE ListPrice > 0.0;
-- (304 row(s) affected)
```

The master Database

The master system database is the nerve center of SQL Server. It contains tables and db objects essential for server operations. System tables are accessible only through read-only views. System tables cannot be changed by users. A subset of the system views are called Dynamic Management Views (DMV) which return server state information for monitoring the operational aspects of a SQL Server instance, diagnosing problems, and performance tuning. Dynamic Management Functions (DMF) are applied in conjunction with DMVs.

```
SELECT TOP 5     ST.text,
                 EQS.*
FROM master.sys.dm_exec_query_stats AS EQS               -- DMV
CROSS APPLY master.sys.dm_exec_sql_text(EQS.sql_handle) as ST    -- DMF
ORDER BY last_worker_time DESC;
```

SQL Server Management Studio Object Explorer display of some objects in the master database and a query listing all databases.

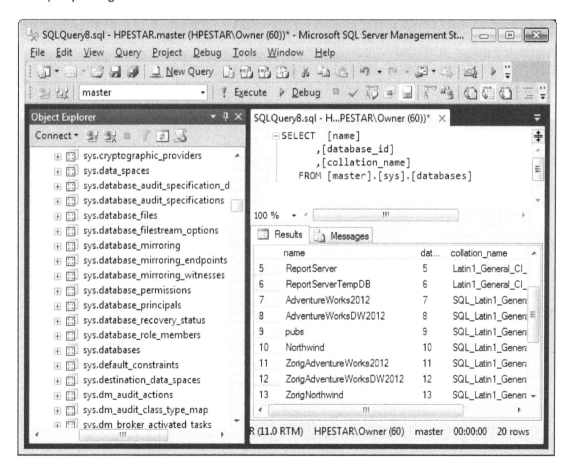

CHAPTER 1: SQL Server Sample & System Databases

An Important System View In master Database: sys.databases

```
SELECT TOP (10) name, database_id
FROM master.sys.databases
ORDER BY database_id;
```

name	database_id
master	1
tempdb	2
model	3
msdb	4
ReportServer	5
ReportServerTempDB	6
AdventureWorks2012	7
AdventureWorksDW2012	8
pubs	9
Northwind	10

spt_values table in master database can be used for integer sequence with a range of 0 - 2047.

```
-- End of the range - BOTTOM
SELECT TOP 5 number FROM master.dbo.spt_values WHERE TYPE='P'
ORDER BY number DESC;
```

number
2047
2046
2045
2044
2043

Example for using the sequence in spt_values to generate DATE and MONTH sequences.

```
SELECT TOP 5 number,  dateadd(day, number, '20000101')      AS "Date",
                      dateadd(mm, number, '20000101')       AS "Month"
FROM master.dbo.spt_values  WHERE type = 'P'  ORDER BY number;
```

number	Date	Month
0	2000-01-01 00:00:00.000	2000-01-01 00:00:00.000
1	2000-01-02 00:00:00.000	2000-02-01 00:00:00.000
2	2000-01-03 00:00:00.000	2000-03-01 00:00:00.000
3	2000-01-04 00:00:00.000	2000-04-01 00:00:00.000
4	2000-01-05 00:00:00.000	2000-05-01 00:00:00.000

The model Database

The model database serves as prototype for a new database. The model database is also the prototype for tempdb when the SQL Server instance started. Upon server shutdown or restart everything is wiped out of tempdb, it starts with a clean slate as a copy of the model database. Therefore we should only place objects into the tempdb can be purged any time.

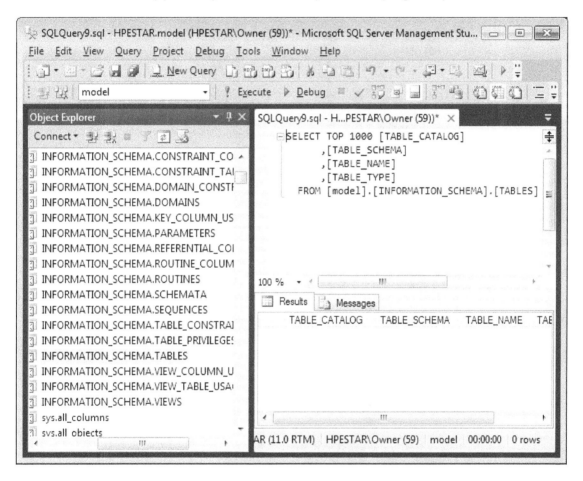

CHAPTER 1: SQL Server Sample & System Databases

The msdb Database

The msdb database is used for server internal operations such as support for SQL Server Agent job scheduling facility or keeping track of database the all important backups and restores.

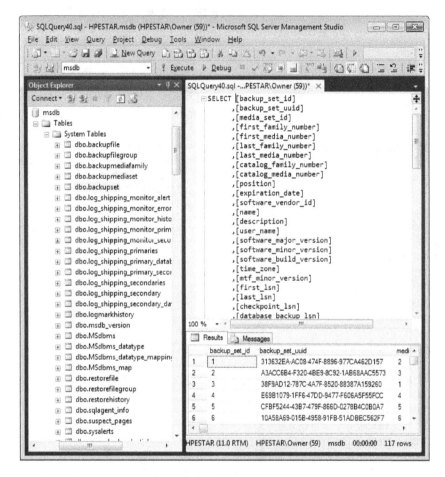

Database backup history query using table in msdb database.

```
SELECT  s.name AS Name, CONVERT(DATE,MAX(b.backup_finish_date)) AS LastGoodBackup,
        b.type AS Type
FROM master.dbo.sysdatabases AS s
LEFT OUTER JOIN msdb.dbo.backupset AS b ON s.name = b.database_name
GROUP BY s.name, b.type ORDER BY Name, Type;
```

Name	LastGoodBackup	Type
Accounting	2016-11-29	D
AdventureWorks	2016-11-29	D
AdventureWorks2008	2016-11-29	D
AdventureWorks2012	2016-11-29	D

The tempdb Database

The tempdb serves as temporary database for system operations such as sorting. Temporary tables (#temp1) and global temporary tables (##globaltemp1) are stored in the tempdb as well. "Permanent" tables can be created in tempdb with a short lifetime which lasts till shutdown or restart.

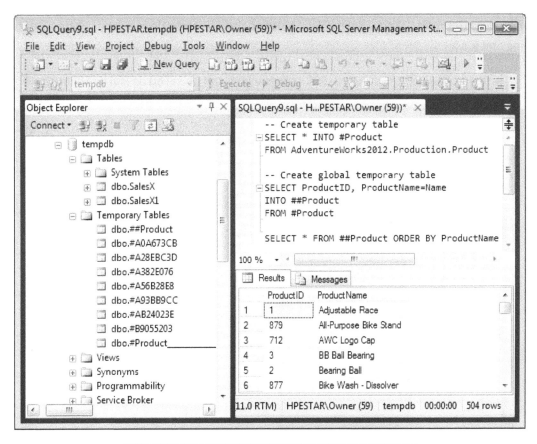

CHAPTER 1: SQL Server Sample & System Databases

Sudden Death in tempdb When Server Restarts

Even though a temporary table and a global temporary table are created and queried in the context setting for AdventureWorks2012 database, they are placed into tempdb automatically. Same consideration when a temporary table is created from a stored procedure which is compiled in an application database. Upon server restart everything is wiped out of tempdb, rebirth follows as a copy of model db. We should not place anything into tempdb we cannot afford to lose. tempdb is also used by SQL Server engine for operations such as version control, sorting and more.

> Instead of GUI & mouse use T-SQL scripts which can be saved as .sql disk files.

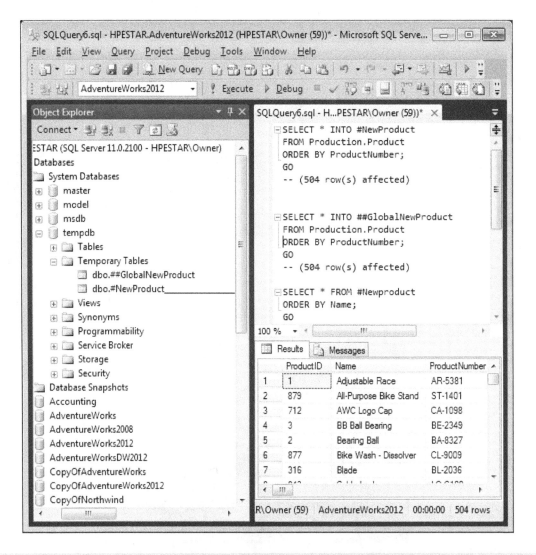

CHAPTER 2: Structure of the SELECT Statement

The SELECT Clause

The SELECT clause is the only required clause in a SELECT statement, all the other clauses are optional. The SELECT columns can be literals (constants), expressions, table columns and even subqueries. Lines can be commented with "--".

```
SELECT 15 * 15;                                              -- 225


SELECT Today = convert(DATE, getdate());                -- 2016-07-27   -- getdate() T-SQL only
SELECT Today = convert(DATE, CURRENT_TIMESTAMP);        -- 2016-07-27   -- ANSI SQL


SELECT          Color,
                ProdCnt              = COUNT(*),
                AvgPrice             = FORMAT(AVG(ListPrice),'c','en-US')
FROM AdventureWorks2012.Production.Product p
WHERE Color is not null
GROUP BY Color
        HAVING count(*) > 10
ORDER BY AvgPrice DESC;
```

Color	ProdCnt	AvgPrice
Yellow	36	$959.09
Blue	26	$923.68
Silver	43	$850.31
Black	93	$725.12
Red	38	$1,401.95

```
-- Equivalent with column aliases on the right
SELECT          Color,
                COUNT(*)                             AS ProdCnt,
                FORMAT(AVG(ListPrice),'c','en-US')   AS AvgPrice
FROM AdventureWorks2012.Production.Product p  WHERE Color is not null
GROUP BY Color HAVING count(*) > 10  ORDER BY AvgPrice DESC;
GO
```

SELECT with Search Expression

SELECT statement can have complex expressions for text or numbers as demonstrated in the next T-SQL query for finding the street name in AddressLine1 column.

```
SELECT AddressID,
       SUBSTRING(AddressLine1, CHARINDEX(' ', AddressLine1+' ', 1) +1,
       CHARINDEX(' ', AddressLine1+' ', CHARINDEX(' ', AddressLine1+' ', 1) +1) -
       CHARINDEX(' ', AddressLine1+' ', 1) -1)                          AS StreetName,
       AddressLine1,
       City
FROM AdventureWorks2012.Person.Address
WHERE ISNUMERIC (LEFT(AddressLine1,1))=1
  AND City = 'Seattle'
ORDER BY AddressLine1;
-- -- (141 row(s) affected)- Partial results.
```

AddressID	StreetName	AddressLine1	City
13079	boulevard	081, boulevard du Montparnasse	Seattle
859	Oak	1050 Oak Street	Seattle
110	Slow	1064 Slow Creek Road	Seattle
113	Ravenwood	1102 Ravenwood	Seattle
95	Bradford	1220 Bradford Way	Seattle
32510	Steven	1349 Steven Way	Seattle
118	Balboa	136 Balboa Court	Seattle
32519	Mazatlan	137 Mazatlan	Seattle
25869	Calle	1386 Calle Verde	Seattle
114	Yorba	1398 Yorba Linda	Seattle
15657	Book	151 Book Ct	Seattle
105	Stillman	1619 Stillman Court	Seattle
18002	Carmel	1635 Carmel Dr	Seattle
19813	Acardia	1787 Acardia Pl.	Seattle
16392	Orchid	1874 Orchid Ct	Seattle
18053	Green	1883 Green View Court	Seattle
13035	Mt.	1887 Mt. Diablo St	Seattle
29864	Valley	1946 Valley Crest Drive	Seattle
13580	Hill	2030 Hill Drive	Seattle
106	San	2144 San Rafael	Seattle

```
-- Search for Crest in the middle of AddessLine1
SELECT * FROM AdventureWorks2012.Person.Address
WHERE AddressLine1 LIKE '% Crest %';
-- (21 row(s) affected)
```

CHAPTER 2: Structure of the SELECT Statement

SELECT Statement with Subquery

Two Northwind category images, Beverages & Dairy Products, from the dbo.Categories table.

The following SELECT statement involves a subquery which is called a derived table. It also demonstrates that INNER JOIN can be performed with a GROUP BY subquery as well not only with another table or view.

```
USE Northwind;
SELECT          c.CategoryName                      AS Category,
                cnum.NoOfProducts                   AS CatProdCnt,
                p.ProductName                       AS Product,
                FORMAT(p.UnitPrice,'c', 'en-US')    AS UnitPrice
FROM    Categories c
                INNER JOIN Products p       ON c.CategoryID = p.CategoryID
                INNER JOIN (    SELECT          c.CategoryID,
                                                NoOfProducts = count(* )
                        FROM    Categories c
                        INNER JOIN Products p
                        ON c.CategoryID = p.CategoryID
                        GROUP BY c.CategoryID
                ) cnum                                  -- derived table
                ON c.CategoryID = cnum.CategoryID
ORDER BY Category, Product;     -- (77 row(s) affected) - Partial results.
```

Category	CatProdCnt	Product	UnitPrice
Dairy Products	10	Mozzarella di Giovanni	$34.80
Dairy Products	10	Queso Cabrales	$21.00
Dairy Products	10	Queso Manchego La Pastora	$38.00
Dairy Products	10	Raclette Courdavault	$55.00
Grains/Cereals	7	Filo Mix	$7.00
Grains/Cereals	7	Gnocchi di nonna Alice	$38.00
Grains/Cereals	7	Gustaf's Knäckebröd	$21.00
Grains/Cereals	7	Ravioli Angelo	$19.50
Grains/Cereals	7	Singaporean Hokkien Fried Mee	$14.00
Grains/Cereals	7	Tunnbröd	$9.00

CHAPTER 2: Structure of the SELECT Statement

Creating Delimited String List (CSV) with XML PATH

The XML PATH clause , the text() function and correlated subquery is used to create a comma delimited string within the SELECT columns. Note: it cannot be done using traditional (without XML) SQL single statement, it can be done with multiple SQL statements only. STUFF() string function is applied to replace the leading comma with an empty string.

```
USE AdventureWorks;

SELECT  Territory        = st.[Name],
        SalesYTD =  FORMAT(floor(SalesYTD), 'c', 'en-US'), -- currency format
        SalesStaffAssignmentHistory =

          STUFF((SELECT CONCAT(', ', c.FirstName, SPACE(1), c.LastName)        AS [text()]
               FROM   Person.Contact c
               INNER JOIN Sales.SalesTerritoryHistory sth
               ON c.ContactID = sth.SalesPersonID
               WHERE  sth.TerritoryID =  st.TerritoryID
               ORDER  BY StartDate
               FOR XML Path ('')), 1, 1, SPACE(0))

FROM   Sales.SalesTerritory st
ORDER  BY SalesYTD DESC;
GO
```

Territory	SalesYTD	SalesStaffAssignmentHistory
Southwest	$8,351,296.00	Shelley Dyck, Jauna Elson
Canada	$6,917,270.00	Carla Eldridge, Michael Emanuel, Gail Erickson
Northwest	$5,767,341.00	Shannon Elliott, Terry Eminhizer, Martha Espinoza
Central	$4,677,108.00	Linda Ecoffey, Maciej Dusza
France	$3,899,045.00	Mark Erickson
Northeast	$3,857,163.00	Maciej Dusza, Linda Ecoffey
United Kingdom	$3,514,865.00	Michael Emanuel
Southeast	$2,851,419.00	Carol Elliott
Germany	$2,481,039.00	Janeth Esteves
Australia	$1,977,474.00	Twanna Evans

```
-- Comma delimited list of column names
SELECT CONCAT(',', c.name) AS [text()]
FROM sys.columns c  WHERE c.[object_id] = OBJECT_ID('Purchasing.PurchaseOrderDetail')
ORDER BY column_id FOR XML PATH('');
```

CHAPTER 2: Structure of the SELECT Statement

Logical Processing Order of the SELECT Statement

The results from the previous step will be available to the next step. The logical processing order for a SELECT statement is the following. Actual processing by the database engine may be different due to performance and other considerations.

1.	FROM
2.	ON
3.	JOIN
4.	WHERE
5.	GROUP BY
6.	WITH CUBE or WITH ROLLUP
7.	HAVING
8.	SELECT
9.	DISTINCT
10.	ORDER BY
11.	TOP

As an example, it is logical to filter with the WHERE clause prior to applying GROUP BY. It is also logical to sort when the final result set is available.

SELECT Color, COUNT(*) AS ColorCount FROM AdventureWorks2012.Production.Product WHERE Color is not NULL GROUP BY Color ORDER BY ColorCount DESC;

Color	ColorCount
Black	93
Silver	43
Red	38
Yellow	36
Blue	26
Multi	8
Silver/Black	7
White	4
Grey	1

CHAPTER 2: Structure of the SELECT Statement

The TOP Clause

The TOP clause filters results according the sorting specified in an ORDER BY clause, otherwise random filtering takes place.

Simple TOP usage to return 10 rows only.

SELECT TOP 10 SalesOrderID, OrderDate, TotalDue
FROM AdventureWorks2012.Sales.SalesOrderHeader ORDER BY TotalDue DESC;

SalesOrderID	OrderDate	TotalDue
51131	2007-07-01 00:00:00.000	187487.825
55282	2007-10-01 00:00:00.000	182018.6272
46616	2006-07-01 00:00:00.000	170512.6689
46981	2006-08-01 00:00:00.000	166537.0808
47395	2006-09-01 00:00:00.000	165028.7482
47369	2006-09-01 00:00:00.000	158056.5449
47355	2006-09-01 00:00:00.000	145741.8553
51822	2007-08-01 00:00:00.000	145454.366
44518	2005-11-01 00:00:00.000	142312.2199
51858	2007-08-01 00:00:00.000	140042.1209

TOP function usage: not known in advance how many rows will be returned due to "TIES".

SELECT   TOP 1 WITH TIES coalesce(Color, 'N/A')   AS Color,
            FORMAT(ListPrice, 'c', 'en-US')   AS ListPrice,
            Name   AS ProductName,
            ProductID
FROM   AdventureWorks2012.Production.Product
ORDER BY ROW_NUMBER() OVER(PARTITION BY Color ORDER BY ListPrice DESC);
.

Color	ListPrice	ProductName	ProductID
N/A	$229.49	HL Fork	804
Black	$3,374.99	Mountain-100 Black, 38	775
Red	$3,578.27	Road-150 Red, 62	749
Silver	$3,399.99	Mountain-100 Silver, 38	771
Blue	$2,384.07	Touring-1000 Blue, 46	966
Grey	$125.00	Touring-Panniers, Large	842
Multi	$89.99	Men's Bib-Shorts, S	855
Silver/Black	$80.99	HL Mountain Pedal	937
White	$9.50	Mountain Bike Socks, M	709
Yellow	$2,384.07	Touring-1000 Yellow, 46	954

The DISTINCT Clause to Omit Duplicates

The DISTINCT clause returns only unique results, omitting duplicates in the result set.

```
USE AdventureWorks2012;
SELECT DISTINCT Color FROM Production.Product
WHERE Color is not NULL
ORDER BY Color;
GO
```

Color
Black
Blue
Grey
Multi
Red
Silver
Silver/Black
White
Yellow

```
SELECT DISTINCT ListPrice
FROM Production.Product
 WHERE ListPrice > 0.0
ORDER BY ListPrice DESC;
GO
-- (102 row(s) affected) - Partial results.
```

ListPrice
3578.27
3399.99
3374.99
2443.35

```
-- Using DISTINCT in COUNT - NULL is counted
SELECT          COUNT(*)                AS TotalRows,
                COUNT(DISTINCT Color)   AS ProductColors,
                COUNT(DISTINCT Size)    AS ProductSizes
FROM AdventureWorks2012.Production.Product;
```

TotalRows	ProductColors	ProductSizes
504	9	18

CHAPTER 2: Structure of the SELECT Statement

The CASE Conditional Expression

The CASE conditional expression evaluates to a **single value of the same data type**, therefore **it can be used anywhere in a query where a single value is required.**

```
SELECT          CASE ProductLine
                    WHEN 'R' THEN 'Road'
                    WHEN 'M' THEN 'Mountain'
                    WHEN 'T' THEN 'Touring'
                    WHEN 'S' THEN 'Other'
                    ELSE 'Parts'
                END                        AS Category,
                Name                       AS ProductName,
                ProductNumber
FROM AdventureWorks2012.Production.Product
ORDER BY ProductName;
GO
-- (504 row(s) affected) - Partial results.
```

Category	ProductName	ProductNumber
Touring	Touring-3000 Blue, 62	BK-T18U-62
Touring	Touring-3000 Yellow, 44	BK-T18Y-44
Touring	Touring-3000 Yellow, 50	BK-T18Y-50
Touring	Touring-3000 Yellow, 54	BK-T18Y-54
Touring	Touring-3000 Yellow, 58	BK-T18Y-58
Touring	Touring-3000 Yellow, 62	BK-T18Y-62
Touring	Touring-Panniers, Large	PA-T100
Other	Water Bottle - 30 oz.	WB-H098
Mountain	Women's Mountain Shorts, L	SH-W890-L

Query to return different result sets for repeated execution due to newid().

```
SELECT  TOP 3 CompanyName,  City=CONCAT(City, ', ', Country),        PostalCode,
        [IsNumeric] =  CASE   WHEN PostalCode like '[0-9][0-9][0-9][0-9][0-9]'
                        THEN '5-Digit Numeric'   ELSE 'Other' END
FROM    Northwind.dbo.Suppliers
ORDER BY NEWID();                -- random sort
GO
```

CompanyName	City	PostalCode	IsNumeric
PB Knäckebröd AB	Göteborg, Sweden	S-345 67	Other
Gai pâturage	Annecy, France	74000	5-Digit Numeric
Heli Süßwaren GmbH & Co. KG	Berlin, Germany	10785	5-Digit Numeric

Same query as above expanded with ROW_NUMBER() and another CASE expression column.

```
SELECT          ROW_NUMBER() OVER (ORDER BY Name)               AS RowNo,
                CASE ProductLine
                  WHEN 'R' THEN 'Road'
                  WHEN 'M' THEN 'Mountain'
                  WHEN 'T' THEN 'Touring'
                  WHEN 'S' THEN 'Other'
                  ELSE 'Parts'
                END                                  AS Category,
                Name                                 AS ProductName,
                CASE WHEN Color is null THEN 'N/A'
                        ELSE Color END               AS Color,
                ProductNumber
FROM Production.Product   ORDER BY ProductName;
-- (504 row(s) affected) - Partial results.
```

RowNo	Category	ProductName	Color	ProductNumber
1	Parts	Adjustable Race	N/A	AR-5381
2	Mountain	All-Purpose Bike Stand	N/A	ST-1401
3	Other	AWC Logo Cap	Multi	CA-1098
4	Parts	BB Ball Bearing	N/A	BE-2349
5	Parts	Bearing Ball	N/A	BA-8327
6	Other	Bike Wash - Dissolver	N/A	CL-9009
7	Parts	Blade	N/A	BL-2036
8	Other	Cable Lock	N/A	LO-C100
9	Parts	Chain	Silver	CH-0234
10	Parts	Chain Stays	N/A	CS-2812

Testing PostalCode with ISNUMERIC and generating a flag with CASE expression.

```
SELECT  TOP (4) AddressID,   City,    PostalCode                        AS Zip,
         CASE WHEN ISNUMERIC(PostalCode) = 1 THEN 'Y'  ELSE 'N'  END    AS IsZipNumeric
FROM    AdventureWorks2008.Person.Address  ORDER BY NEWID();
```

AddressID	City	Zip	IsZipNumeric
16704	Paris	75008	Y
26320	Grossmont	91941	Y
27705	Matraville	2036	Y
18901	Kirkby	KB9	N

CHAPTER 2: Structure of the SELECT Statement

The OVER Clause

The OVER clause defines the partitioning and sorting of a rowset (intermediate result set) preceding the application of an associated window function, such as ranking. Window functions are also dubbed as ranking functions.

```
USE AdventureWorks2012;
-- Query with three different OVER clauses
SELECT   ROW_NUMBER() OVER ( ORDER BY SalesOrderID, ProductID)          AS RowNum
         ,SalesOrderID, ProductID, OrderQty
         ,RANK() OVER(PARTITION BY SalesOrderID ORDER BY OrderQty DESC)  AS Ranking
         ,SUM(OrderQty) OVER(PARTITION BY SalesOrderID)                  AS TotalQty
         ,AVG(OrderQty) OVER(PARTITION BY SalesOrderID)                  AS AvgQty
         ,COUNT(OrderQty) OVER(PARTITION BY SalesOrderID)  AS "Count"  -- T-SQL keyword, use "" or []
         ,MIN(OrderQty) OVER(PARTITION BY SalesOrderID)                  AS "Min"
         ,MAX(OrderQty) OVER(PARTITION BY SalesOrderID)                  AS "Max"
FROM Sales.SalesOrderDetail
WHERE SalesOrderID BETWEEN 61190 AND 61199
ORDER BY RowNum;
-- (143 row(s) affected) - Partial results.
```

RowNum	SalesOrderID	ProductID	OrderQty	Ranking	TotalQty	AvgQty	Count	Min	Max
1	61190	707	4	13	159	3	40	1	17
2	61190	708	3	18	159	3	40	1	17
3	61190	711	5	8	159	3	40	1	17
4	61190	712	12	2	159	3	40	1	17
5	61190	714	3	18	159	3	40	1	17
6	61190	715	5	8	159	3	40	1	17
7	61190	716	5	8	159	3	40	1	17
8	61190	858	4	13	159	3	40	1	17
9	61190	859	7	6	159	3	40	1	17
10	61190	864	8	4	159	3	40	1	17
11	61190	865	3	18	159	3	40	1	17
12	61190	870	9	3	159	3	40	1	17
13	61190	876	4	13	159	3	40	1	17
14	61190	877	5	8	159	3	40	1	17
15	61190	880	1	34	159	3	40	1	17
16	61190	881	5	8	159	3	40	1	17
17	61190	883	2	26	159	3	40	1	17
18	61190	884	17	1	159	3	40	1	17
19	61190	885	3	18	159	3	40	1	17
20	61190	886	1	34	159	3	40	1	17
21	61190	889	2	26	159	3	40	1	17
22	61190	892	4	13	159	3	40	1	17
23	61190	893	3	18	159	3	40	1	17
24	61190	895	1	34	159	3	40	1	17

FROM Clause: Specifies the Data Source

The FROM clause specifies the source data sets for the query such as tables, views, derived tables and table-valued functions. Typically the tables are JOINed together. The most common JOIN is INNER JOIN which is based on equality between FOREIGN KEY and PRIMARY KEY values in the two tables.

PERFORMANCE NOTE
All FOREIGN KEYs should be indexed. PRIMARY KEYs are indexed automatically with unique index.

```
USE AdventureWorks2012;
GO
SELECT
 ROW_NUMBER() OVER(ORDER BY SalesYTD DESC)                        AS RowNo,
 ROW_NUMBER() OVER(PARTITION BY PostalCode ORDER BY SalesYTD DESC)   AS SeqNo,
           CONCAT(p.FirstName, SPACE(1), p.LastName)          AS SalesStaff,
           FORMAT(s.SalesYTD,'c','en-US')                     AS YTDSales,
           City,
           a.PostalCode                                       AS ZipCode
FROM Sales.SalesPerson AS s
   INNER JOIN Person.Person AS p
     ON s.BusinessEntityID = p.BusinessEntityID
   INNER JOIN Person.Address AS a
     ON a.AddressID = p.BusinessEntityID
WHERE TerritoryID IS NOT NULL   AND SalesYTD <> 0 ORDER BY ZipCode, SeqNo;
```

RowNo	SeqNo	SalesStaff	YTDSales	City	ZipCode
1	1	Linda Mitchell	$4,251,368.55	Issaquah	98027
3	2	Michael Blythe	$3,763,178.18	Issaquah	98027
4	3	Jillian Carson	$3,189,418.37	Issaquah	98027
8	4	Tsvi Reiter	$2,315,185.61	Issaquah	98027
12	5	Garrett Vargas	$1,453,719.47	Issaquah	98027
14	6	Pamela Ansman-Wolfe	$1,352,577.13	Issaquah	98027
2	1	Jae Pak	$4,116,871.23	Renton	98055
5	2	Ranjit Varkey Chudukatil	$3,121,616.32	Renton	98055
6	3	José Saraiva	$2,604,540.72	Renton	98055
7	4	Shu Ito	$2,458,535.62	Renton	98055
9	5	Rachel Valdez	$1,827,066.71	Renton	98055
10	6	Tete Mensa-Annan	$1,576,562.20	Renton	98055
11	7	David Campbell	$1,573,012.94	Renton	98055
13	8	Lynn Tsoflias	$1,421,810.92	Renton	98055

The WHERE Clause to Filter Records (Rows)

The WHERE clause filters the rows generated by the query. Only rows satisfying (TRUE) the WHERE clause predicates are returned.

PERFORMANCE NOTE
All columns in WHERE clause should be indexed.

USE AdventureWorks2012;

String equal match predicate - equal is TRUE, not equal is FALSE.

SELECT ProductID, Name, ListPrice, Color
FROM Production.Product WHERE Name = 'Mountain-100 Silver, 38' ;

ProductID	Name	ListPrice	Color
771	Mountain-100 Silver, 38	3399.99	Silver

-- Function equality predicate
SELECT * FROM Sales.SalesOrderHeader WHERE YEAR(OrderDate) = 2008;
-- (13951 row(s) affected)

PERFORMANCE NOTE
When a column is used as a parameter in a function (e.g. YEAR(OrderDate)), index (if any) usage is voided. Instead of random SEEK, all rows are SCANned in the table. The predicate is not SARGable.

-- String wildcard match predicate
SELECT ProductID, Name, ListPrice, Color
FROM Production.Product WHERE Name LIKE ('%touring%');

-- Integer range predicate
SELECT ProductID, Name, ListPrice, Color
FROM Production.Product WHERE ProductID >= 997 ;

-- Double string wildcard match predicate
SELECT ProductID, Name, ListPrice, Color
FROM Production.Product WHERE Name LIKE ('%bike%') AND Name LIKE ('%44%');

-- String list match predicate
SELECT ProductID, Name, ListPrice, Color FROM Production.Product
WHERE Name IN ('Mountain-100 Silver, 44', 'Mountain-100 Black, 44');

The GROUP BY Clause to Aggregate Results

The GROUP BY clause is applied to partition the rows and calculate aggregate values. An extremely powerful way of looking at the data from a summary point of view.

```
SELECT
                V.Name                                      AS Vendor,
                FORMAT(SUM(TotalDue), 'c', 'en-US')         AS TotalPurchase,
                A.City,
                SP.Name                                     AS State,
                CR.Name                                     AS Country
FROM Purchasing.Vendor AS V
    INNER JOIN Purchasing.VendorAddress AS VA
                ON VA.VendorID = V.VendorID
    INNER JOIN Person.Address AS A
                ON A.AddressID = VA.AddressID
    INNER JOIN Person.StateProvince AS SP
                ON SP.StateProvinceID =  A.StateProvinceID
    INNER JOIN Person.CountryRegion AS CR
                ON CR.CountryRegionCode = SP.CountryRegionCode
    INNER JOIN Purchasing.PurchaseOrderHeader POH
                ON POH.VendorID = V.VendorID
GROUP BY  V.Name, A.City, SP.Name, CR.Name
ORDER BY SUM(TotalDue) DESC,  Vendor;   -- TotalPurchase does a string sort instead of numeric
GO
-- (79 row(s) affected) - Partial results.
```

Vendor	TotalPurchase	City	State	Country
Superior Bicycles	$5,034,266.74	Lynnwood	Washington	United States
Professional Athletic Consultants	$3,379,946.32	Burbank	California	United States
Chicago City Saddles	$3,347,165.20	Daly City	California	United States
Jackson Authority	$2,821,333.52	Long Beach	California	United States
Vision Cycles, Inc.	$2,777,684.91	Glendale	California	United States
Sport Fan Co.	$2,675,889.22	Burien	Washington	United States
Proseware, Inc.	$2,593,901.31	Lebanon	Oregon	United States
Crowley Sport	$2,472,770.05	Chicago	Illinois	United States
Greenwood Athletic Company	$2,472,770.05	Lemon Grove	Arizona	United States
Mitchell Sports	$2,424,284.37	Everett	Washington	United States
First Rate Bicycles	$2,304,231.55	La Mesa	New Mexico	United States
Signature Cycles	$2,236,033.80	Coronado	California	United States
Electronic Bike Repair & Supplies	$2,154,773.37	Tacoma	Washington	United States
Vista Road Bikes	$2,090,857.52	Salem	Oregon	United States
Victory Bikes	$2,052,173.62	Issaquah	Washington	United States
Bicycle Specialists	$1,952,375.30	Lake Oswego	Oregon	United States

The HAVING Clause to Filter Aggregates

The HAVING clause is similar to the WHERE clause filtering but applies to GROUP BY aggregates.

```
USE AdventureWorks;
SELECT
          V.Name                                    AS Vendor,
          FORMAT(SUM(TotalDue), 'c', 'en-US')       AS TotalPurchase,
          A.City,
          SP.Name                                   AS State,
          CR.Name                                   AS Country
FROM Purchasing.Vendor AS V
   INNER JOIN Purchasing.VendorAddress AS VA
          ON VA.VendorID = V.VendorID
   INNER JOIN Person.Address AS A
          ON A.AddressID = VA.AddressID
   INNER JOIN Person.StateProvince AS SP
          ON SP.StateProvinceID =  A.StateProvinceID
   INNER JOIN Person.CountryRegion AS CR
          ON CR.CountryRegionCode = SP.CountryRegionCode
   INNER JOIN Purchasing.PurchaseOrderHeader POH
          ON POH.VendorID = V.VendorID
GROUP BY  V.Name, A.City, SP.Name, CR.Name
HAVING SUM(TotalDue) < $26000   -- HAVING clause predicate
ORDER BY SUM(TotalDue) DESC,  Vendor;
```

Vendor	TotalPurchase	City	State	Country
Speed Corporation	$25,732.84	Anacortes	Washington	United States
Gardner Touring Cycles	$25,633.64	Altadena	California	United States
National Bike Association	$25,513.90	Sedro Woolley	Washington	United States
Australia Bike Retailer	$25,060.04	Bellingham	Washington	United States
WestAmerica Bicycle Co.	$25,060.04	Houston	Texas	United States
Ready Rentals	$23,635.06	Kirkland	Washington	United States
Morgan Bike Accessories	$23,146.99	Albany	New York	United States
Continental Pro Cycles	$22,960.07	Long Beach	California	United States
American Bicycles and Wheels	$9,641.01	West Covina	California	United States
Litware, Inc.	$8,553.32	Santa Cruz	California	United States
Business Equipment Center	$8,497.80	Everett	Montana	United States
Bloomington Multisport	$8,243.95	West Covina	California	United States
International	$8,061.10	Salt Lake City	Utah	United States
Wide World Importers	$8,025.60	Concord	California	United States
Midwest Sport, Inc.	$7,328.72	Detroit	Michigan	United States
Wood Fitness	$6,947.58	Philadelphia	Pennsylvania	United States
Metro Sport Equipment	$6,324.53	Lebanon	Oregon	United States
Burnett Road Warriors	$5,779.99	Corvallis	Oregon	United States
Lindell	$5,412.57	Lebanon	Oregon	United States
Consumer Cycles	$3,378.17	Torrance	California	United States
Northern Bike Travel	$2,048.42	Anacortes	Washington	United States

The ORDER BY Clause to Sort Results

The ORDER BY clause sorts the result set. It guarantees ordering according to the columns or expressions listed from major to minor keys. Unique ordering requires a set of keys which generate unique data rows. The major key, YEAR(HireDate), in the first example is not sufficient for uniqueness.

```
USE AdventureWorks2012;          -- Sort on 2 keys
SELECT BusinessEntityID AS EmployeeID, JobTitle, HireDate
FROM HumanResources.Employee  ORDER BY YEAR(HireDate) DESC, EmployeeID;
-- (290 row(s) affected) - Partial results.
```

EmployeeID	JobTitle	HireDate
285	Pacific Sales Manager	2007-04-15
286	Sales Representative	2007-07-01
288	Sales Representative	2007-07-01

```
-- Sort on CASE conditional expression
SELECT   BusinessEntityID AS SalesStaffID, CONCAT(LastName, ', ', FirstName) AS FullName,
         CASE CountryRegionName WHEN 'United States' THEN TerritoryName
             ELSE '' END AS TerritoryName, CountryRegionName
FROM Sales.vSalesPerson   WHERE TerritoryName IS NOT NULL        -- view
ORDER BY CASE WHEN CountryRegionName != 'United States' THEN  CountryRegionName
             ELSE TerritoryName  END;
```

SalesStaffID	FullName	TerritoryName	CountryRegionName
286	Tsoflias, Lynn		Australia
278	Vargas, Garrett		Canada
282	Saraiva, José		Canada

The EXCEPT & INTERSECT Set Operators

The EXCEPT operator & the INTERSECT operator require the column lists are compatible for the comparison.

```
USE tempdb;  -- Prepare two tables with 400 random(newid()) picks from the Product table
SELECT TOP (400) * INTO Prod1 FROM AdventureWorks2012.Production.Product ORDER BY NEWID();
SELECT TOP (400) * INTO Prod2 FROM AdventureWorks2012.Production.Product ORDER BY NEWID();

-- EXCEPT SET OPERATOR - no match rows
SELECT * FROM PROD1 EXCEPT SELECT * FROM PROD2;  -- (81 row(s) affected)

-- INTERSECT SET OPERATOR - matching rows
SELECT * FROM PROD1 INTERSECT SELECT * FROM PROD2;  -- (319 row(s) affected)
```

CHAPTER 2: Structure of the SELECT Statement

CTE - Common Table Expression

CTE helps with structured programming by the definition of named subqueries at the beginning of the query. It supports nesting and recursion.

```
USE AdventureWorks;
-- Testing CTE
WITH CTE (SalesPersonID, NumberOfOrders, MostRecentOrderDate)
    AS  (       SELECT SalesPersonID, COUNT(*), CONVERT(date, MAX(OrderDate))
                FROM Sales.SalesOrderHeader
                GROUP BY SalesPersonID  )
SELECT * FROM CTE;
-- (18 row(s) affected) - Partial results.
```

SalesPersonID	NumberOfOrders	MostRecentOrderDate
284	39	2004-05-01
278	234	2004-06-01
281	242	2004-06-01

```
-- Using CTE in a query
;WITH CTE (SalesPersonID, NumberOfOrders, MostRecentOrderDate)
    AS  ( SELECT SalesPersonID, COUNT(*), CONVERT(date, MAX(OrderDate))
        FROM Sales.SalesOrderHeader   GROUP BY SalesPersonID        )
-- Start of outer (main) query
  SELECT        E.EmployeeID,
                OE.NumberOfOrders               AS EmpOrders,
                OE.MostRecentOrderDate          AS EmpLastOrder,
                E.ManagerID,
                OM.NumberOfOrders               AS MgrOrders,
                OM.MostRecentOrderDate          AS MgrLastOrder
  FROM   HumanResources.Employee AS E
            INNER JOIN CTE AS OE                ON E.EmployeeID = OE.SalesPersonID
            LEFT OUTER JOIN CTE AS OM           ON E.ManagerID = OM.SalesPersonID
ORDER BY EmployeeID;
-- (17 row(s) affected) - Partial results.
```

EmployeeID	EmpOrders	EmpLastOrder	ManagerID	MgrOrders	MgrLastOrder
268	48	2004-06-01	273	NULL	NULL
275	450	2004-06-01	268	48	2004-06-01
276	418	2004-06-01	268	48	2004-06-01
277	473	2004-06-01	268	48	2004-06-01
278	234	2004-06-01	268	48	2004-06-01

Combining Results of Multiple Queries with UNION

UNION and UNION ALL (no duplicates elimination) operators can be used to **stack result sets from two or more queries into a single result set**.

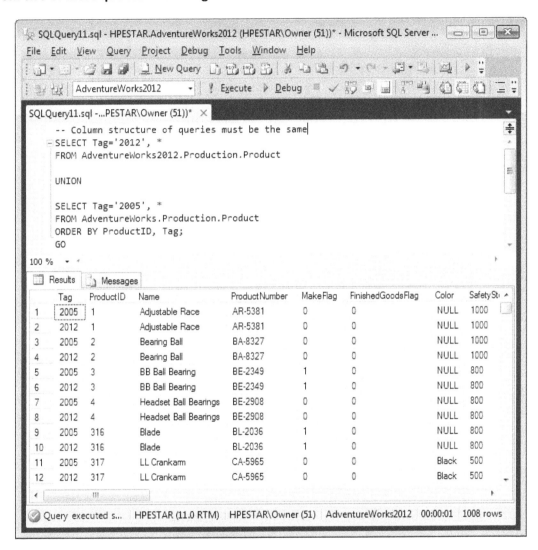

```
-- Combining data from OLTP & data warehouse databases
SELECT FirstName,LastName, 0 AS TotalChildren
FROM AdventureWorks2012.Person.Person
UNION ALL
SELECT FirstName,LastName, TotalChildren
FROM AdventureWorksDW2012..DimCustomer;
```

TOP n by Group Query with OVER PARTITION BY

OVER PARTITION BY method is very convenient for TOP n by group selection. List of top 3 orders placed by resellers (customers of AdventureWorks Cycles).

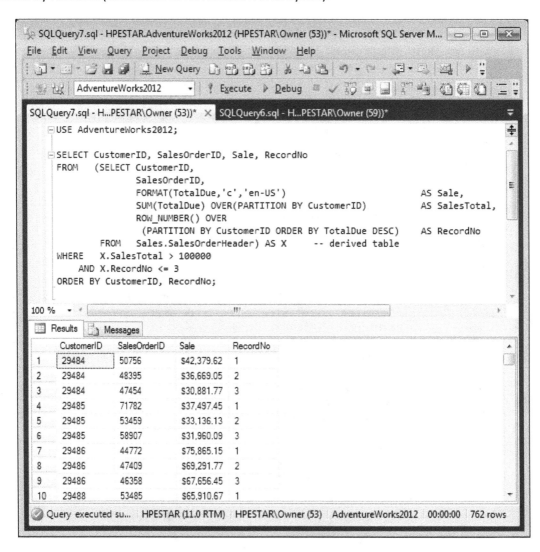

-- Row numbering by partitioning view results
```
SELECT ROW_NUMBER() OVER(PARTITION BY PhoneNumberType ORDER BY SalesYTD DESC) RN,
       CONCAT(FirstName, ' ', LastName) as Name, ROUND(SalesYTD,2,1) AS YTDSales,
       PhoneNumberType
FROM AdventureWorks2012.Sales.vSalesPerson
ORDER BY PhoneNumberType, RN;
```

CHAPTER 2: Structure of the SELECT Statement

CHAPTER 3: Basic Concepts of Client-Server Computing

Client - Server Relational Database Management System

The "server" is SQL Server, operating on a powerful hardware platform, managing databases and related items. The client is application software. The real client is naturally a human user who runs the application software. Automated software which uses the database for one thing or another is also considered a "client". The client computer, in the next room or thousands of miles away, is connected to the server through communications link. The client software sends a request, a query, to SQL Server, after execution the server returns the results to the client. An example for a query sent by the client to the server:

SELECT ListPrice FROM AdventureWorks2012.Production.Product WHERE ProductID = 800;

SQL Server executes the query and returns "1120.49" to the client with a flag indicating successful query execution. A tempting analogy is a restaurant: kitchen is the server, patrons are the clients and the communications / delivery done by waiters & waitresses.

Screenshot displays SQL Server (highlighted) along with other related software such as SQL Server Agent (job scheduling facility) , SSIS (data transformation & transfer), SSRS (Reporting), SSAS (OLAP Cube) and other auxiliary software.

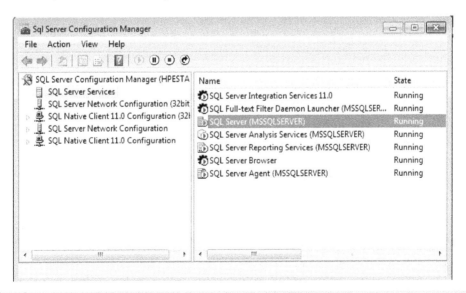

CHAPTER 3: Basic Concepts of Client-Server Computing

Database Objects on Server-Side

Screenshot of Object Explorer displays almost all important database objects with the exception of constraints, triggers and indexes.

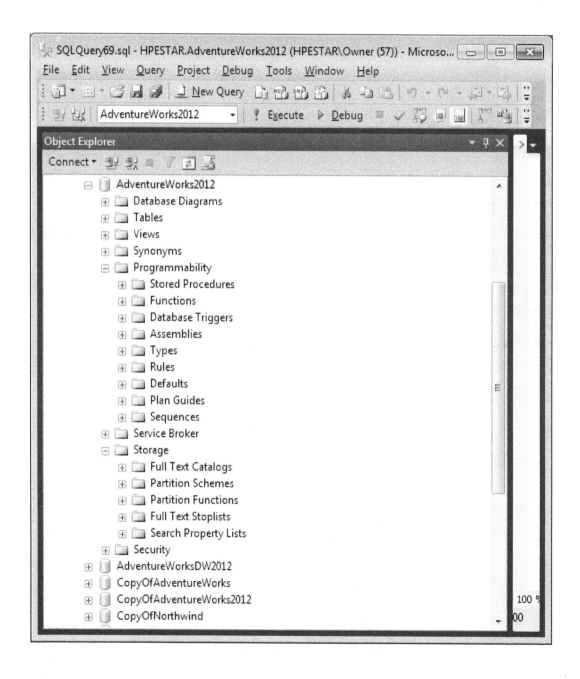

Database Related Items on Client-Side

On the client side the following items:

- ➢ SQL Server client libraries to access the server and database
- ➢ SQL queries imbedded in application programs
- ➢ Stored procedure calls imbedded in application software

Queries by themselves are not database object. To make them database objects we have to build stored procedures, functions or views around them.

The following code segment illustrates database connection and query from ASP to Inventory database. In ANSI SQL terminology catalog means database.

```
' Connect
<%
Dim StrConnInventory
Dim ConnInventory

StrConnInventory = "Provider=SQLOLEDB.1;Data Source=LONDONHEADOFFICE;Initial
Catalog=Inventory;User ID=finance;Password=fa$nAnCe#9*"

Set ConnInventory = Server.CreateObject("ADODB.Connection")

ConnInventory.ConnectionTimeout = 4000
ConnInventory.CommandTimeout = 4000
ConnInventory.Open StrConnInventory

' Query
Dim YourQuery As String = "SELECT Name, Price FROM Product"
 Dim YourCommand As New SqlCommand(YourQuery)
 YourCommand.Connection = ConnInventory
 YourConnection.Open()
 YourCommand.ExecuteNonQuery()
 Response.Write(YourCommand)
 YourCommand.Connection.Close()
%>
' Disconnect
<%
ConnInventory.Close
Set ConnInventory = Nothing
%>
```

SQL Server Profiler to Monitor Client-Server Communications

SQL Server Profiler, a tool in SSMS, has two modes of operations: interactive GUI and silent T-SQL script based operation. The simplest use of the Profiler is to check what queries are sent to the server (SQL Server) from the client and how long does processing take (duration). The client software sending the queries is SSMS. Even though SSMS appears as the "face of SQL Server", it is only a client software.

```
USE pubs;
GO
SELECT * FROM titles;
GO


USE Northwind;
GO
SELECT * FROM Products ORDER BY ProductName;
GO


USE AdventureWorks2012;
GO
SELECT * FROM Sales.SalesOrderHeader WHERE OrderDate='20080201';
GO
```

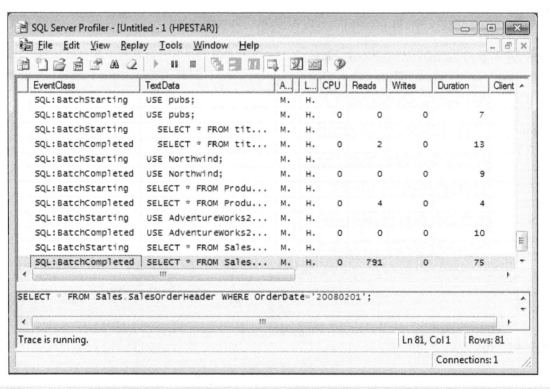

Table - Database Object

A database table holds data in tabular format by rows and columns. The main method of connecting tables is FOREIGN KEY referencing PRIMARY KEY. A set of connected tables makes up the database. Screenshot displays the structure and partial content of Northwind database Products table.

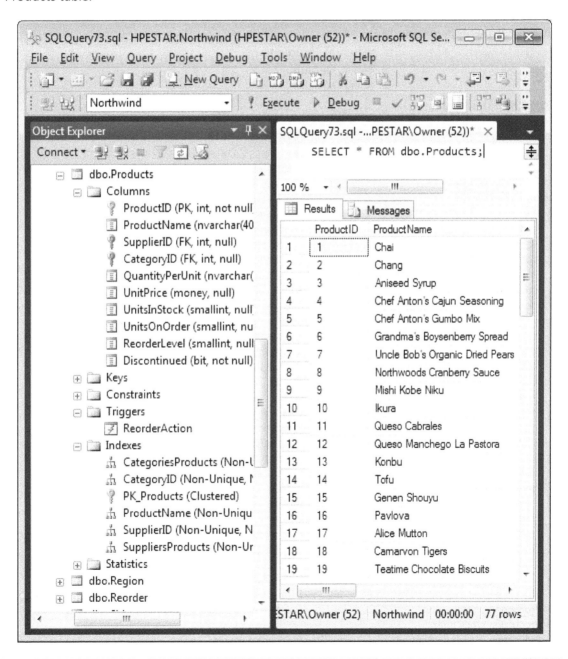

CHAPTER 3: Basic Concepts of Client-Server Computing

Tables in Production Schema

The listing and data dictionary description of tables in AdventureWorks2012 Production schema.

```
USE AdventureWorks2012;

SELECT  CONCAT('Production.', objname COLLATE DATABASE_DEFAULT) AS TableName,
        value                                                   AS [Description]
FROM fn_listextendedproperty (          NULL,
                              'schema', 'Production',
                              'table', default,
                              NULL, NULL)
ORDER BY TableName;
```

TableName	Description
Production.BillOfMaterials	Items required to make bicycles and bicycle subassemblies. It identifies the hierarchical relationship between a parent product and its components.
Production.Culture	Lookup table containing the languages in which some AdventureWorks data is stored.
Production.Document	Product maintenance documents.
Production.Illustration	Bicycle assembly diagrams.
Production.Location	Product inventory and manufacturing locations.
Production.Product	Products sold or used in the manfacturing of sold products.
Production.ProductCategory	High-level product categorization.
Production.ProductCostHistory	Changes in the cost of a product over time.
Production.ProductDescription	Product descriptions in several languages.
Production.ProductDocument	Cross-reference table mapping products to related product documents.
Production.ProductInventory	Product inventory information.
Production.ProductListPriceHistory	Changes in the list price of a product over time.
Production.ProductModel	Product model classification.
Production.ProductModelIllustration	Cross-reference table mapping product models and illustrations.
Production.ProductModelProductDescriptionCulture	Cross-reference table mapping product descriptions and the language the description is written in.
Production.ProductPhoto	Product images.
Production.ProductProductPhoto	Cross-reference table mapping products and product photos.
Production.ProductReview	Customer reviews of products they have purchased.
Production.ProductSubcategory	Product subcategories. See ProductCategory table.
Production.ScrapReason	Manufacturing failure reasons lookup table.
Production.TransactionHistory	Record of each purchase order, sales order, or work order transaction year to date.
Production.TransactionHistoryArchive	Transactions for previous years.
Production.UnitMeasure	Unit of measure lookup table.
Production.WorkOrder	Manufacturing work orders.
Production.WorkOrderRouting	Work order details.

Index - Database Object

An index on a table is a B-tree based structure which speeds up random searches. **Typically PRIMARY KEY (automatic), FOREIGN KEY and WHERE clause columns have indexes.** If the index is constructed on more than one column, it is called **composite index**. If all the columns in a query are in the index, it is called **covering index**. Properties dialog box displays the PRIMARY KEY composite index of the EmployeeDepartmentHistory table.

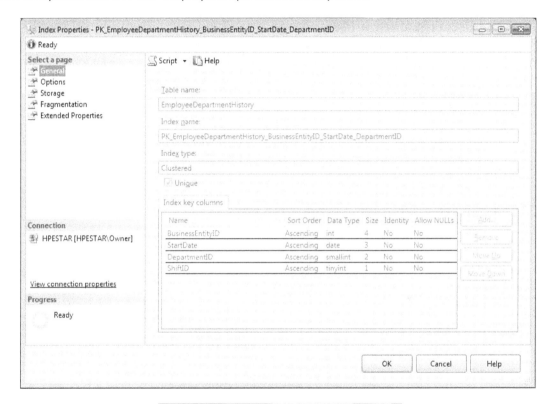

CHAPTER 3: Basic Concepts of Client-Server Computing

Diagram of EmployeeDepartmentHistory and Related Tables

EmployeeDepartmentHistory is a simple junction table with three FOREIGN KEYs to the Employee, Shift and Department tables respectively.

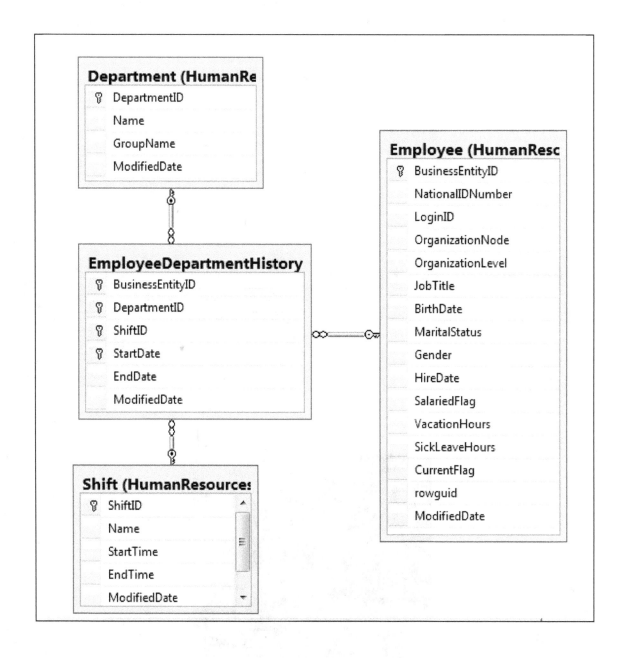

Index Description in Data Dictionary

The indexes listing for Product, SalesOrderHeader & SalesOrderDetail tables.

```
USE AdventureWorks2012;

SELECT  objtype                     AS ObjectType,
        'Sales.SalesOrderHeader'    AS TableName,
        objname                     AS ObjectName,
        value                       AS [Description]
FROM fn_listextendedproperty (NULL, 'schema', 'Sales', 'table', 'SalesOrderHeader', 'index', default)


UNION


SELECT objtype, 'Sales.SalesOrderDetail', objname, value
FROM fn_listextendedproperty (NULL, 'schema', 'Sales', 'table', 'SalesOrderDetail', 'index', default)


UNION


SELECT objtype, 'Production.Product', objname,  value
FROM fn_listextendedproperty (NULL, 'schema', 'Production', 'table', 'Product', 'index', default)
ORDER BY TableName;
GO
```

ObjectType	TableName	ObjectName	Description
INDEX	Production.Product	AK_Product_Name	Unique nonclustered index.
INDEX	Production.Product	AK_Product_ProductNumber	Unique nonclustered index.
INDEX	Production.Product	AK_Product_rowguid	Unique nonclustered index. Used to support replication samples.
INDEX	Production.Product	PK_Product_ProductID	Clustered index created by a primary key constraint.
INDEX	Sales.SalesOrderDetail	AK_SalesOrderDetail_rowguid	Unique nonclustered index. Used to support replication samples.
INDEX	Sales.SalesOrderDetail	IX_SalesOrderDetail_ProductID	Nonclustered index.
INDEX	Sales.SalesOrderDetail	PK_SalesOrderDetail_SalesOrderID_SalesOrderDetailID	Clustered index created by a primary key constraint.
INDEX	Sales.SalesOrderHeader	AK_SalesOrderHeader_rowguid	Unique nonclustered index. Used to support replication samples.
INDEX	Sales.SalesOrderHeader	AK_SalesOrderHeader_SalesOrderNumber	Unique nonclustered index.
INDEX	Sales.SalesOrderHeader	IX_SalesOrderHeader_CustomerID	Nonclustered index.
INDEX	Sales.SalesOrderHeader	IX_SalesOrderHeader_SalesPersonID	Nonclustered index.
INDEX	Sales.SalesOrderHeader	PK_SalesOrderHeader_SalesOrderID	Clustered index created by a primary key constraint.

Constraint - Database Object

The PRIMARY KEY constraint ensures that each row has a unique ID. The FOREIGN KEY constraint ensures that the FK points to (references) a valid PK. CHECK constraint enforces formulas (check clauses) defined for a column such as OrderQty > 0. If the formula evaluates to TRUE, the CHECK constraint satisfied, otherwise ERROR condition is generated by the database engine. SSMS screenshot shows a CHECK constraints listing query and results in the Northwind database.

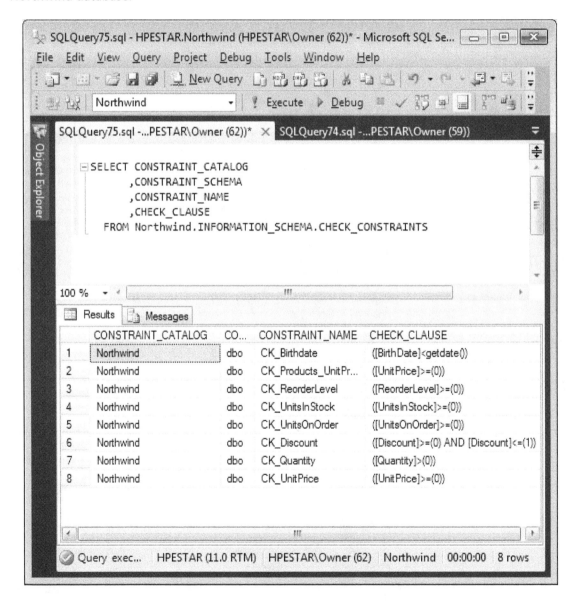

PRIMARY KEY & FOREIGN KEY Constraint Descriptions in Data Dictionary

Query to retrieve constraint descriptions (extended properties) for Product, SalesOrderHeader & SalesOrderDetail tables. Note: *description* not definition.

```
USE AdventureWorks2012;

-- UNION of 3 result sets
SELECT objtype AS ObjectType, 'Sales.SalesOrderHeader' AS TableName,
        objname as ObjectName, value AS [Description]
FROM fn_listextendedproperty (NULL, 'schema', 'Sales', 'table', 'SalesOrderHeader', 'constraint', default)
WHERE left(convert(varchar,value),7)='Foreign' or left(convert(varchar,value),7)='Primary'
UNION
SELECT objtype, 'Sales.SalesOrderDetail', objname,  value
FROM fn_listextendedproperty (NULL, 'schema', 'Sales', 'table', 'SalesOrderDetail', 'constraint', default)
WHERE left(convert(varchar,value),7)='Foreign' or left(convert(varchar,value),7)='Primary'
UNION
SELECT objtype, 'Production.Product', objname,  value
FROM fn_listextendedproperty (NULL, 'schema', 'Production', 'table', 'Product', 'constraint', default)
WHERE left(convert(varchar,value),7)='Foreign' or left(convert(varchar,value),7)='Primary'
ORDER BY TableName, ObjectName DESC;
GO
```

ObjectType	TableName	ObjectName	Description
CONSTRAINT	Production.Product	PK_Product_ProductID	Primary key (clustered) constraint
CONSTRAINT	Production.Product	FK_Product_UnitMeasure_WeightUnitMeasureCode	Foreign key constraint referencing UnitMeasure.UnitMeasureCode.
CONSTRAINT	Production.Product	FK_Product_UnitMeasure_SizeUnitMeasureCode	Foreign key constraint referencing UnitMeasure.UnitMeasureCode.
CONSTRAINT	Production.Product	FK_Product_ProductSubcategory_ProductSubcategoryID	Foreign key constraint referencing ProductSubcategory.ProductSubcategoryID.
CONSTRAINT	Production.Product	FK_Product_ProductModel_ProductModelID	Foreign key constraint referencing ProductModel.ProductModelID.
CONSTRAINT	Sales.SalesOrderDetail	PK_SalesOrderDetail_SalesOrderID_SalesOrderDetailID	Primary key (clustered) constraint
CONSTRAINT	Sales.SalesOrderDetail	FK_SalesOrderDetail_SpecialOfferProduct_SpecialOfferIDProductID	Foreign key constraint referencing SpecialOfferProduct.SpecialOfferIDProductID.
CONSTRAINT	Sales.SalesOrderDetail	FK_SalesOrderDetail_SalesOrderHeader_SalesOrderID	Foreign key constraint referencing SalesOrderHeader.PurchaseOrderID.
CONSTRAINT	Sales.SalesOrderHeader	PK_SalesOrderHeader_SalesOrderID	Primary key (clustered) constraint
CONSTRAINT	Sales.SalesOrderHeader	FK_SalesOrderHeader_ShipMethod_ShipMethodID	Foreign key constraint referencing ShipMethod.ShipMethodID.
CONSTRAINT	Sales.SalesOrderHeader	FK_SalesOrderHeader_SalesTerritory_TerritoryID	Foreign key constraint referencing SalesTerritory.TerritoryID.
CONSTRAINT	Sales.SalesOrderHeader	FK_SalesOrderHeader_SalesPerson_SalesPersonID	Foreign key constraint referencing SalesPerson.SalesPersonID.
CONSTRAINT	Sales.SalesOrderHeader	FK_SalesOrderHeader_Customer_CustomerID	Foreign key constraint referencing Customer.CustomerID.
CONSTRAINT	Sales.SalesOrderHeader	FK_SalesOrderHeader_CurrencyRate_CurrencyRateID	Foreign key constraint referencing CurrencyRate.CurrencyRateID.
CONSTRAINT	Sales.SalesOrderHeader	FK_SalesOrderHeader_CreditCard_CreditCardID	Foreign key constraint referencing CreditCard.CreditCardID.
CONSTRAINT	Sales.SalesOrderHeader	FK_SalesOrderHeader_Address_ShipToAddressID	Foreign key constraint referencing Address.AddressID.
CONSTRAINT	Sales.SalesOrderHeader	FK_SalesOrderHeader_Address_BillToAddressID	Foreign key constraint referencing Address.AddressID.

View - Database Object

A SELECT query, with some restrictions, can be repackaged as view and thus become a server-side object, a coveted status, from "homeless" to "mansion". The creation of view is very simple, basically a name assignment is required as shown in the following demonstration. As soon as the CREATE VIEW statement is executed successfully the query, unknown to the SQL Server so far, becomes an "official" SQL Server database object, stored in the database. A view, a virtual table, can be used just like a table in SELECT queries. A note about the query: **the column aliases FirstAuthor and SecondAuthor cannot be used in the WHERE clause, only in the ORDER BY clause if present.**

SELECT results from views require ORDER BY if sorting is desired. There is no way around it.

```
USE pubs;
GO
```

```
CREATE VIEW vAuthorsInSameCity
AS
SELECT          FirstAuthor      = CONCAT(au1.au_fname,' ', au1.au_lname),
                SecondAuthor     = CONCAT(au2.au_fname,' ', au2.au_lname),
                FirstCity        = au1.city,
                SecondCity       = au2.city
FROM    authors au1
     INNER JOIN authors au2
     ON au1.city = au2.city
WHERE   CONCAT(au1.au_fname,' ', au1.au_lname) < CONCAT(au2.au_fname,' ', au2.au_lname)
GO
```

```
SELECT * FROM vAuthorsInSameCity
ORDER BY FirstAuthor, SecondAuthor
GO
-- (13 row(s) affected) - Partial results.
```

FirstAuthor	SecondAuthor	FirstCity	SecondCity
Abraham Bennet	Cheryl Carson	Berkeley	Berkeley
Albert Ringer	Anne Ringer	Salt Lake City	Salt Lake City
Ann Dull	Sheryl Hunter	Palo Alto	Palo Alto
Dean Straight	Dirk Stringer	Oakland	Oakland
Dean Straight	Livia Karsen	Oakland	Oakland
Dean Straight	Marjorie Green	Oakland	Oakland
Dean Straight	Stearns MacFeather	Oakland	Oakland
Dirk Stringer	Livia Karsen	Oakland	Oakland

View Descriptions in Data Dictionary

Query to list view descriptions in selected schemas.

```
USE AdventureWorks2012;
SELECT   CONCAT('Sales.', objname COLLATE DATABASE_DEFAULT)          AS ViewName,
         value                                                        AS [Description]
FROM fn_listextendedproperty (NULL, 'schema', 'Sales', 'view', default, NULL, NULL)
UNION
SELECT   CONCAT('Production.', objname COLLATE DATABASE_DEFAULT),  value
FROM fn_listextendedproperty (NULL, 'schema', 'Production', 'view', default, NULL, NULL)
UNION
SELECT   CONCAT('HumanResources.', objname COLLATE DATABASE_DEFAULT),  value
FROM fn_listextendedproperty (NULL, 'schema', 'HumanResources', 'view', default, NULL, NULL)
UNION
SELECT   CONCAT('Person.', objname COLLATE DATABASE_DEFAULT),   value
FROM fn_listextendedproperty (NULL, 'schema', 'Person', 'view', default, NULL, NULL)
ORDER BY ViewName;  -- (18 row(s) affected) - Partial results.
```

ViewName	Description
HumanResources.vEmployee	Employee names and addresses.
HumanResources.vEmployeeDepartment	Returns employee name, title, and current department.
HumanResources.vEmployeeDepartmentHistory	Returns employee name and current and previous departments.
HumanResources.vJobCandidate	Job candidate names and resumes.

CREATE Indexed View for Business Critical Queries

An indexed view is stored like a table unlike a standard view which is a virtual table with a query
that is evaluated upon view invocation. Performance is the main benefit of an indexed view, but
it comes at a cost: it slows down INSERTs and other operations in the underlying tables.

```
IF OBJECT_ID ('Sales.vSalesByDateByProduct', 'V') IS NOT NULL DROP VIEW Sales.vSalesByDateByProduct ;
GO
CREATE VIEW Sales.vSalesByDateByProduct WITH SCHEMABINDING  AS
   SELECT OrderDate, ProductNumber, SUM(LineTotal) AS TotalSales, COUNT_BIG(*) AS Items
   FROM Sales.SalesOrderDetail AS sod INNER JOIN Sales.SalesOrderHeader AS soh
     ON soh.SalesOrderID = sod.SalesOrderID   INNER JOIN Production.Product p ON sod.ProductID=p.ProductID
     GROUP BY OrderDate, ProductNumber;
GO
CREATE UNIQUE CLUSTERED INDEX idxVSalesCI ON Sales.vSalesByDateByProduct (OrderDate, ProductNumber);
GO
SELECT * FROM Sales.vSalesByDateByProduct ORDER BY OrderDate, ProductNumber;
GO  -- (26878 row(s) affected) - Partial results.
```

OrderDate	ProductNumber	TotalSales	Items
2005-07-01 00:00:00.000	BK-M82B-38	44549.868000	7
2005-07-01 00:00:00.000	BK-M82B-42	32399.904000	8
2005-07-01 00:00:00.000	BK-M82B-44	46574.862000	7

CHAPTER 3: Basic Concepts of Client-Server Computing

Graphical View Designer

A view can be designed graphically or an existing view altered by using the Design option on the View drop-down menu in SSMS Object Explorer. First we create a view, then enter the graphical view designer to take a look.

```
USE [Northwind];
GO
CREATE VIEW [dbo].[ListOfProducts] AS
SELECT Categories.CategoryName as Category, ProductName, CompanyName AS Supplier
FROM Categories          INNER JOIN Products  ON Categories.CategoryID = Products.CategoryID
                         INNER JOIN Suppliers  ON Suppliers.SupplierID = Products.SupplierID
WHERE (((Products.Discontinued)=0));
GO
```

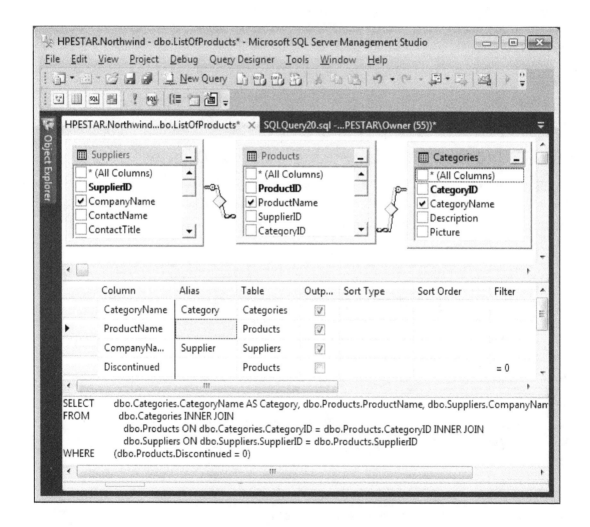

Stored Procedure: Server-Side Program

Stored procedures are T-SQL programs with optional input/output parameters. They vary from very simply to extremely complex. Following is the query which we will transform into a stored procedure, a server-side database object. Typical stored procedure returns table-like results to the client application software just like a SELECT query. That is though not a requirement.

```
USE AdventureWorks2012;
GO
SELECT       P.Name                    AS Product,
             L.Name                    AS [Inventory Location],
             SUM(PI.Quantity)          AS [Qty Available]
FROM Production.Product AS P
   INNER JOIN Production.ProductInventory AS PI
             ON P.ProductID = PI.ProductID
   INNER JOIN Production.Location AS L
             ON PI.LocationID = L.LocationID
   INNER JOIN Production.ProductSubcategory SC
             ON P.ProductSubcategoryID = SC.ProductSubcategoryID
WHERE SC.Name = 'Touring Bikes'
GROUP BY P.Name, L.Name
ORDER BY P.Name;
GO
-- (44 row(s) affected) - Partial results.
```

Product	Inventory Location	Qty Available
Touring-1000 Blue, 46	Final Assembly	86
Touring-1000 Blue, 46	Finished Goods Storage	99
Touring-1000 Blue, 50	Final Assembly	81
Touring-1000 Blue, 50	Finished Goods Storage	67
Touring-1000 Blue, 54	Final Assembly	60
Touring-1000 Blue, 54	Finished Goods Storage	73
Touring-1000 Blue, 60	Final Assembly	99
Touring-1000 Blue, 60	Finished Goods Storage	30
Touring-1000 Yellow, 46	Final Assembly	83
Touring-1000 Yellow, 46	Finished Goods Storage	65
Touring-1000 Yellow, 50	Final Assembly	62
Touring-1000 Yellow, 50	Finished Goods Storage	75
Touring-1000 Yellow, 54	Final Assembly	40
Touring-1000 Yellow, 54	Finished Goods Storage	35
Touring-1000 Yellow, 60	Final Assembly	100

Stored Procedure with Input Parameters

To make the stored procedure even more useful, we replace the literal 'Touring Bikes' with an input parameter.

```
CREATE PROC uspProductInventoryLocation @Subcategory nvarchar(50)
AS
BEGIN
SELECT          P.Name                          AS Product,
                L.Name                          AS [Inventory Location],
                SUM(PI.Quantity)                AS [Qty Available]
FROM Production.Product AS P
    INNER JOIN Production.ProductInventory AS PI
            ON P.ProductID = PI.ProductID
    INNER JOIN Production.Location AS L
            ON PI.LocationID = L.LocationID
    INNER JOIN Production.ProductSubcategory SC
            ON P.ProductSubcategoryID = SC.ProductSubcategoryID
WHERE SC.Name = @Subcategory
GROUP BY P.Name, L.Name
ORDER BY P.Name;
END
GO
```

```
-- Execute stored procedure with parameter
EXEC uspProductInventoryLocation 'Touring Bikes';
-- (44 row(s) affected)
```

```
EXEC uspProductInventoryLocation 'Mountain Bikes';        -- (64 row(s) affected) - Partial results.
```

Product	Inventory Location	Qty Available
Mountain-100 Black, 38	Final Assembly	56
Mountain-100 Black, 38	Finished Goods Storage	99
Mountain-100 Black, 42	Final Assembly	116
Mountain-100 Black, 42	Finished Goods Storage	78
Mountain-100 Black, 44	Final Assembly	100
Mountain-100 Black, 44	Finished Goods Storage	49
Mountain-100 Black, 48	Final Assembly	65
Mountain-100 Black, 48	Finished Goods Storage	88
Mountain-100 Silver, 38	Final Assembly	100
Mountain-100 Silver, 38	Finished Goods Storage	49
Mountain-100 Silver, 42	Final Assembly	65
Mountain-100 Silver, 42	Finished Goods Storage	88
Mountain-100 Silver, 44	Final Assembly	75
Mountain-100 Silver, 44	Finished Goods Storage	83
Mountain-100 Silver, 48	Final Assembly	102

Stored Procedure Descriptions in Data Dictionary

Query to list stored procedure descriptions in selected schemas.

```
USE AdventureWorks2012;

SELECT
        CONCAT('dbo.', objname COLLATE DATABASE_DEFAULT)              AS SprocName,
        value                                                        AS [Description]
FROM fn_listextendedproperty (NULL, 'schema', 'dbo', 'procedure', default, NULL, NULL)
WHERE LEN(convert(nvarchar(max),value)) > 4
UNION
SELECT
        CONCAT('dbo.', objname COLLATE DATABASE_DEFAULT),
        value
FROM fn_listextendedproperty (NULL, 'schema', 'HumanResources', 'procedure', default, NULL, NULL)
ORDER BY SprocName;
```

SprocName	Description
dbo.uspGetBillOfMaterials	Stored procedure using a recursive query to return a multi-level bill of material for the specified ProductID.
dbo.uspGetEmployeeManagers	Stored procedure using a recursive query to return the direct and indirect managers of the specified employee.
dbo.uspGetManagerEmployees	Stored procedure using a recursive query to return the direct and indirect employees of the specified manager.
dbo.uspGetWhereUsedProductID	Stored procedure using a recursive query to return all components or assemblies that directly or indirectly use the specified ProductID.
dbo.uspLogError	Logs error information in the ErrorLog table about the error that caused execution to jump to the CATCH block of a TRY...CATCH construct. Should be executed from within the scope of a CATCH block otherwise it will return without inserting error information.
dbo.uspPrintError	Prints error information about the error that caused execution to jump to the CATCH block of a TRY...CATCH construct. Should be executed from within the scope of a CATCH block otherwise it will return without printing any error information.
dbo.uspUpdateEmployeeHireInfo	Updates the Employee table and inserts a new row in the EmployeePayHistory table with the values specified in the input parameters.
dbo.uspUpdateEmployeeLogin	Updates the Employee table with the values specified in the input parameters for the given BusinessEntityID.
dbo.uspUpdateEmployeePersonalInfo	Updates the Employee table with the values specified in the input parameters for the given EmployeeID.

Trigger: Event Fired Server-Side Program

Trigger is like a stored procedure with four differences:

➢ Trigger is fired by an event such as table insert not by a call like a stored procedure.
➢ Trigger has the deleted (old row copy) and inserted (new row copy) tables available.
➢ Trigger does not have input/output parameter option.
➢ Trigger never returns table-like results.

Trigger to synchronize data in StateTaxFreeBondArchive table if data is inserted or updated in the StateTaxFreeBond table.

```
CREATE TRIGGER trgFillInMissingCouponRate

ON [dbo].StateTaxFreeBond

FOR INSERT,UPDATE

AS

BEGIN

    UPDATE StateTaxFreeBondArchive

        SET CouponRate = isnull(i.CouponRate,m.CouponRate)

    FROM StateTaxFreeBondArchive m

        INNER JOIN inserted i

            ON m.MBCID = i.MBCID

END
GO
```

Once a trigger is compiled, it is active and working silently in the background whenever insert, update or delete event fires it up.

It is important to note that there is a downside to the trigger "stealth" operation: if a trigger is dropped , it may not be noticed as part of the day-to-day operation. This behaviour is unlike stored procedure whereby if dropped, it causes error in the calling application software which can be noticed by users.

Function: Read-Only Server-Side Program

A user-defined function is also a program like a stored procedure, however, **no database change can be performed within a function, read only**. The database can be changed both in a trigger and a stored procedure. The following T-SQL script demonstrates the creation and use of a table-valued user-defined function. The other function type is scalar-valued, returns only a single value.

```
CREATE FUNCTION dbo.ufnSplitCommaDelimitedIntegerString (@NumberList nvarchar(max))
RETURNS @SplitList TABLE ( Element INT )
AS
 BEGIN
    DECLARE @Pointer   int,
         @Element nvarchar(32)
    SET @NumberList = LTRIM(RTRIM(@NumberList))
    IF ( RIGHT(@NumberList, 1) != ',' )
     SET @NumberList=@NumberList + ','
    SET @Pointer = CHARINDEX(',', @NumberList, 1)
    IF REPLACE(@NumberList, ',', '') <> ''
     BEGIN
       WHILE ( @Pointer > 0 )
        BEGIN
          SET @Element = LTRIM(RTRIM(LEFT(@NumberList, @Pointer - 1)))
          IF ( @Element <> '' )
           INSERT INTO @SplitList
           VALUES    (CONVERT(int, @Element))
          SET @NumberList = RIGHT(@NumberList,
                  LEN(@NumberList) - @Pointer  )
          SET @Pointer = CHARINDEX(',', @NumberList, 1)
        END
     END
    RETURN
 END;
GO
SELECT * FROM  dbo.ufnSplitCommaDelimitedIntegerString ('1, 2, 4, 8, 16, 32, 64, 128, 256');
```

Element
1
2
4
8
16
32
64
128
256

CHAPTER 3: Basic Concepts of Client-Server Computing

User-Defined Function Descriptions in Data Dictionary

Query to list user-defined function descriptions in the default "dbo" schema. "dbo" stands for database owner, a database role.

```
USE AdventureWorks2012;
GO

SELECT
        CONCAT('dbo.', objname COLLATE DATABASE_DEFAULT)              AS UDFName,
        value                                                        AS [Description]
FROM fn_listextendedproperty (NULL, 'schema', 'dbo', 'function', default, NULL, NULL)
WHERE LEN(convert(nvarchar(max),value)) > 4
ORDER BY UDFName;
GO
```

UDFName	Description
dbo.ufnGetAccountingEndDate	Scalar function used in the uSalesOrderHeader trigger to set the starting account date.
dbo.ufnGetAccountingStartDate	Scalar function used in the uSalesOrderHeader trigger to set the ending account date.
dbo.ufnGetContactInformation	Table value function returning the first name, last name, job title and contact type for a given contact.
dbo.ufnGetDocumentStatusText	Scalar function returning the text representation of the Status column in the Document table.
dbo.ufnGetProductDealerPrice	Scalar function returning the dealer price for a given product on a particular order date.
dbo.ufnGetProductListPrice	Scalar function returning the list price for a given product on a particular order date.
dbo.ufnGetProductStandardCost	Scalar function returning the standard cost for a given product on a particular order date.
dbo.ufnGetPurchaseOrderStatusText	Scalar function returning the text representation of the Status column in the PurchaseOrderHeader table.
dbo.ufnGetSalesOrderStatusText	Scalar function returning the text representation of the Status column in the SalesOrderHeader table.
dbo.ufnGetStock	Scalar function returning the quantity of inventory in LocationID 6 (Miscellaneous Storage)for a specified ProductID.
dbo.ufnLeadingZeros	Scalar function used by the Sales.Customer table to help set the account number

Sequence - Database Object

The INT IDENTITY(1,1) function commonly used as **SURROGATE PRIMARY KEY** is limited to the host table. Sequence object, new in SQL Server 2012, can be shared by tables and programs. T-SQL script to demonstrate how two tables can share an integer sequence.

```
USE AdventureWorks2012;
GO
CREATE SEQUENCE CustomerSequence as INT
START WITH 1  INCREMENT BY 1;
GO
CREATE TABLE LONDONCustomer
(
        CustomerID       INT PRIMARY KEY,
        Name             NVARCHAR(64) UNIQUE,
        ModifiedDate     DATE default (CURRENT_TIMESTAMP)    );
GO
CREATE TABLE NYCCustomer
(
        CustomerID       INT PRIMARY KEY,
        Name             NVARCHAR(64) UNIQUE,
        ModifiedDate     DATE default (CURRENT_TIMESTAMP)    );
GO
INSERT NYCCustomer (CustomerID, Name)
VALUES
        (NEXT VALUE FOR CustomerSequence, 'Richard Blackstone'),
        (NEXT VALUE FOR CustomerSequence, 'Anna Smithfield');
GO
SELECT * FROM NYCCustomer;
```

CustomerID	Name	ModifiedDate
1	Richard Blackstone	2016-07-18
2	Anna Smithfield	2016-07-18

```
INSERT LONDONCustomer (CustomerID, Name)
VALUES
        (NEXT VALUE FOR CustomerSequence, 'Kevin Lionheart'),
        (NEXT VALUE FOR CustomerSequence, 'Linda Wakefield');
GO

SELECT * FROM LONDONCustomer;
```

CustomerID	Name	ModifiedDate
3	Kevin Lionheart	2016-07-18
4	Linda Wakefield	2016-07-18

ROW_NUMBER() and Ranking Functions

Ranking functions (window functions), introduced with SQL Server 2005, provide sequencing and ranking items in a partition or all. ROW_NUMBER() (sequence) function is the most used.

```
SELECT   CustomerID,
         CONVERT(date, OrderDate)                          AS OrderDate,
         RANK() OVER (    PARTITION BY CustomerID
                          ORDER BY OrderDate DESC)          AS RankNo
FROM   AdventureWorks2012.Sales.SalesOrderHeader
ORDER  BY CustomerID,  RankNo;
GO
-- (31465 row(s) affected) - Partial results.
```

CustomerID	OrderDate	RankNo
11014	2007-11-01	1
11014	2007-09-24	2
11015	2007-07-22	1
11016	2007-08-13	1
11017	2008-04-16	1
11017	2007-07-05	2
11017	2005-07-15	3
11018	2008-04-26	1
11018	2007-07-20	2
11018	2005-07-20	3
11019	2008-07-15	1
11019	2008-07-14	2
11019	2008-06-12	3
11019	2008-06-02	4
11019	2008-06-01	5
11019	2008-04-28	6
11019	2008-04-19	7
11019	2008-03-22	8
11019	2008-03-11	9
11019	2008-02-23	10
11019	2008-01-24	11
11019	2007-11-26	12
11019	2007-11-09	13
11019	2007-10-30	14
11019	2007-09-14	15
11019	2007-09-05	16
11019	2007-08-16	17
11020	2007-07-02	1

Partition data by CustomerID and rank it OrderDate DESC (most recent orders first).

```
SELECT *
FROM   (SELECT CustomerID,
          CONVERT(date, OrderDate)        AS OrderDate,
          RANK() OVER (
            PARTITION BY CustomerID
            ORDER BY OrderDate DESC)       AS RankNo
        FROM   AdventureWorks2012.Sales.SalesOrderHeader)  x -- derived table
WHERE  RankNo  BETWEEN 1 AND 4
ORDER  BY CustomerID;
GO
-- (29383 row(s) affected)  - Partial results.
```

CustomerID	OrderDate	RankNo
11675	2007-08-13	1
11675	2006-04-27	2
11676	2008-06-11	1
11676	2008-02-21	2
11677	2008-06-02	1
11677	2008-03-24	2
11677	2008-03-17	3
11677	2008-03-07	4
11678	2007-08-09	1
11678	2006-04-12	2
11679	2008-06-01	1
11679	2008-04-15	2
11680	2008-07-22	1
11680	2008-03-04	2
11681	2008-05-28	1
11681	2007-09-08	2
11682	2008-06-11	1
11682	2008-03-08	2
11683	2007-08-11	1
11683	2006-04-07	2
11684	2008-06-14	1
11684	2008-01-02	2
11685	2008-06-15	1
11685	2007-09-12	2
11686	2007-10-26	1
11686	2007-09-09	2
11687	2007-12-23	1
11687	2007-10-14	2
11688	2007-08-18	1
11688	2006-04-04	2
11689	2008-03-05	1
11689	2008-02-27	2

Query to compare RANK, DENSE_RANK and NTILE.

```
USE AdventureWorks;

SELECT c.AccountNumber                              AS CustAccount,
    FLOOR(h.SubTotal / 1000)                        AS [SubTotal (Thousands $)],
    ROW_NUMBER() OVER(
        ORDER BY FLOOR(h.SubTotal /1000) DESC)       AS RowNumber,
    RANK()  OVER(
        ORDER BY FLOOR(h.SubTotal /1000) DESC)      AS Rank,
    DENSE_RANK()  OVER(
        ORDER BY FLOOR(h.SubTotal /1000) DESC)      AS DenseRank,
    NTILE(5)  OVER(
        ORDER BY FLOOR(h.SubTotal /1000) DESC)      AS NTile
FROM   Sales.Customer c
    INNER JOIN Sales.SalesOrderHeader h
        ON c.CustomerID = h.CustomerID
    INNER JOIN Sales.SalesTerritory t
        ON h.TerritoryID = t.TerritoryID
WHERE  t.Name = 'Germany'
        AND OrderDate >= '20040101' AND OrderDate  <  DATEADD(yy, 1, '20040101' )
        AND SubTotal >= 4000.0
ORDER  BY RowNumber;
```

CustAccount	SubTotal (Thousands $)	RowNumber	Rank	DenseRank	NTile
AW00000230	100.00	1	1	1	1
AW00000230	88.00	2	2	2	1
AW00000302	77.00	3	3	3	1
AW00000320	68.00	4	4	4	1
AW00000536	68.00	5	4	4	1
AW00000536	64.00	6	6	5	1
AW00000266	58.00	7	7	6	1
AW00000302	44.00	8	8	7	2
AW00000687	43.00	9	9	8	2
AW00000482	36.00	10	10	9	2
AW00000176	36.00	11	10	9	2
AW00000464	35.00	12	12	10	2
AW00000320	35.00	13	12	10	2
AW00000176	34.00	14	14	11	2
AW00000464	34.00	15	14	11	3

Dynamic SQL To Soar Beyond the Limits of Static SQL

Static (regular) T-SQL syntax does not accept variables at all places in a query. With dynamic SQL we can overcome the limitation. Dynamic SQL script uses table list metadata from the INFORMATION_SCHEMA.TABLES system view to build a COUNT() query for all tables. COUNT(*) returns 4 bytes integer. For large values COUNT_BIG() returns an 8 bytes integer.

```
DECLARE @SQL nvarchar(max) = '', @Schema sysname, @Table sysname;
SELECT TOP 20 @SQL = CONCAT(@SQL , 'SELECT "',QUOTENAME(TABLE_SCHEMA),'.',
      QUOTENAME(TABLE_NAME),'"',
        '= COUNT(*) FROM ', QUOTENAME(TABLE_SCHEMA),'.',QUOTENAME(TABLE_NAME) , ';',
      CHAR(10))
FROM INFORMATION_SCHEMA.TABLES
WHERE TABLE_TYPE='BASE TABLE';
PRINT @SQL;          -- Test & debug - Partial results.
```

```
SELECT "[Production].[BillOfMaterials]"= COUNT(*) FROM [Production].[BillOfMaterials];
SELECT "[Production].[Culture]"= COUNT(*) FROM [Production].[Culture];
```

```
EXEC sp_executesql @SQL   -- Dynamic SQL query execution
-- Partial results.
```

```
[Production].[ScrapReason]
16
```

```
[HumanResources].[Shift]
3
```

Parameterized Dynamic SQL Query Execution

The dynamic SQL string has a parameterized query. It can only be executed if the parameter(s) is supplied when dynamic execution is called.

```
DECLARE @LastName varchar(30) = 'O''Brien';
DECLARE @DynamicSQL nvarchar(max)= 'SELECT BusinessEntityID, FirstName, LastName
              FROM AdventureWorks2012.Person.Person ';
SET @DynamicSQL = CONCAT(@DynamicSQL, 'WHERE LastName = @pLastName');
PRINT @DynamicSQL;   -- testing & debugging
```

```
EXEC sp_executesql  @DynamicSQL, N'@pLastName varchar(40)', @pLastName = @LastName;
```

BusinessEntityID	FirstName	LastName
1553	Tim	O'Brien

CHAPTER 3: Basic Concepts of Client-Server Computing

Built-in System Functions

SQL Server T-SQL language has a large collection of system functions such as date & time, string and math function. The nested REPLACE string function can be used to remove unwanted characters from a string.

```
DECLARE @text nvarchar(128) = '#1245! $99^@';
SELECT REPLACE(REPLACE(REPLACE(REPLACE(REPLACE(REPLACE(REPLACE(REPLACE(REPLACE(@text,
    '!',''),'@',''),'#',''),'$',''),'%',''),'^',''),'&',''),'*',''),' ','');    -- 124599
```

All the system function are listed in SSMS Object Explorer under the Programmability tab.

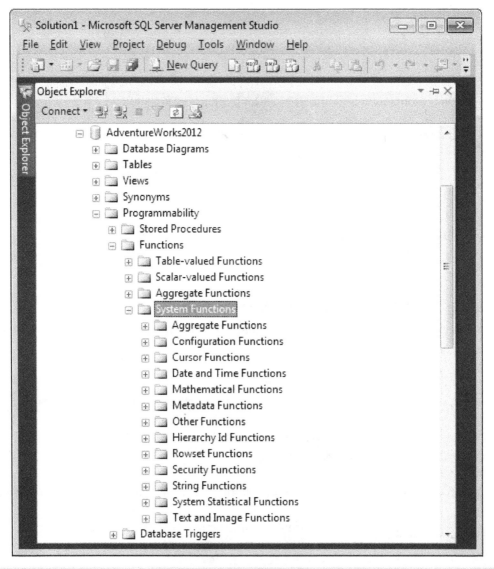

Local Variables & Table Variables in T-SQL

Local variables with different data types have scope of a batch or a stored procedure/trigger/function. Note that a "GO" in T-SQL script indicates end of batch, therefore the end of scope for local variables. Table variable is a virtual table with similar scope to local variable. Script to demonstrate local and table variables.

```
DECLARE @i INT;  SET @i = 999;

SELECT @i + @i;
-- 1998

SELECT @i = 555;  -- assignment
SELECT @i + @i;
GO
-- 1110

DECLARE @i INT = 999;              -- new in SQL Server 2008
SET @i += 1;                       -- new in SQL Server 2008

SELECT @i;
GO
-- 1000

DECLARE @OrderShipperJunction TABLE                    -- Table variable
  (
    ShipperID          SMALLINT IDENTITY ( 1, 1 ) PRIMARY KEY,
    ShipperName        NVARCHAR(64),
    PurchaseOrderID    INT,
    ShipDate           DATE DEFAULT (CURRENT_TIMESTAMP),
    FreightCost        SMALLMONEY
  ) ;
INSERT @OrderShipperJunction
    (ShipperName,
     PurchaseOrderID,
     FreightCost)
VALUES('Custom Motor Bike Distributor',     11111,    177.34)

SELECT * FROM   @OrderShipperJunction
GO
```

ShipperID	ShipperName	PurchaseOrderID	ShipDate	FreightCost
1	Custom Motor Bike Distributor	11111	2016-07-18	177.34

CHAPTER 3: Basic Concepts of Client-Server Computing

Metadata Visibility Through System Views

The system views provide SQL Server and database metadata which can be used just for viewing in SSMS Object Explorer or programmatically in T-SQL scripts. The system views are based on system tables which are no longer accessible since SQL Server 2005. The system view sys.objects contains all the basic info on each and every user objects in the database with the exception of indexes. Query to retrieve partial data form sys.objects system view.

```
select
    s.name                  as [Schema],
    o.name                  as [Name],
    o.type_desc             as [Type],
    o.create_date           as CreateDate
from    sys.objects o
        inner join sys.schemas s
        on s.schema_id = o.schema_id
where is_ms_shipped = 0
order by [Type], [Schema], [Name]
-- (722 row(s) affected)  -  Partial results.
```

Schema	Name	Type	CreateDate
HumanResources	Department	USER_TABLE	2012-03-14 13:14:19.267
HumanResources	Employee	USER_TABLE	2012-03-14 13:14:19.303
HumanResources	EmployeeDepartmentHistory	USER_TABLE	2012-03-14 13:14:19.313
HumanResources	EmployeePayHistory	USER_TABLE	2012-03-14 13:14:19.320
HumanResources	JobCandidate	USER_TABLE	2012-03-14 13:14:19.337
HumanResources	Shift	USER_TABLE	2012-03-14 13:14:19.593
Person	Address	USER_TABLE	2012-03-14 13:14:19.140
Person	AddressType	USER_TABLE	2012-03-14 13:14:19.150
Person	BusinessEntity	USER_TABLE	2012-03-14 13:14:19.183
Person	BusinessEntityAddress	USER_TABLE	2012-03-14 13:14:19.190
Person	BusinessEntityContact	USER_TABLE	2012-03-14 13:14:19.197
Person	ContactType	USER_TABLE	2012-03-14 13:14:19.207
Person	CountryRegion	USER_TABLE	2012-03-14 13:14:19.220
Person	EmailAddress	USER_TABLE	2012-03-14 13:14:19.290
Person	Password	USER_TABLE	2012-03-14 13:14:19.350
Person	Person	USER_TABLE	2012-03-14 13:14:19.357
Person	PersonPhone	USER_TABLE	2012-03-14 13:14:19.370
Person	PhoneNumberType	USER_TABLE	2012-03-14 13:14:19.377
Person	StateProvince	USER_TABLE	2012-03-14 13:14:19.623
Production	BillOfMaterials	USER_TABLE	2012-03-14 13:14:19.170
Production	Culture	USER_TABLE	2012-03-14 13:14:19.237

Constructing T-SQL Identifiers

Identifiers are the names given to SQL Server & database objects such as linked servers, tables, views or stored procedures.

Very simple rule: **do not include any special character in an identifier other than single underscore (_). Double underscore in an identifier inevitably leads to confusion, loss of database developer productivity.**

Creating good identifiers helps with productivity in database development, administration and maintenance. Using names AccountsPayable1 and AccountsPayable2 as variations for AccountsPayable is not good because the 1,2 suffixes are meaningless. On the other hand AccountsPayableLondon & AccountsPayableNYC are good, meaningful names. The list of identifiers can be enumerated from AdventureWorks2012.sys.objects.

SELECT name FROM AdventureWorks2012.sys.objects ORDER BY name; -- (820 row(s) affected)

Selected results with comments.

Identifier(name)	Style Comment
Account	single word
AddressType	double words CamelCase style
BillOfMaterials	CamelCase (also known as Pascal case)
BusinessEntityContact	CamelCase
CK__ImageStore__67152DD3	double underscore separator, CK prefix for CHECK CONSTRAINT
CK_Document_Status	single underscore separator
CK_EmployeeDepartmentHistory_EndDate	mixed - CamelCase and underscore
DF__ImageStor__is_sy__75634D2A	database engine (system) generated name
sp_creatediagram	old-fashioned, sp prefix for system procedure
syscscolsegments	old-fashioned with abbreviations
ufnGetProductDealerPrice	Hungarian naming, ufn stands for user(-defined) function
vSalesPersonSalesByFiscalYears	Hungarian naming, v prefix is for view

The Use of [] - Square Brackets in Identifiers

Each identifier can be enclosed in square brackets, but not required. If the identifier is the same as a T-SQL reserved keyword, then it is required. Square brackets are also required when the identifier includes a special character such as space. Double quotes can be used also but that becomes very confusing when single quotes are present. The use of brackets is demonstrated in the following T-SQL script.

```
USE Northwind;
```

```
-- Syntax error without brackets since table name has space
SELECT * FROM Order Details;
/* ERROR
Msg 156, Level 15, State 1, Line 3
Incorrect syntax near the keyword 'Order'.
*/
```

```
-- Valid statement with brackets around table name
SELECT * FROM [Order Details];
-- (2155 row(s) affected)
```

```
-- Create and populate table with SELECT INTO
-- Error since ORDER is a reserved keyword
SELECT * INTO Order FROM Orders;
/* ERROR
Msg 156, Level 15, State 1, Line 1
Incorrect syntax near the keyword 'Order'.
*/
```

```
-- With brackets, query is valid
SELECT * INTO [Order] FROM Orders;
-- (830 row(s) affected)
```

When a database object is scripted out in SSMS Object Explore, the identifiers are surrounded with square brackets even when not needed as shown in the following demonstration.

```
CREATE TABLE [dbo].[Order Details](
        [OrderID] [int] NOT NULL,
        [ProductID] [int] NOT NULL,
        [UnitPrice] [money] NOT NULL,
        [Quantity] [smallint] NOT NULL,
        [Discount] [real] NOT NULL,
 CONSTRAINT [PK_Order_Details] PRIMARY KEY CLUSTERED
 (       [OrderID] ASC,
        [ProductID] ASC));
```

CHAPTER 4: Fundamentals of Relational Database Design

Logical Data Modeling

Logical data modeling is the first step in database design. The task can be carried out by systems analysts, subject-matter experts, database designers or lead database developers. Small budget projects usually settle for an experienced database developer in the design role. The database design team spends time with the future users (stakeholders) of the database to find out the expectations and requirements for the new database. As soon as the design team has some basic idea of functional requirements, the iterative process continues with discussing entities (corresponds to tables in the database) and their relationships with the users. For example the Order entity has many to many relationship to the Product entity. A Product occurs in many orders, and an Order may hold many products.

Physical Data Modeling

Physical Data Modeling is the process of translating the logical data model into actual database tables and related objects such as PRIMARY KEY and FOREIGN KEY constraints. If a software tool was used to design the logical data model then the forward engineering feature can be applied to generate SQL scripts to create tables and related database objects. **An important step in this process is the design of indexes to support SQL query performance**. Example for Data Warehouse dimension table implementation.

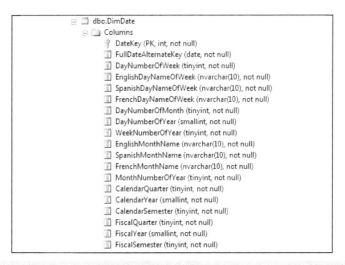

CHAPTER 4: Fundamentals of Relational Database Design

Column Definitions for the FactInternetSales Table

Table columns for a fact table in AdventureWorksDW2012 database. PK stands for PRIMARY KEY, FK for FOREGN KEY. The PRIMARY KEY is a composite of 2 columns: SalesOrderNumber and SalesOrderLineNumber.

The screen image is from SSMS Object Explorer.

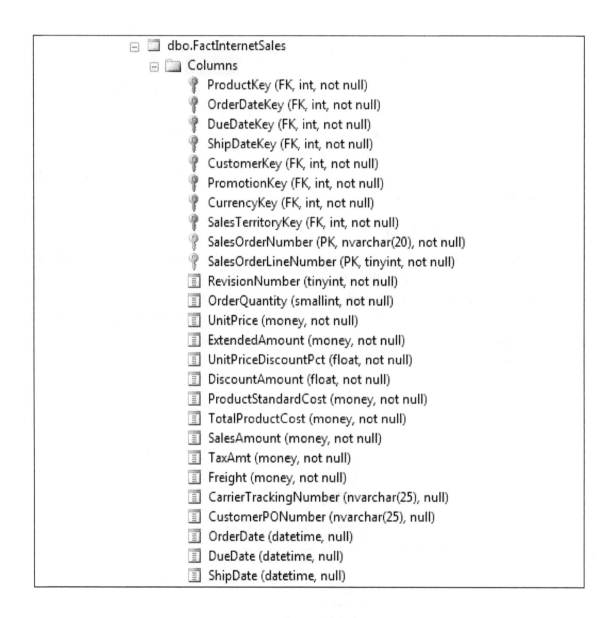

Table Column Data Types

Exact Numerics

bigint	8 byte signed integer	-- Exact Numerics
bit	Boolean	
decimal	5 - 17 bytes decimal number with variable precision	
int	4 byte signed integer	
money	8 byte with ten-thousandth accuracy	
numeric	Same as decimal	
smallint	2 byte signed integer	
smallmoney	4 byte with ten-thousandth accuracy	
tinyint	1 byte signed integer	

Approximate Numerics

float	4 - 8 byte floating point	-- Approximate Numerics
real	4 byte floating point	

Date and Time

date	3 byte date only
datetime	8 byte date & time
datetime2	6 - 8 byte date & time
datetimeoffset	10 byte date & time with time zone
smalldatetime	4 byte date & time
time	5 byte time only

Character Strings

char	Fixed length ASCII character storage - 1 byte for each character	-- Character String
text	Variable-length ASCII data with a maximum string length of 2^31-1 (deprecated)	
varchar	Variable length ASCII character storage	

Unicode Character Strings

nchar	Fixed length UNICODE character storage - 2 bytes for each character
ntext	Variable-length UNICODE data with a maximum string length of 2^30-1 (deprecated)
nvarchar	Variable length UNICODE character storage

Binary Strings

binary	Fixed-length binary data with maximum storage size of 2^31-1 bytes	-- Binary String
image	Variable-length binary data with maximum storage size of 2^31-1 bytes (deprecated)	
varbinary	Variable-length binary data with maximum storage size of 2^31-1 bytes	

Other Data Types

cursor	Contains a reference to a cursor - not for column use
hierarchyid	Represents a position in a tree hierarchy, typically a few bytes up to 892 bytes
sql_variant	Stores values of various SQL Server data types, maximum length of 8016 bytes
table	Store a result set for processing at a later time, not for columns
timestamp	8 byte generated binary number, mechanism for version-stamping table rows
uniqueidentifier	16 byte GUID - Globally Unique Identifier
xml	Stores XML data up to 2GB in size

CHAPTER 4: Fundamentals of Relational Database Design

Date Type max_length, precision, scale & collation_name Listing
Database metadata on data types can be found in types system view.

```
SELECT          name, system_type_id, max_length, precision, scale,
                isnull(collation_name, SPACE(0)) AS collation_name
FROM AdventureWorks2012.sys.types WHERE schema_id = 4 ORDER BY name;
```

name	system_type_id	max_length	precision	scale	collation_name
bigint	127	8	19	0	
binary	173	8000	0	0	
bit	104	1	1	0	
char	175	8000	0	0	SQL_Latin1_General_CP1_CI_AS
date	40	3	10	0	
datetime	61	8	23	3	
datetime2	42	8	27	7	
datetimeoffset	43	10	34	7	
decimal	106	17	38	38	
float	62	8	53	0	
geography	240	-1	0	0	
geometry	240	-1	0	0	
hierarchyid	240	892	0	0	
image	34	16	0	0	
int	56	4	10	0	
money	60	8	19	4	
nchar	239	8000	0	0	SQL_Latin1_General_CP1_CI_AS
ntext	99	16	0	0	SQL_Latin1_General_CP1_CI_AS
numeric	108	17	38	38	
nvarchar	231	8000	0	0	SQL_Latin1_General_CP1_CI_AS
real	59	4	24	0	
smalldatetime	58	4	16	0	
smallint	52	2	5	0	
smallmoney	122	4	10	4	
sql_variant	98	8016	0	0	
sysname	231	256	0	0	SQL_Latin1_General_CP1_CI_AS
text	35	16	0	0	SQL_Latin1_General_CP1_CI_AS
time	41	5	16	7	
timestamp	189	8	0	0	
tinyint	48	1	3	0	
uniqueidentifier	36	16	0	0	
varbinary	165	8000	0	0	
varchar	167	8000	0	0	SQL_Latin1_General_CP1_CI_AS
xml	241	-1	0	0	

U.S. Default Collation SQL_Latin1_General_CP1_CI_AS

Interpretation:

- SQL collation not Windows
- Latin 1 alphabet
- Code page 1 for sorting
- Case insensitive
- Accent sensitive

SQL_Latin1_General_CP1_CI_AS is the default collation of SQL Server 2012 in the United States. Only a handful of experts around the world really understand collations. You first encounter with collation will probably be like the following error.

```
SELECT CONCAT('Production.', objname) AS TableName, value AS [Description]
FROM fn_listextendedproperty (NULL, 'schema', 'Production', 'table', default, NULL, NULL);
GO
/*  Msg 468, Level 16, State 9, Line 1
Cannot resolve the collation conflict between "SQL_Latin1_General_CP1_CI_AS" and
"Latin1_General_CI_AI" in the concat operation.
*/
```

The easiest fix in most collation error cases is placing COLLATE DATABASE_DEFAULT following the right most operator.

```
SELECT CONCAT('Production.', objname COLLATE DATABASE_DEFAULT) AS TableName,
                value AS [Description]
FROM fn_listextendedproperty (NULL, 'schema', 'Production', 'table', default, NULL, NULL);
```

There are a number of articles on the web which deal extensively with collations.

Collation is a column level property. Server and database collations are only defaults. To change the collation of a column, use ALTER TABLE.

```
-- SQL Server Change Column Collation
SELECT * INTO Product FROM AdventureWorks2012.Production.Product;
GO
ALTER TABLE Product ALTER COLUMN Name nvarchar(50) COLLATE SQL_Latin1_General_CP1_CS_AS null;
GO  -- (504 row(s) affected)
```

CHAPTER 4: Fundamentals of Relational Database Design

DATE & DATETIME Temporal Data Types

DATE data type has been introduced with SQL Server 2008. DATETIME on the other hand is around since the inception of SQL Server. A good deal of programming effort goes into supporting hundreds of different string date & time formats. Each country has its own string date formats adding more to the general confusion. As an example in the United States the mdy string date format is used. In the United Kingdom, the dmy format is used. When one looks at a date like 10/11/2015, it is not apparent which date format is it. In a globalized world the data flows freely from one country to another, frequently without adequate documentation, hence the loss of database developer productivity as related to date & time data issues. List of century (CCYY or YYYY) datetime conversions styles (stylenumber >= 100).

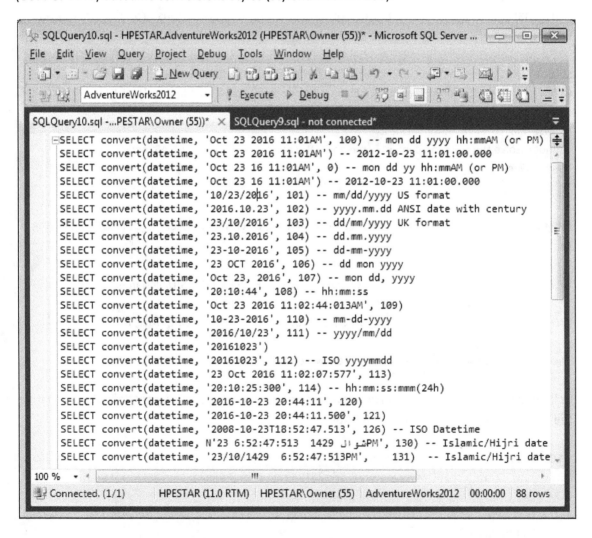

Two Ways of Commenting in T-SQL Scripts

Line comment is prefixed by "--". Multiple lines comment has to be enclosed with "/*" and "*/".

Exploring Database Schemas

A schema - introduced in SQL Server 2005 - is a single-level container of database objects to replace database object "owner" in previous SQL Server versions. **The default schema is "dbo", database owner**. Schemas can be used for functional separation of objects which may be essential in large databases with thousands of tables. The application schemas in AdventureWorks: HumanResources, Production, Purchasing, Sales, and Person. The word "schemas" also used in database terminology to mean table definition scripts or database diagram. Screenshot to display all the schemas in AdventureWorks2012 and to demonstrate the use of the CREATE SCHEMA statement. Database object reference in SQL Server 2012 is: "dbname.schemaname.objectname" like "AdventureWorks2012.Sales.SalesOrderheader".

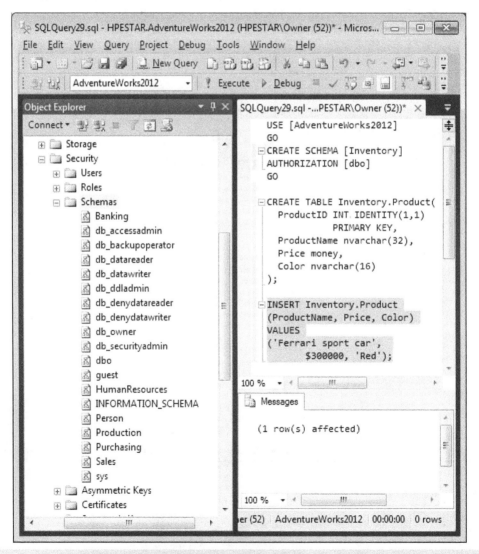

SCHEMA_NAME() Function

The SCHEMA_NAME() function can be used to obtain the name of a schema based on the schema_id parameter. Query to list all 3 database objects with the name "Product" in 3 different schemas.

```
SELECT          CONCAT(SCHEMA_NAME(schema_id),'.',name) as ObjectName,
                name, object_id, schema_id, type, type_desc
FROM sys.objects
WHERE name = 'Product' ORDER BY ObjectName;
```

ObjectName	name	object_id	schema_id	type	type_desc
dbo.Product	Product	264388011	1	U	USER_TABLE
Inventory.Product	Product	1533964541	11	U	USER_TABLE
Production.Product	Product	1973582069	7	U	USER_TABLE

T-SQL query to display all the schemas in AdventureWorks2012.

```
SELECT s.*,  p.name as PrincipalName
FROM AdventureWorks2012.sys.schemas s
 INNER JOIN AdventureWorks2012.sys.database_principals p    ON s.principal_id = p.principal_id
ORDER BY principal_id, s.name;
```

name	schema_id	principal_id	PrincipalName
Banking	10	1	dbo
dbo	1	1	dbo
HumanResources	5	1	dbo
Inventory	11	1	dbo
Person	6	1	dbo
Production	7	1	dbo
Purchasing	8	1	dbo
Sales	9	1	dbo
guest	2	2	guest
INFORMATION_SCHEMA	3	3	INFORMATION_SCHEMA
sys	4	4	sys
db_owner	16384	16384	db_owner
db_accessadmin	16385	16385	db_accessadmin
db_securityadmin	16386	16386	db_securityadmin
db_ddladmin	16387	16387	db_ddladmin
db_backupoperator	16389	16389	db_backupoperator
db_datareader	16390	16390	db_datareader
db_datawriter	16391	16391	db_datawriter
db_denydatareader	16392	16392	db_denydatareader
db_denydatawriter	16393	16393	db_denydatawriter

CHAPTER 4: Fundamentals of Relational Database Design

Tables in HumanResources, Person & Purchasing Schemas

Query to list tables in the above schemas with data dictionary description.

```
USE AdventureWorks2012;
SELECT   CONCAT('Purchasing.', objname COLLATE DATABASE_DEFAULT)      AS TableName,
         value                                                        AS [Description]
FROM fn_listextendedproperty (NULL, 'schema', 'Purchasing', 'table', default, NULL, NULL)
UNION
SELECT   CONCAT('Person.', objname COLLATE DATABASE_DEFAULT)          AS TableName,
         value                                                        AS [Description]
FROM fn_listextendedproperty (NULL, 'schema', 'Person', 'table', default, NULL, NULL)
UNION
SELECT   CONCAT('HumanResources.', objname COLLATE DATABASE_DEFAULT)  AS TableName,
         value                                                        AS [Description]
FROM fn_listextendedproperty (NULL, 'schema', 'HumanResources', 'table', default, NULL, NULL)
ORDER BY TableName;
```

TableName	Description
HumanResources.Department	Lookup table containing the departments within the Adventure Works Cycles company.
HumanResources.Employee	Employee information such as salary, department, and title.
HumanResources.EmployeeDepartmentHistory	Employee department transfers.
HumanResources.EmployeePayHistory	Employee pay history.
HumanResources.JobCandidate	Résumés submitted to Human Resources by job applicants.
HumanResources.Shift	Work shift lookup table.
Person.Address	Street address information for customers, employees, and vendors.
Person.AddressType	Types of addresses stored in the Address table.
Person.BusinessEntity	Source of the ID that connects vendors, customers, and employees with address and contact information.
Person.BusinessEntityAddress	Cross-reference table mapping customers, vendors, and employees to their addresses.
Person.BusinessEntityContact	Cross-reference table mapping stores, vendors, and employees to people
Person.ContactType	Lookup table containing the types of business entity contacts.
Person.CountryRegion	Lookup table containing the ISO standard codes for countries and regions.
Person.EmailAddress	Where to send a person email.
Person.Password	One way hashed authentication information
Person.Person	Human beings involved with AdventureWorks: employees, customer contacts, and vendor contacts.
Person.PersonPhone	Telephone number and type of a person.
Person.PhoneNumberType	Type of phone number of a person.
Person.StateProvince	State and province lookup table.
Purchasing.ProductVendor	Cross-reference table mapping vendors with the products they supply.
Purchasing.PurchaseOrderDetail	Individual products associated with a specific purchase order. See PurchaseOrderHeader.
Purchasing.PurchaseOrderHeader	General purchase order information. See PurchaseOrderDetail.
Purchasing.ShipMethod	Shipping company lookup table.
Purchasing.Vendor	Companies from whom Adventure Works Cycles purchases parts or other goods.

The CREATE TABLE Statement

Creates a table based on column name, data type & size specifications. Constraint and default information can be included as well, or alternately given as a separate ALTER TABLE statement.

Branch Banking Database with ON DELETE CASCADE

T-SQL script to create basic banking application tables. Preceding the first CREATE TABLE, we execute a CREATE SCHEMA to group the tables within one schema.

```
USE AdventureWorks2012;
GO


CREATE SCHEMA Banking;
GO



CREATE TABLE Banking.Branch
 (
    BranchID    INT IDENTITY ( 1, 1 ),
    BranchName   CHAR(32) NOT NULL UNIQUE,
    BranchCity   CHAR(32) NOT NULL,
    Assets     MONEY NOT NULL,
    ModifiedDate DATETIME DEFAULT (getdate()),
    PRIMARY KEY ( BranchID ),
 );

CREATE TABLE Banking.Account
 (
    AccountID     INT IDENTITY ( 1, 1 ) UNIQUE,
    BranchID     INT NOT NULL,
    AccountNumber CHAR(20) NOT NULL UNIQUE,
    AccountType   CHAR(12) NOT NULL CONSTRAINT ATC CHECK (AccountType IN ('C',  'S')),
    Balance     MONEY NOT NULL,
    ModifiedDate  DATETIME DEFAULT (getdate()),
    PRIMARY KEY ( AccountID ),
    FOREIGN KEY ( BranchID ) REFERENCES Banking.Branch(BranchID) ON DELETE   CASCADE
 );
```

-- T-SQL script continued

```sql
CREATE TABLE Banking.[Transaction]
 (
   TransactionID INT IDENTITY ( 1, 1 ) PRIMARY KEY,
   AccountID    INT NOT NULL  REFERENCES Banking.Account   ON DELETE  CASCADE, -- FK
   TranType     CHAR(1),
   Amount       MONEY,
   ModifiedDate  DATETIME DEFAULT (getdate()),
   UNIQUE ( AccountID, ModifiedDate)
 );

CREATE TABLE Banking.Customer
 (
   CustomerID   INT IDENTITY ( 1, 1 ) PRIMARY KEY,
   Name        CHAR(32) NOT NULL,
   SSNo        CHAR(9) NOT NULL UNIQUE,
   [Type]      CHAR(20) NOT NULL,
   Street      VARCHAR(32) NOT NULL,
   City        CHAR(32) NOT NULL,
   [State]     CHAR(32) NOT NULL,
   Zip         CHAR(10) NOT NULL,
   Country     CHAR(32) NOT NULL,
   ModifiedDate DATETIME DEFAULT (getdate())
  );

CREATE TABLE Banking.Loan
 (
   LoanID      INT IDENTITY ( 1, 1 ) PRIMARY KEY,
   BranchID    INT NOT NULL REFERENCES Banking.Branch ON DELETE   CASCADE,  -- FK
   LoanNumber  CHAR(20) NOT NULL UNIQUE,
   LoanType    VARCHAR(30) NOT NULL,
   Amount      MONEY NOT NULL,
   ModifiedDate DATETIME DEFAULT (getdate())
 );
```

-- T-SQL script continued

```
CREATE TABLE Banking.Depositor
 (
   CustomerID   INT NOT NULL,
   AccountID    INT NOT NULL,
   ModifiedDate DATETIME DEFAULT (getdate()),
   PRIMARY KEY ( CustomerID, AccountID ),
   FOREIGN KEY ( AccountID ) REFERENCES Banking.Account(AccountID) ON DELETE   CASCADE,
   FOREIGN KEY ( CustomerID ) REFERENCES Banking.Customer(CustomerID)
 );

CREATE TABLE Banking.Borrower
 (
   CustomerID   INT NOT NULL,
   LoanID       INT NOT NULL,
   ModifiedDate DATETIME DEFAULT (getdate()),
   PRIMARY KEY ( CustomerID, LoanID ),
   FOREIGN KEY ( CustomerID ) REFERENCES Banking.Customer(CustomerID),
   FOREIGN KEY ( LoanID ) REFERENCES Banking.Loan(LoanID)
 );
```

CHAPTER 4: Fundamentals of Relational Database Design

Temporary Tables: Workhorses of SQL Server

So much so that they even have their own database: tempdb. Temporary tables (example: #Product1) can be applied in queries just like permanent tables. The differences are:

> ➢ Temporary tables are created in tempdb.

> ➢ Temporary tables have limited life.

There are two versions:

> ➢ Temporary tables (#tempA) are multi-user automatically, cannot be shared among connections.

> ➢ Global temporary tables (##gtempB) is single-user, can be shared among connections.

Global temporary tables are used only for special purposes since they make stored procedures single user only.

Temporary tables can be created by CREATE TABLE or SELECT INTO methods.

```
USE AdventureWorks2012;
GO
-- Command(s) completed successfully.
```

```
-- Create temporary table with CREATE TABLE
CREATE TABLE #Product
(
        ProductID INT,
        ProductName nvarchar(50),
        ListPrice money,
        Color varchar(16)
);
GO
-- Command(s) completed successfully.
```

```
INSERT INTO #Product
SELECT   ProductID,
         Name,
         ListPrice,
         Color
FROM Production.Product ORDER BY Name;
GO  --(504 row(s) affected)
```

Temporary Tables Are Handy When Developing Scripts Or Stored Procedures

```
SELECT TOP 10 * FROM #Product
ORDER BY ProductName;
GO
```

ProductID	ProductName	ListPrice	Color
1	Adjustable Race	0.00	NULL
879	All-Purpose Bike Stand	159.00	NULL
712	AWC Logo Cap	8.99	Multi
3	BB Ball Bearing	0.00	NULL
2	Bearing Ball	0.00	NULL
877	Bike Wash - Dissolver	7.95	NULL
316	Blade	0.00	NULL
843	Cable Lock	25.00	NULL
952	Chain	20.24	Silver
324	Chain Stays	0.00	NULL

```
DROP TABLE #Product;
GO


-- CREATE temporary table with SELECT INTO
SELECT ProductID, ProductName = Name, ListPrice, StandardCost, Color
INTO #ProductA
FROM Production.Product
ORDER BY ProductName;
GO


SELECT TOP 10 * FROM #ProductA
ORDER BY ProductName;
```

ProductID	ProductName	ListPrice	StandardCost	Color
1	Adjustable Race	0.00	0.00	NULL
879	All-Purpose Bike Stand	159.00	59.466	NULL
712	AWC Logo Cap	8.99	6.9223	Multi
3	BB Ball Bearing	0.00	0.00	NULL
2	Bearing Ball	0.00	0.00	NULL
877	Bike Wash - Dissolver	7.95	2.9733	NULL
316	Blade	0.00	0.00	NULL
843	Cable Lock	25.00	10.3125	NULL
952	Chain	20.24	8.9866	Silver
324	Chain Stays	0.00	0.00	NULL

```
DROP TABLE #ProductA;
GO
```

CHAPTER 4: Fundamentals of Relational Database Design

ALTER TABLE for Changing Table Definition

An empty table can easily be altered by ALTER TABLE. A populated table change (alter) may require additional operations such as data conversion to the new column data type. Generally increasing the size of a column is a safe change even if the table is populated. If we were to change size from 25 to 10, truncation may occur (data loss), for which we would have to plan by examining what will be lost if any. When decreasing string column size, we can use the LEFT function to truncate the string. T-SQL script to increase the size of a column from 25 to 32, then decrease it 9.

```
 USE CopyOfAdventureWorks2012;
-- Sales.SalesOrderDetail columns
/*Name    Policy Health State
SalesOrderID (PK, FK, int, not null)
SalesOrderDetailID (PK, int, not null)
CarrierTrackingNumber (nvarchar(25), null) ..... */
```

```
-- Increase column size of CarrierTrackingNumber
ALTER TABLE Sales.SalesOrderDetail   ALTER COLUMN CarrierTrackingNumber nvarchar(32)  null;
```

```
/* Columns after ALTER TABLE
Name      Policy Health State
SalesOrderID (PK, FK, int, not null)
SalesOrderDetailID (PK, int, not null)
CarrierTrackingNumber (nvarchar(32), null) .....          */
```

```
SELECT TOP (1) SalesOrderID, CarrierTrackingNumber FROM  Sales.SalesOrderDetail ORDER BY SalesOrderID;
```

SalesOrderID	CarrierTrackingNumber
43659	4911-403C-98

We shall now decrease the size to 9 characters, but first truncate the extra characters. Without the UPDATE, the following error happens.
/* Msg 8152, Level 16, State 13, Line 1 String or binary data would be truncated. The statement has been terminated.*/

```
UPDATE Sales.SalesOrderDetail SET CarrierTrackingNumber = LEFT (CarrierTrackingNumber,9);
-- (121317 row(s) affected)
```

```
-- Decrease column size of CarrierTrackingNumber
ALTER TABLE Sales.SalesOrderDetail   ALTER COLUMN CarrierTrackingNumber nvarchar(9)  null;
-- Command(s) completed successfully.
```

```
SELECT TOP (1) SalesOrderID, CarrierTrackingNumber FROM  Sales.SalesOrderDetail  ORDER BY SalesOrderID;
```

SalesOrderID	CarrierTrackingNumber
43659	4911-403C

Renaming Tables & Columns with sp_rename

The system stored procedure sp_rename can be used to rename tables, columns and other user-created database objects.

```
USE tempdb;
GO


-- Create test table
SELECT * INTO Department FROM AdventureWorks2012.HumanResources.Department;
GO
-- (16 row(s) affected)

SELECT TOP 1 * FROM Department;
GO
```

DepartmentID	Name	GroupName	ModifiedDate
1	Engineering	Research and Development	2002-06-01 00:00:00.000

```
-- Rename table column
EXEC sp_rename "Department.Name", "Department";
GO


SELECT TOP 1 * FROM Department;
GO
```

DepartmentID	Department	GroupName	ModifiedDate
1	Engineering	Research and Development	2002-06-01 00:00:00.000

```
-- Rename table
EXEC sp_rename "dbo.Department", "ProfitCenter"
GO

SELECT * FROM ProfitCenter;
GO
```

DepartmentID	Department	GroupName	ModifiedDate
1	Engineering	Research and Development	2002-06-01 00:00:00.000

```
DROP TABLE tempdb.dbo.ProfitCenter;
GO
```

DROP TABLE: A Dangerous Statement

The DROP TABLE statement is to delete a table, including content, for good. It is a very dangerous statement which we don't want to execute accidentally. Therefore, if appropriate we should comment it out in a T-SQL script to prevent unintentional execution.

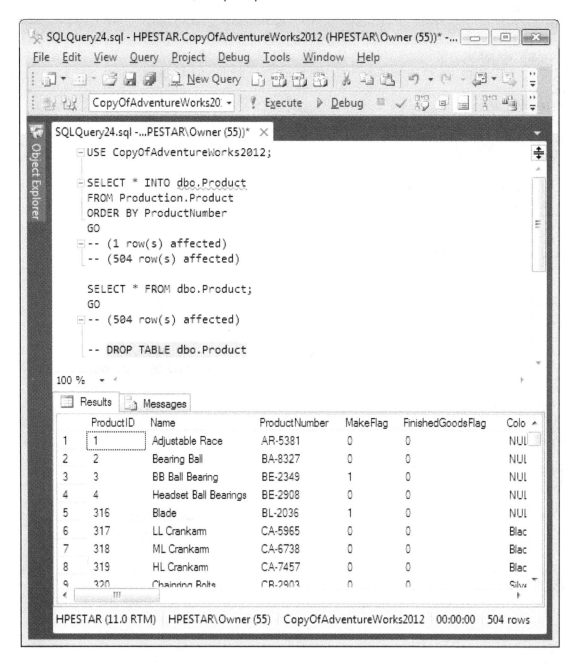

Table Constraints Inclusion in CREATE TABLE

Table constraints are user-defined database objects that restricts the behaviors of columns. PRIMARY KEY, UNIQUE KEY, FOREIGN KEY, or CHECK constraint, or a DEFAULT constraint can be included in the CREATE TABLE statement on the same line as the column or added as a separate line. In the definition of the Banking.Branch table UNIQUE and DEFAULT constraints are included in the same line while the PRIMARY KEY constraint has its own line at the end of column list. In the definition of Banking.Loan table, the PRIMARY KEY constraint is included with the column definition. FOREIGN KEY constraint definition can include ON DELETE CASCADE action option, meaning if the PRIMARY KEY is deleted all FOREIGN KEYs in the table referencing it should also be deleted.

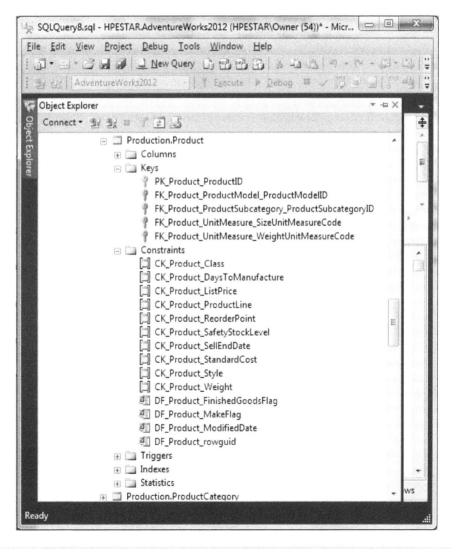

Nullability Column-Level Constraints in CREATE TABLE

The default is NULL, the column can contain NULL entries, the column is nullable. We have to specifically declare NOT NULL on the column line in CREATE TABLE if we want to add the cardinality constraint to the column. The NULL / NOT NULL constraint cannot be declared on a separate line. In the Production.Product table the Color column is nullable. The ListPrice column is not nullable instead has 0.0 price where there is no price.

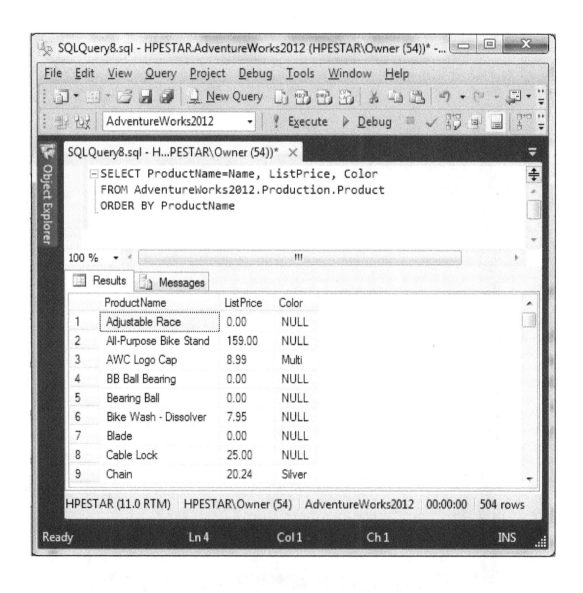

PRIMARY KEY constraint on a column automatically implies NOT NULL

The UNIQUE KEY CONSTRAINT allows only one NULL entry in a column since two or more NULL entries would not be unique. Demonstration script:

```
USE tempdb;
CREATE TABLE Product     (   ProductID INT UNIQUE,
                             ProductName varchar(64) PRIMARY KEY
                         );


INSERT Product (ProductName) VALUES ('Mobile Phone xZing');
-- (1 row(s) affected)


-- One NULL is OK in ProductID column
-- Second NULL insert attempt errors out


INSERT Product (ProductName) VALUES ('Motor Bike');


/* Msg 2627, Level 14, State 1, Line 7
Violation of UNIQUE KEY constraint 'UQ__Product__B40CC6ECDF4DC6D3'.
Cannot insert duplicate key in object 'dbo.Product'.
The duplicate key value is (<NULL>).
The statement has been terminated. */


-- NULL value in PRIMARY KEY column not allowed


INSERT Product (ProductID) VALUES (2);


/* Msg 515, Level 16, State 2, Line 2
Cannot insert the value NULL into column
'ProductName', table 'tempdb.dbo.Product';
column does not allow nulls. INSERT fails.
The statement has been terminated. */

SELECT * FROM Product;
```

ProductID	ProductName
NULL	Mobile Phone xZing

The PRIMARY KEY constraint is a combination of UNIQUE and NOT NULL constraints.

CHAPTER 4: Fundamentals of Relational Database Design

PRIMARY KEY & FOREIGN KEY Constraints

The PRIMARY KEY constraint is to ensure a referenceable unique address for each row in a table. PK column value cannot be NULL. The underlying mechanism to carry out the enforcement action is a unique index which is clustered by default but in can be nonclustered. PRIMARY KEY constraint can be considered as a UNIQUE constraint with NOT NULL on the column. The typical PRIMARY KEY is the SURROGATE PRIMARY KEY INT IDENTITY(1,1) column. There can only be one PRIMARY KEY defined per table. A PRIMARY KEY can consist of multiple columns, a composite PRIMARY KEY. A PRIMARY KEY cannot be based on part of a column. Production.ProductSubcategory table PRIMARY KEY setup.

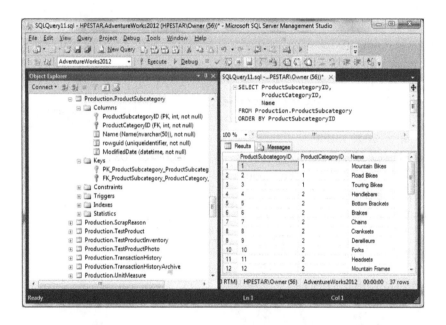

The ProductSubcategoryID is the PRIMARY KEY constraint. It is an INT IDENTITY(1,1) surrogate key. ProductCategoryID is a FOREIGN KEY referencing the Production.ProductCategory table ProductCategoryID column. "Name" is the NATURAL KEY. rowguid (used in replication) & ModifiedDate are row maintenance columns. The NATURAL KEY column Name has NOT NULL constraint and unique index defined. As such it can serve as PRIMARY KEY for the table, but we shall see why a meaningless integer number (INT IDENTITY) is better for PRIMARY KEY. Related to this topic: A heap is a table without a clustered index. The implication is if we choose nonclustered PRIMARY KEY, we have to define a clustered index on other column(s) so that the database engine can work with the table as normal. Clustered index speeds up range searches.

> The SURROGATE PRIMARY KEY should not be exposed to end-users, it is for programming use only.

FOREIGN KEY constraint requires that the referenced PK value exists.
FOREIGN KEY column is nullable. FOREIGN KEY can be named differently from the referenced PRIMARY KEY, although for readability purposes usually the same. **Multiple FK columns can reference the same PK column**. In such a case only one FK column can have the same name as the PK column. Invalid FK reference results in error.

```
USE [AdventureWorks2012]
GO


INSERT INTO Production.ProductSubcategory
    (ProductCategoryID
    ,Name)
  VALUES
    (99
    ,'Inner Tube')


/*
Msg 547, Level 16, State 0, Line 2
The INSERT statement conflicted with the FOREIGN KEY constraint
"FK_ProductSubcategory_ProductCategory_ProductCategoryID".
The conflict occurred in database "AdventureWorks2012",
table "Production.ProductCategory", column 'ProductCategoryID'.
The statement has been terminated.
*/
```

DELETE attempt on a referenced PRIMARY KEY will give an error unless DELETE CASCADE is defined on the FK:

```
DELETE FROM Production.ProductSubcategory
WHERE ProductSubCategoryID = 4
GO


/* Msg 547, Level 16, State 0, Line 1
The DELETE statement conflicted with the REFERENCE constraint
"FK_Product_ProductSubcategory_ProductSubcategoryID".
The conflict occurred in database "AdventureWorks2012",
table "Production.Product", column 'ProductSubcategoryID'.
The statement has been terminated. */
```

CHAPTER 4: Fundamentals of Relational Database Design

Single Column & Composite PRIMARY KEY List with XML PATH

Query to form delimited list for composite PRIMARY KEY columns. STUFF function deletes the leading comma.

```
-- Show composite PRIMARY KEYs as a comma-delimited list
USE AdventureWorks2012;
SELECT  K.TABLE_SCHEMA,
        T.TABLE_NAME,
        PK_COLUMN_NAMES =
                STUFF(( SELECT
                                CONCAT(', ',   KK.COLUMN_NAME)            AS [text()]
                                FROM  INFORMATION_SCHEMA.KEY_COLUMN_USAGE kk
                        WHERE  K.CONSTRAINT_NAME = KK.CONSTRAINT_NAME
                        ORDER BY  KK.ORDINAL_POSITION
                        FOR XML Path ('')), 1, 1, '')
FROM    INFORMATION_SCHEMA.TABLE_CONSTRAINTS T
   INNER JOIN    INFORMATION_SCHEMA.KEY_COLUMN_USAGE K
        ON T.CONSTRAINT_NAME = K.CONSTRAINT_NAME
WHERE           T.CONSTRAINT_TYPE = 'PRIMARY KEY'
                AND K.ORDINAL_POSITION = 1
ORDER BY        K.TABLE_SCHEMA,
                T.TABLE_NAME;
-- (71 row(s) affected) - Partial results
```

TABLE_SCHEMA	TABLE_NAME	PK_COLUMN_NAMES
dbo	AWBuildVersion	SystemInformationID
dbo	DatabaseLog	DatabaseLogID
dbo	ErrorLog	ErrorLogID
HumanResources	Department	DepartmentID
HumanResources	Employee	BusinessEntityID
HumanResources	EmployeeDepartmentHistory	BusinessEntityID, StartDate, DepartmentID, ShiftID
HumanResources	EmployeePayHistory	BusinessEntityID, RateChangeDate
HumanResources	JobCandidate	JobCandidateID
HumanResources	Shift	ShiftID
Person	Address	AddressID
Person	AddressType	AddressTypeID
Person	BusinessEntity	BusinessEntityID
Person	BusinessEntityAddress	BusinessEntityID, AddressID, AddressTypeID
Person	BusinessEntityContact	BusinessEntityID, PersonID, ContactTypeID
Person	ContactType	ContactTypeID
Person	CountryRegion	CountryRegionCode
Person	EmailAddress	BusinessEntityID, EmailAddressID
Person	Password	BusinessEntityID
Person	Person	BusinessEntityID
Person	PersonPhone	BusinessEntityID, PhoneNumber, PhoneNumberTypeID

SSMS GUI Table Designer

SSMS Object Explorer includes a GUI Table Designer which can be launched the following ways for new or existing table from the right-click drop-down menus.

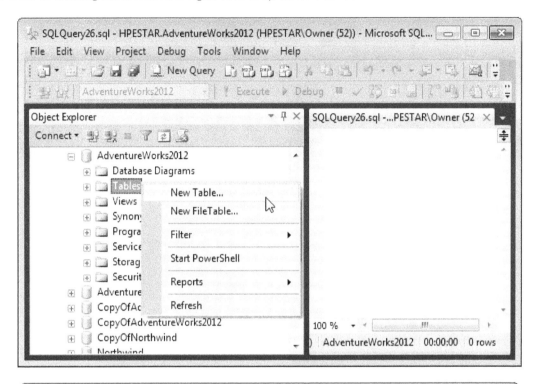

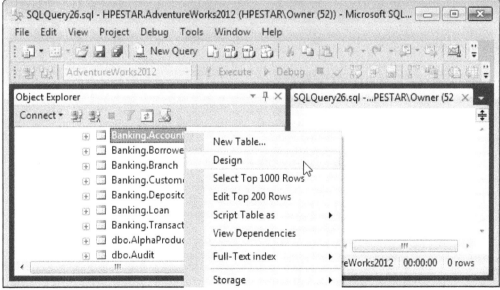

Basic GUI Table Design

The Table Designer provides line-by-line row design including all properties (bottom of dialog box) such as defaults, computed columns, identity and so on.

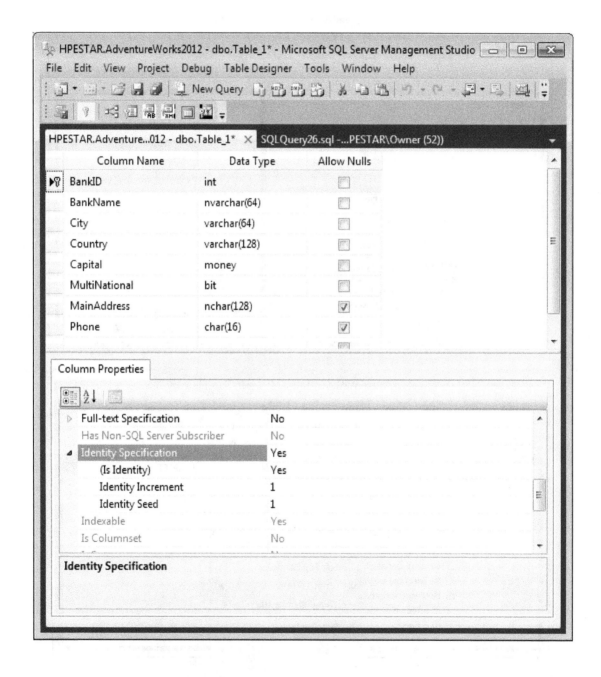

CHECK Constraint Definition

CHECK Constraint design window can be launched from toolbox icon: Manage Check Constraints or right-click drop-down menu. We create a constraint on Capital to be greater or equal to $5 billion.

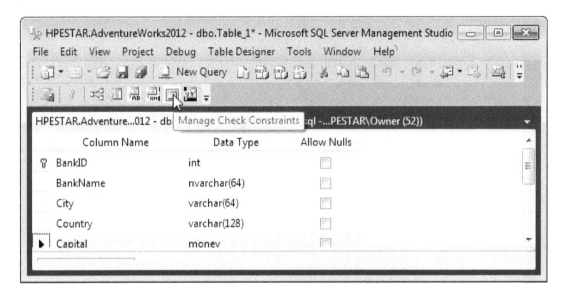

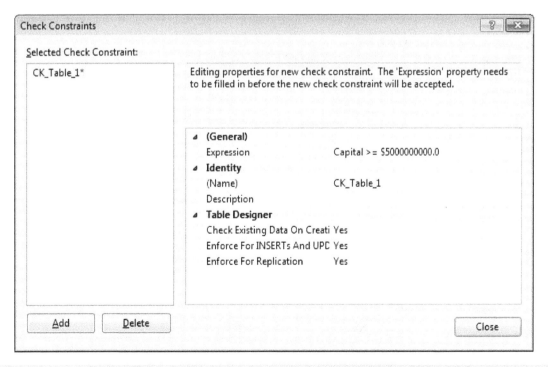

Managing Indexes and Keys

The Manage Indexes and Keys window can be launched by toolbox icon or right-click menu. We add UNIQUE KEY property to the BankName column.

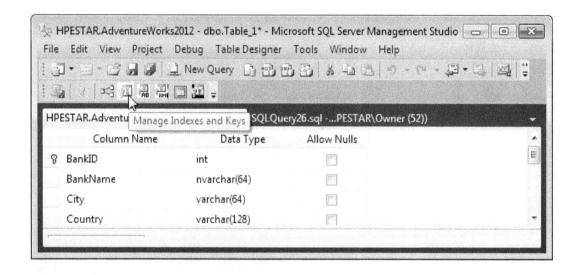

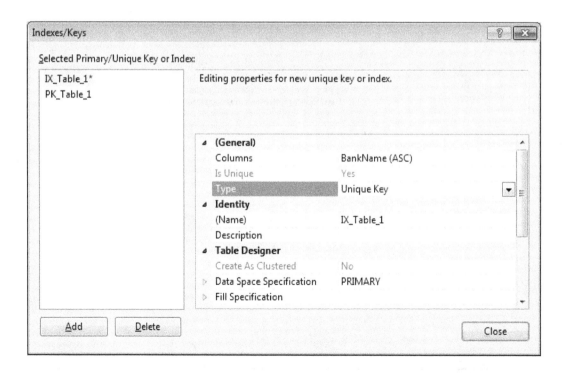

Setting PRIMARY KEY with a Single Click

PRIMARY KEY can simply be configured just by clicking on the gold key icon. A PRIMARY KEY constraint is created automatically.

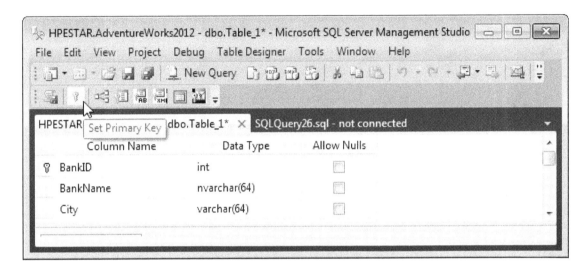

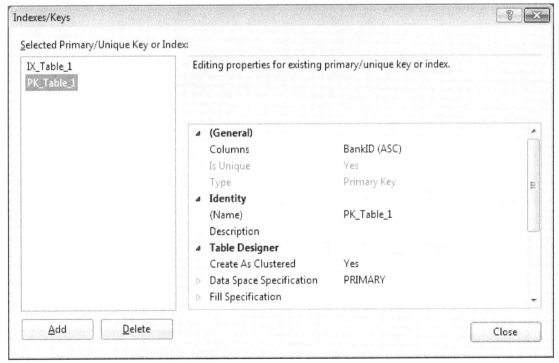

Configuring FOREIGN KEY: Declarative Referential Integrity

The Relationships facility can be used to create a FOREIGN KEY link (constraint). NOTE: demo only, BusinessEntityID column in the demo table has no relationship to AdventureWorks tables.

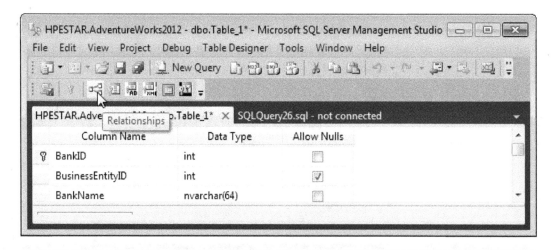

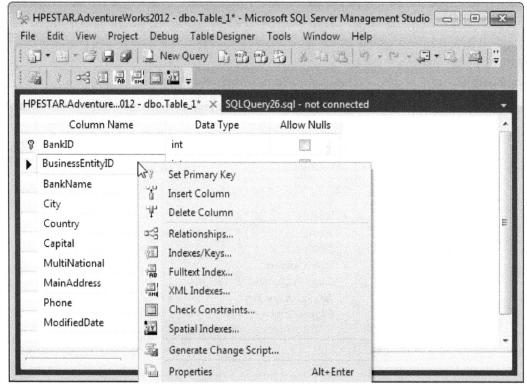

Tables And Columns Specific Tab Is To Define Mapping From FK To PK

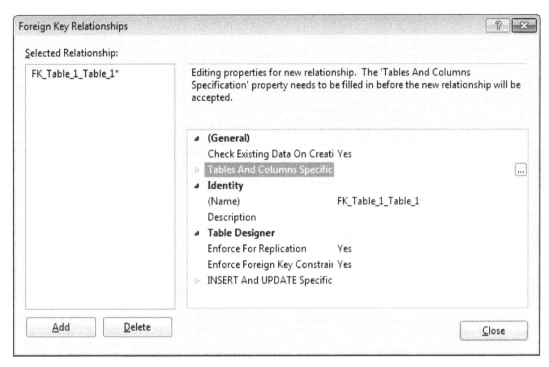

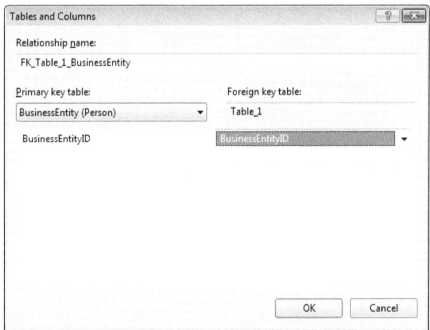

CHAPTER 4: Fundamentals of Relational Database Design

T-SQL Script Generation from GUI Table Designer

T-SQL code can be generated any time prior to saving the changes.

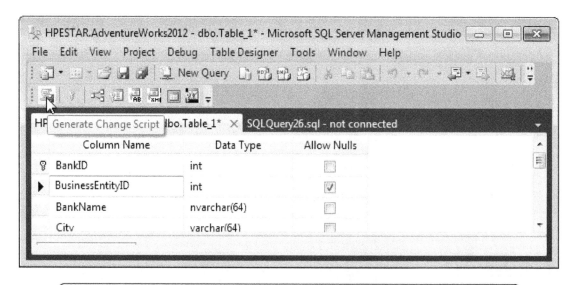

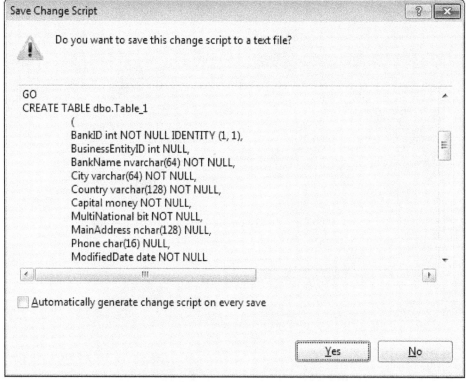

Generated CREATE TABLE & Related Objects Script

Code generated by the Table Designer.

```
/* To prevent any potential data loss issues, you should review this script in detail before running it
outside the context of the database designer.*/
BEGIN TRANSACTION
SET QUOTED_IDENTIFIER ON
SET ARITHABORT ON
SET NUMERIC_ROUNDABORT OFF
SET CONCAT_NULL_YIELDS_NULL ON
SET ANSI_NULLS ON
SET ANSI_PADDING ON
SET ANSI_WARNINGS ON
COMMIT
BEGIN TRANSACTION
GO
CREATE TABLE dbo.Table_1
        (
        BankID int NOT NULL IDENTITY (1, 1),
        BusinessEntityID int NULL,
        BankName nvarchar(64) NOT NULL,
        City varchar(64) NOT NULL,
        Country varchar(128) NOT NULL,
        Capital money NOT NULL,
        MultiNational bit NOT NULL,
        MainAddress nchar(128) NULL,
        Phone char(16) NULL,
        ModifiedDate date NOT NULL
        ) ON [PRIMARY]
GO
ALTER TABLE dbo.Table_1 ADD CONSTRAINT
        CK_Table_1 CHECK (Capital >= $5000000000.0)
GO
ALTER TABLE dbo.Table_1 ADD CONSTRAINT
        DF_Table_1_ModifiedDate DEFAULT CURRENT_TIMESTAMP FOR ModifiedDate
GO
ALTER TABLE dbo.Table_1 ADD CONSTRAINT
        PK_Table_1 PRIMARY KEY CLUSTERED
        (
        BankID
        ) WITH( STATISTICS_NORECOMPUTE = OFF, IGNORE_DUP_KEY = OFF, ALLOW_ROW_LOCKS = ON,
ALLOW_PAGE_LOCKS = ON) ON [PRIMARY]

GO
```

-- T-SQL script continues

```
ALTER TABLE dbo.Table_1 ADD CONSTRAINT
        IX_Table_1 UNIQUE NONCLUSTERED
        (
        BankName
        ) WITH( STATISTICS_NORECOMPUTE = OFF, IGNORE_DUP_KEY = OFF, ALLOW_ROW_LOCKS = ON,
ALLOW_PAGE_LOCKS = ON) ON [PRIMARY]

GO
ALTER TABLE dbo.Table_1 ADD CONSTRAINT
        FK_Table_1_Table_1 FOREIGN KEY
        (
        BankID
        ) REFERENCES dbo.Table_1
        (
        BankID
        ) ON UPDATE  NO ACTION
         ON DELFTE  NO ACTION

GO
ALTER TABLE dbo.Table_1 SET (LOCK_ESCALATION = TABLE)
GO
COMMIT
```

Upon Exit or Save, a name can be assigned to the table. In this instance, the Table_1 is changed to MultiNationalBank. The Table Designer automatically replaces all the "Table_1" occurrences in the script with "MultiNationalBank".

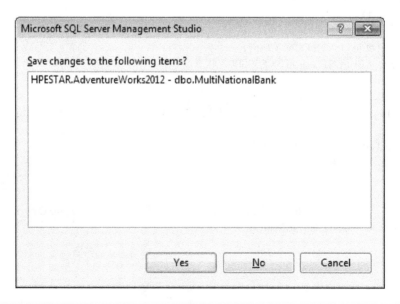

CHAPTER 4: Fundamentals of Relational Database Design

One-to-Many Relationship Implementation

The cardinality of relationship implemented with PRIMARY KEY & FOREIGN KEY constraints is one-to-many. Many FKs can reference a single PK value. In the following demo, many products map to a single subcategory value 'Touring Bike'. The matching is not done on the name between tables, rather on the surrogate PK value 3.

FOREIGN KEY Referencing A UNIQUE KEY

A FOREIGN KEY can reference a UNIQUE KEY or UNIQUE index column in another table in addition to the PRIMARY KEY. In the following demonstration a FOREIGN KEY is created from ProdNumber column pointing to Production.Product ProductNumber (UNIQUE index) column.

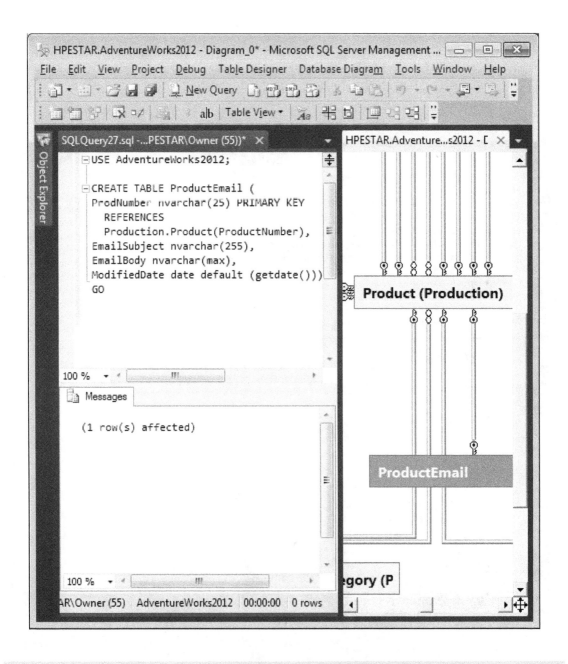

FOREIGN KEY Relationship Without Constraint

A table can have a FOREIGN KEY which is not supported by server-side constraint. In such instance the client-side application software has to ensure that the relationship is valid. Generally it is undesirable. **Whatever can be done on the server-side should be done there because it is more efficient development wise, maintenance wise and performance wise.** Demonstration to remove the FK constraint on the ProductID column in the [Order Details] table of the CopyOfNorthwind database.

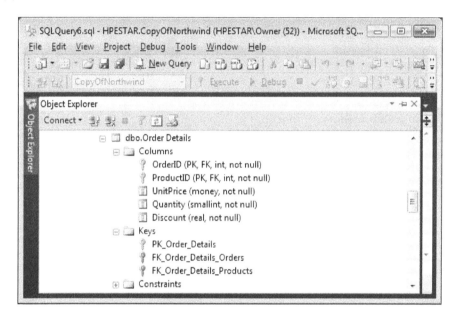

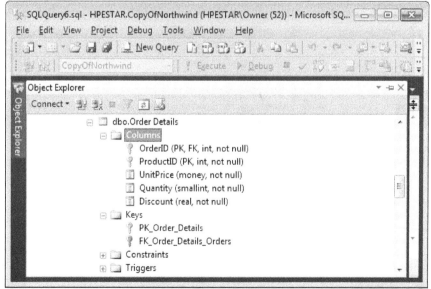

CHAPTER 4: Fundamentals of Relational Database Design

Database Diagram Design Tool in SSMS

Management Studio Object Explorer includes a diagramming tool for tables and their relationships with each other. While not as sophisticated as independent database design tools, it is excellent for working with a small number of tables.

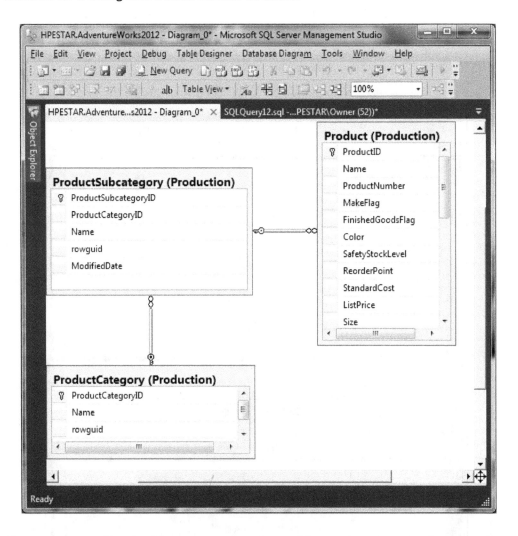

The diagramming tool has both reverse engineering and forward engineering features. **Reverse engineering**: it creates a diagram based on table and PK/FK constraints definitions. **Forward engineering**: it can change table and constraint setup in the database based on diagram changes. The Gold Key (PRIMARY KEY symbol) end of the connection line points to the PRIMARY KEY table, while the double "o" (infinite symbol in mathematics, here meaning many) end to the FOREIGN KEY table.

CHAPTER 4: Fundamentals of Relational Database Design

PRIMARY KEY & FOREIGN KEY as JOIN ON Keys

When we need data from two related tables we have to JOIN the tables. The typical JOIN keys
are the PRIMARY KEY and FOREIGN KEY. In the following demonstration, we want to display the
subcategory for each Touring Bike product from the Product table. Since the 'Touring Bike'
subcategory value is in the ProductSubcategory table, we have to JOIN it to the Product table.
The JOIN keys are: ProductSubcategoryID PRIMARY KEY in the ProductSubcategory table and
ProductSubcategoryID FOREIGN KEY in the Product table. Naming the FK same as the PK is
helpful with readability, therefore developer productivity.

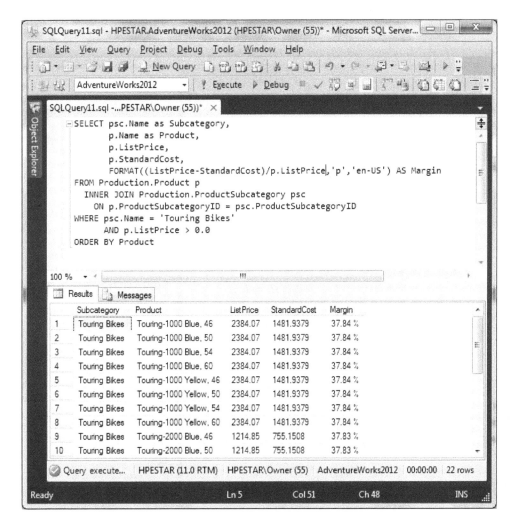

The Margin column is calculated with an expression. It is also formatted as percentage with US
English culture.

CHAPTER 4: Fundamentals of Relational Database Design

Composite & Indirect FOREIGN KEY

A composite (more than one column) PRIMARY KEY requires matching composite FOREIGN KEY references. In the Sales.SalesOrderDetail table SpecialOfferID & ProductID constitute a composite FOREIGN KEY which references the SpecialOfferProduct table composite PRIMARY KEY. Thus ProductID indirectly references the Production.Product table.

NATURAL KEY is a Must in Every Table

NATURAL KEY is a unique key which can serve as PRIMARY KEY for identifying data. A product name is a natural key in a product table. A product number is also a NATURAL KEY in a product table. Note that product "number" should better be called product identification since it is frequently not a number rather it is alphanumeric like: AB342BL where BL stands for blue. The Name and ProductNumber columns are NATURAL KEYs in the Production.Product table. **Every table should have a NATURAL KEY**. If it does not, there is a definition problem. Naturally, test tables, work tables and staging tables are exceptions to this rule.

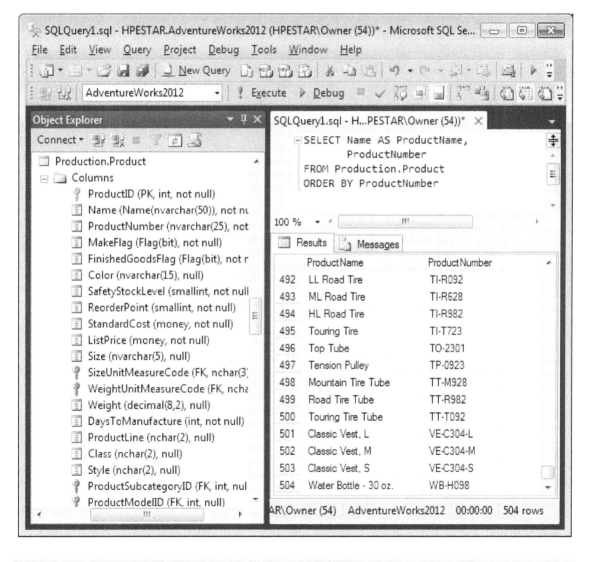

CANDIDATE KEY

A CANDIDATE KEY can be any column or a combination of columns that can qualify as UNIQUE
KEY in a table with no NULL value. The ProductID, Name, ProductNumber, rowguid (16 byte
random value like FA3C65CD-0A22-47E3-BDF6-53F1DC138C43, hyphens are for readability) are
all CANDIDATE KEYs in the Production.Product table. Only one of them can be the PRIMARY KEY.
In this instance the selected PRIMARY KEY is ProductID, a SURROGATE (to NATURAL KEY) INT
IDENTITY (1,1) PRIMARY KEY.

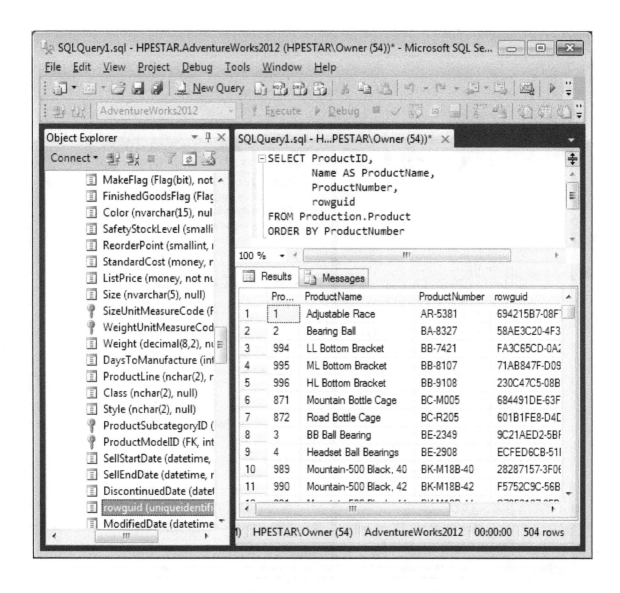

Logical Data Modeling in Visio

The following screenshots demonstrate logical / conceptual data modeling in Visio using the ORM diagram tool.

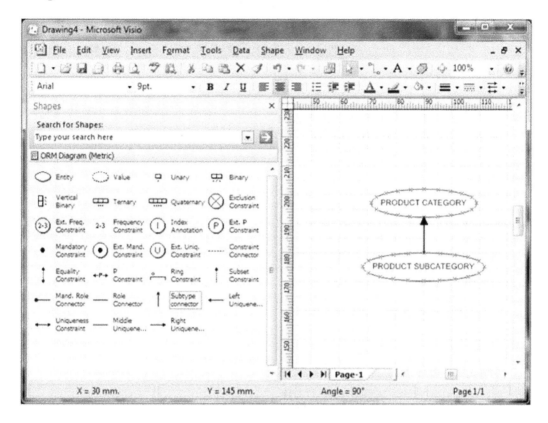

Following is the actual implementation of the above relationship.

```
CREATE TABLE [Production].[ProductCategory](
        [ProductCategoryID] [int] IDENTITY(1,1) PRIMARY KEY,
        [Name] [dbo].[Name] NOT NULL,
        [rowguid] [uniqueidentifier] ROWGUIDCOL  NOT NULL,
        [ModifiedDate] [datetime] NOT NULL          );

CREATE TABLE [Production].[ProductSubcategory](
        [ProductSubcategoryID] [int] IDENTITY(1,1) PRIMARY KEY,
        [ProductCategoryID] [int] NOT NULL REFERENCES
Production.ProductCategory(ProductCategoryID) ,
        [Name] [dbo].[Name] NOT NULL,
        [rowguid] [uniqueidentifier] ROWGUIDCOL  NOT NULL,
        [ModifiedDate] [datetime] NOT NULL          );
```

CHAPTER 4: Fundamentals of Relational Database Design

Branch Banking Conceptual Diagram Preparation In Visio ORM Diagram Tool

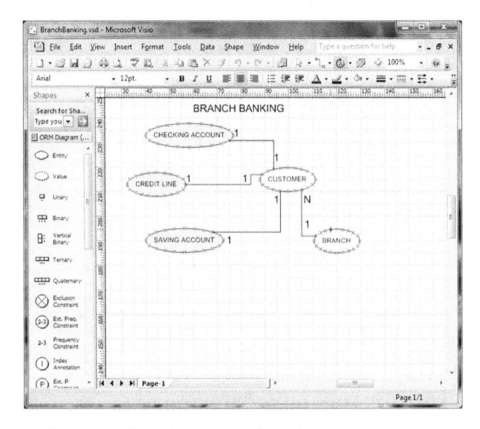

The actual implementation of Branch - Customer relationship.

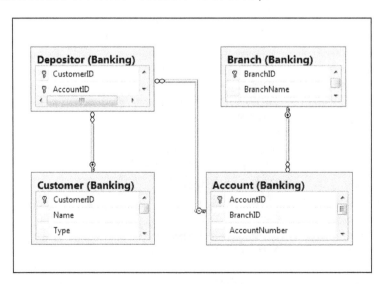

Relational Database Design with Visio

Office Visio can be used for physical database modeling and design. Another widely used database modeling tool is ERWIN.

A sample database design diagram in Visio. Lines represent FOREIGN KEY constraints, arrowheads point to the referenced table.

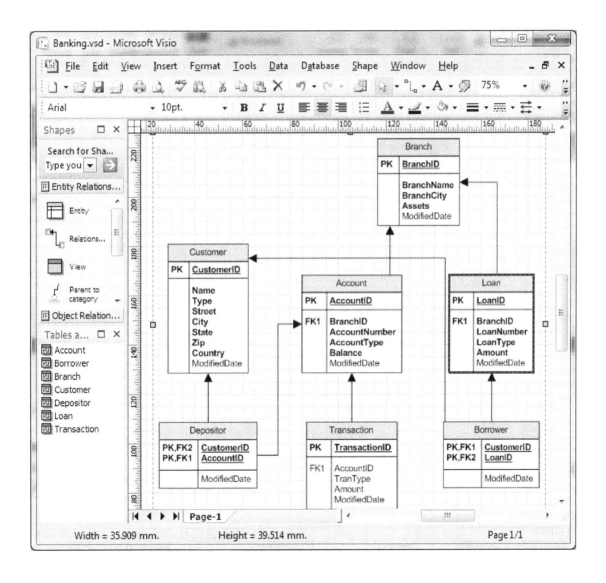

AdventureWorks Database Model in Visio

A segment of the AdventureWorks database design model in Visio. U indicates UNIQUE KEY or unique index.

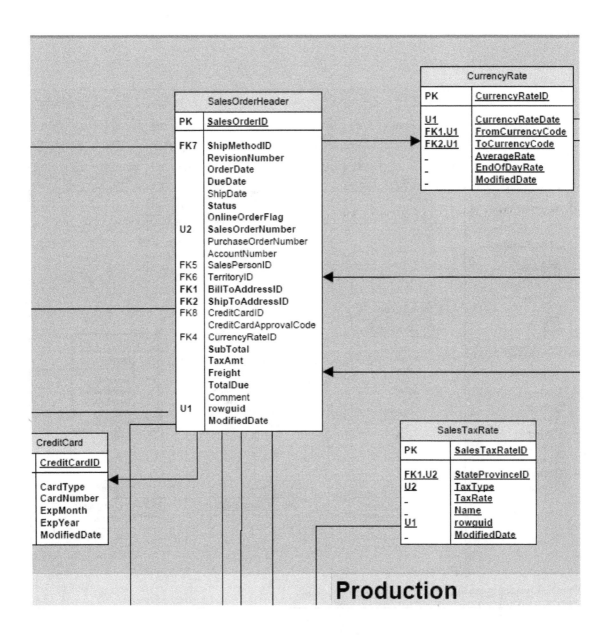

Reverse Engineering a Database with Visio

Visio can reverse engineer a database. Based on PRIMARY KEY & FOREIGN KEY constraints and table definitions, it can construct a database diagram automatically. Here are the first and an intermediate steps.

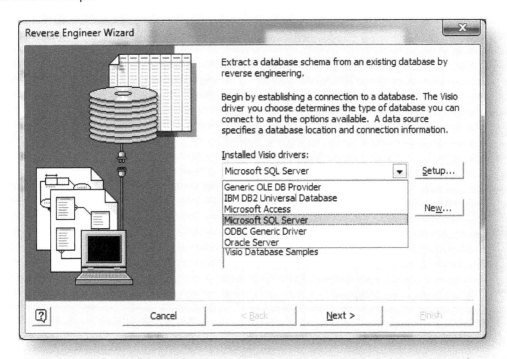

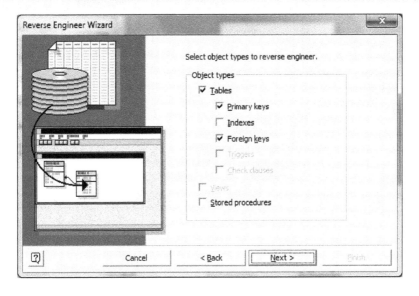

CHAPTER 4: Fundamentals of Relational Database Design

Reverse Engineered Diagram of Northwind

A section display from the reverse engineered diagram of Northwind sample database(not clear why "Discontinued" displays in bold):

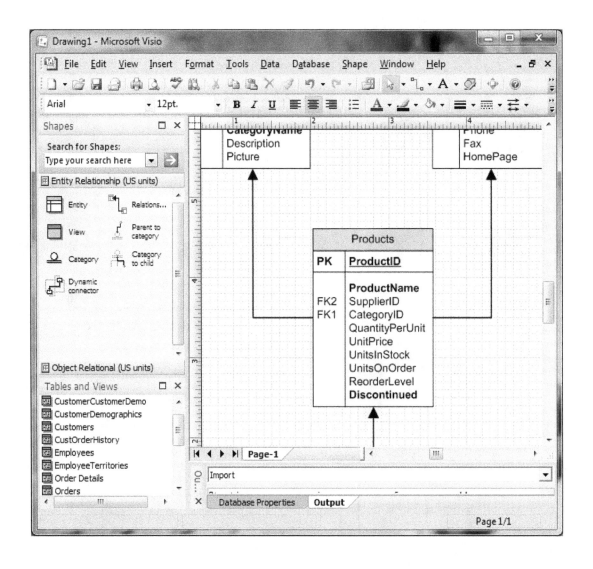

Forward Engineering a Database with Visio

Visio product itself does not have forward engineering feature. Alberto Ferrari developed an Office Addin for generating database scripts from a Visio database model diagram: Visio Forward Engineer Addin for Office 2010 (http://sqlblog.com/blogs/alberto_ferrari/archive/2010/04/16/visio-forward-engineer-addin-for-office-2010.aspx).

Codeplex blog post and free download for the same: Visio Forward Engineer Addin (http://forwardengineer.codeplex.com/).

Forward Engineering from SSMS Diagram Tool

The Database Diagram Tool in SSMS Object Explorer support graphical design and forward engineering.

Screenshot to show the creation of a new table "Automobile" in the Diagram Tool.

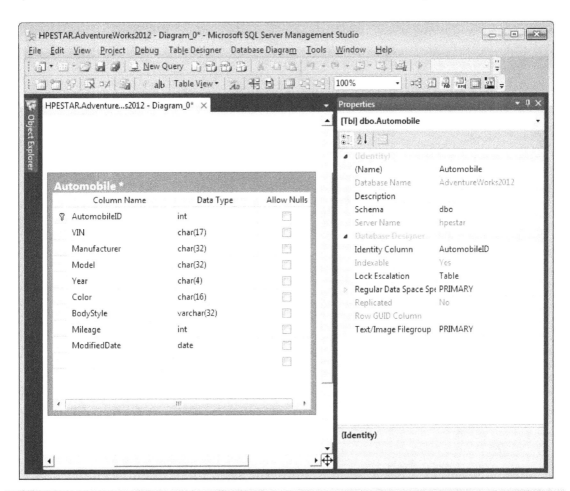

CHAPTER 4: Fundamentals of Relational Database Design

The Properties Dialog Box Allows The Individual Configuration Of Each Column

The Right Click drop-down menu has options to Add Indexes/Keys, Add XML Indexes, Add Spatial Indexes, Add Fulltext Indexes, Delete Tables from Database (DANGEROUS!), CHECK constraint and other table related database objects.

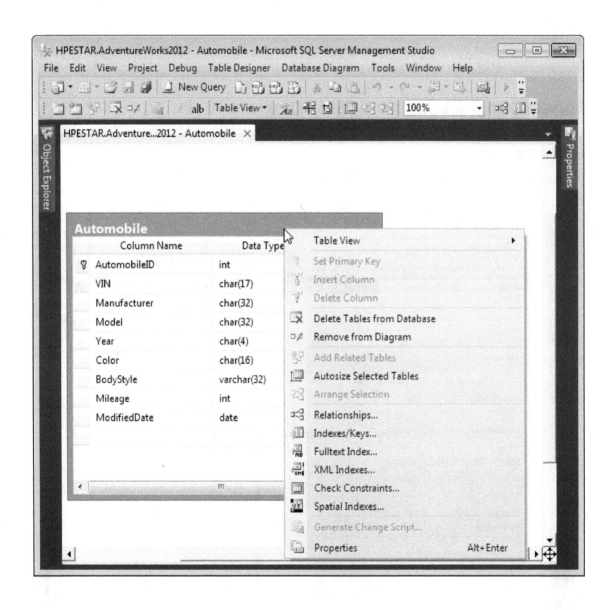

Forward Engineering Can Be Initiated By Exiting / Saving The Diagram

The save option dialog box activates automatically upon exit.

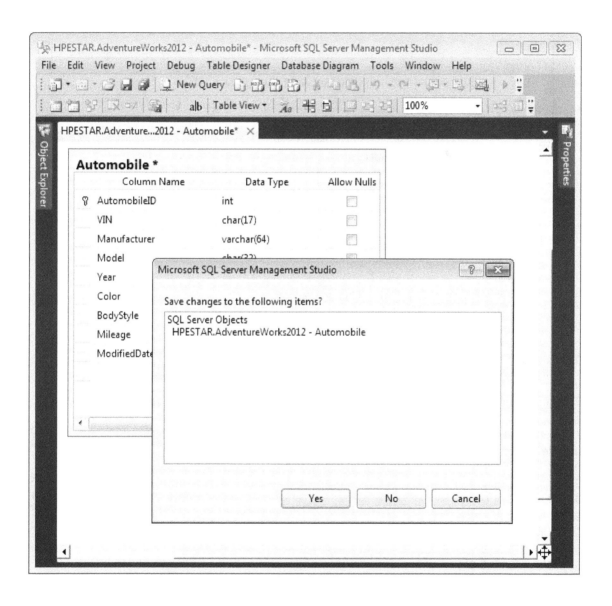

Save Change Script Panel Pops Up With The Generated T-SQL Change Script

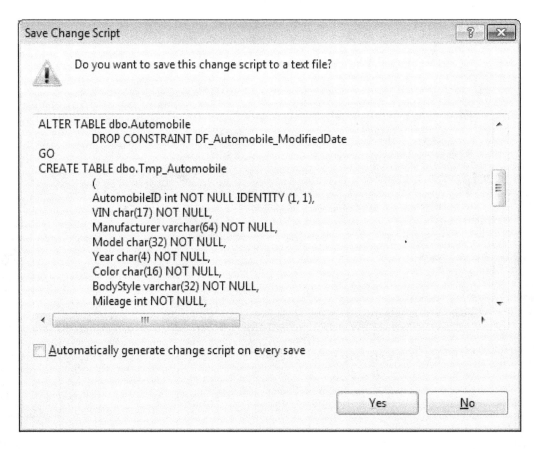

The generated T-SQL change script for changing Manufacturer data type to varchar(64).

```
/* To prevent any potential data loss issues, you should review this script in detail before running it
outside the context of the database designer.*/
BEGIN TRANSACTION
SET QUOTED_IDENTIFIER ON
SET ARITHABORT ON
SET NUMERIC_ROUNDABORT OFF
SET CONCAT_NULL_YIELDS_NULL ON
SET ANSI_NULLS ON
SET ANSI_PADDING ON
SET ANSI_WARNINGS ON
COMMIT
BEGIN TRANSACTION
GO
```

```
-- T-SQL script continued

ALTER TABLE dbo.Automobile
        DROP CONSTRAINT DF_Automobile_ModifiedDate
GO


CREATE TABLE dbo.Tmp_Automobile          (

        AutomobileID int NOT NULL IDENTITY (1, 1),
        VIN char(17) NOT NULL,
        Manufacturer varchar(64) NOT NULL,
        Model char(32) NOT NULL,
        Year char(4) NOT NULL,
        Color char(16) NOT NULL,
        BodyStyle varchar(32) NOT NULL,
        Mileage int NOT NULL,
        ModifiedDate date NOT NULL )  ON [PRIMARY]
GO
ALTER TABLE dbo.Tmp_Automobile SET (LOCK_ESCALATION = TABLE)
GO
ALTER TABLE dbo.Tmp_Automobile ADD CONSTRAINT
        DF_Automobile_ModifiedDate DEFAULT (getdate()) FOR ModifiedDate
GO
SET IDENTITY_INSERT dbo.Tmp_Automobile ON
GO
IF EXISTS(SELECT * FROM dbo.Automobile)
        EXEC('INSERT INTO dbo.Tmp_Automobile (AutomobileID, VIN, Manufacturer, Model, Year,
Color, BodyStyle, Mileage, ModifiedDate)
                SELECT AutomobileID, VIN, CONVERT(varchar(64), Manufacturer), Model, Year, Color,
BodyStyle, Mileage, ModifiedDate FROM dbo.Automobile WITH (HOLDLOCK TABLOCKX)')
GO
SET IDENTITY_INSERT dbo.Tmp_Automobile OFF
GO
DROP TABLE dbo.Automobile
GO
EXECUTE sp_rename N'dbo.Tmp_Automobile', N'Automobile', 'OBJECT'
GO
ALTER TABLE dbo.Automobile ADD CONSTRAINT
        PK_Automobile PRIMARY KEY CLUSTERED
        ( AutomobileID
        ) WITH( STATISTICS_NORECOMPUTE = OFF, IGNORE_DUP_KEY = OFF, ALLOW_ROW_LOCKS = ON,
ALLOW_PAGE_LOCKS = ON) ON [PRIMARY]
GO
COMMIT
```

CHAPTER 4: Fundamentals of Relational Database Design

Generate Change Script Option

Forward Engineering can also be initiated by the Generate Change Script option. The same option can be used when making any changes to the Diagram using the Diagram Tool.

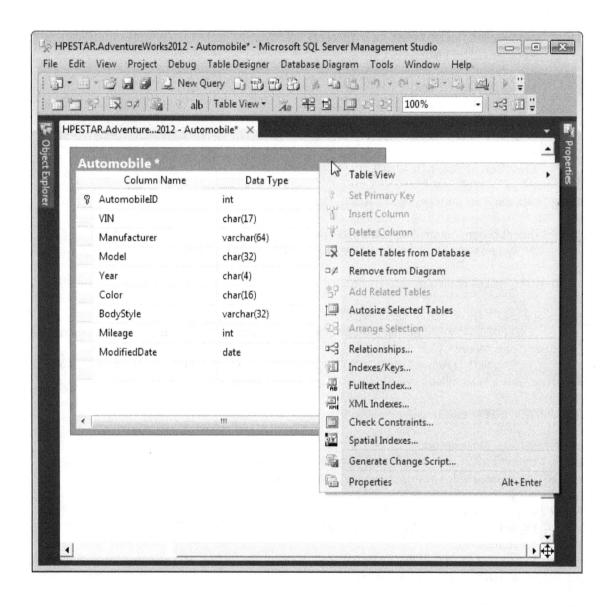

The Generated Script Of The Automobile Table By The Diagram Tool

```
USE [AdventureWorks2012]
GO

/****** Object:  Table [dbo].[Automobile]    Script Date: 7/22/2016 11:20:17 AM ******/
SET ANSI_NULLS ON
GO

SET QUOTED_IDENTIFIER ON
GO

SET ANSI_PADDING ON
GO

CREATE TABLE [dbo].[Automobile](
        [AutomobileID] [int] IDENTITY(1,1) NOT NULL,
        [VIN] [char](17) NOT NULL,
        [Manufacturer] [char](32) NOT NULL,
        [Model] [char](32) NOT NULL,
        [Year] [char](4) NOT NULL,
        [Color] [char](16) NOT NULL,
        [BodyStyle] [varchar](32) NOT NULL,
        [Mileage] [int] NOT NULL,
        [ModifiedDate] [date] NOT NULL,
 CONSTRAINT [PK_Automobile] PRIMARY KEY CLUSTERED
(
        [AutomobileID] ASC
)WITH (PAD_INDEX = OFF, STATISTICS_NORECOMPUTE = OFF, IGNORE_DUP_KEY = OFF,
ALLOW_ROW_LOCKS = ON, ALLOW_PAGE_LOCKS = ON) ON [PRIMARY]
) ON [PRIMARY]

GO

SET ANSI_PADDING ON
GO

ALTER TABLE [dbo].[Automobile] ADD  CONSTRAINT [DF_Automobile_ModifiedDate]
DEFAULT (getdate()) FOR [ModifiedDate]
GO
```

Scripting Single Database Object with Related Objects

The scripting feature works only through the graphical user interface (GUI) in SSMS Object Explorer. **There is no command to script a table.** Start with Right Click on the Banking.Account table.

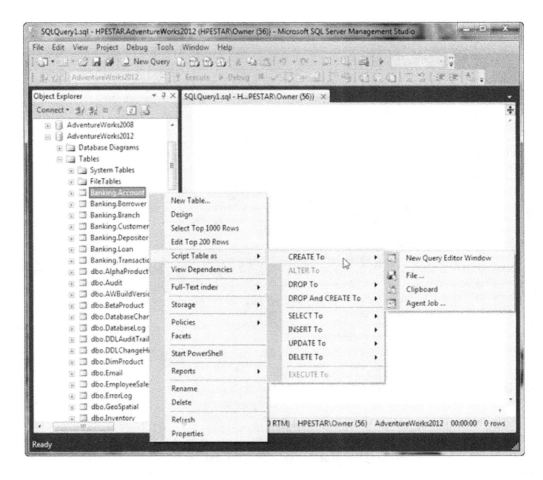

Generated script for the Banking.Account table and related objects.

USE [AdventureWorks2012]
GO
SET ANSI_NULLS ON
GO
SET QUOTED_IDENTIFIER ON
GO
SET ANSI_PADDING ON
GO

-- T-SQL script continued

```
CREATE TABLE [Banking].[Account](
        [AccountID] [int] IDENTITY(1,1) NOT NULL,
        [BranchID] [int] NOT NULL,
        [AccountNumber] [char](20) NOT NULL,
        [AccountType] [char](12) NOT NULL,
        [Balance] [money] NOT NULL,
        [ModifiedDate] [datetime] NULL,
PRIMARY KEY CLUSTERED
(
        [AccountID] ASC
)WITH (PAD_INDEX = OFF, STATISTICS_NORECOMPUTE = OFF, IGNORE_DUP_KEY = OFF,
ALLOW_ROW_LOCKS = ON,
ALLOW_PAGE_LOCKS = ON) ON [PRIMARY],
UNIQUE NONCLUSTERED
(       [AccountID] ASC
)WITH (PAD_INDEX = OFF, STATISTICS_NORECOMPUTE = OFF, IGNORE_DUP_KEY = OFF,
ALLOW_ROW_LOCKS = ON,
ALLOW_PAGE_LOCKS = ON) ON [PRIMARY],
UNIQUE NONCLUSTERED
(
        [AccountNumber] ASC
)WITH (PAD_INDEX = OFF, STATISTICS_NORECOMPUTE = OFF, IGNORE_DUP_KEY = OFF,
ALLOW_ROW_LOCKS = ON,
ALLOW_PAGE_LOCKS = ON) ON [PRIMARY]   ) ON [PRIMARY]
GO
SET ANSI_PADDING ON
GO
ALTER TABLE [Banking].[Account] ADD  DEFAULT (getdate()) FOR [ModifiedDate]
GO


ALTER TABLE [Banking].[Account]  WITH CHECK ADD FOREIGN KEY([BranchID])
REFERENCES [Banking].[Branch] ([BranchID])
ON DELETE CASCADE
GO


ALTER TABLE [Banking].[Account]  WITH CHECK ADD  CONSTRAINT [ATC]
CHECK  (([AccountType]='S' OR [AccountType]='C'))
GO
```

CHAPTER 4: Fundamentals of Relational Database Design

Scripting DB Objects With Script Wizard

The Script Wizard is a sophisticated tool for scripting out multiple objects, in fact all objects can be scripted in a single setup and execution. The generated script can be saved to single/multiple files, new query window or the Clipboard. The launching sequence of menus starts with Right Click on the database.

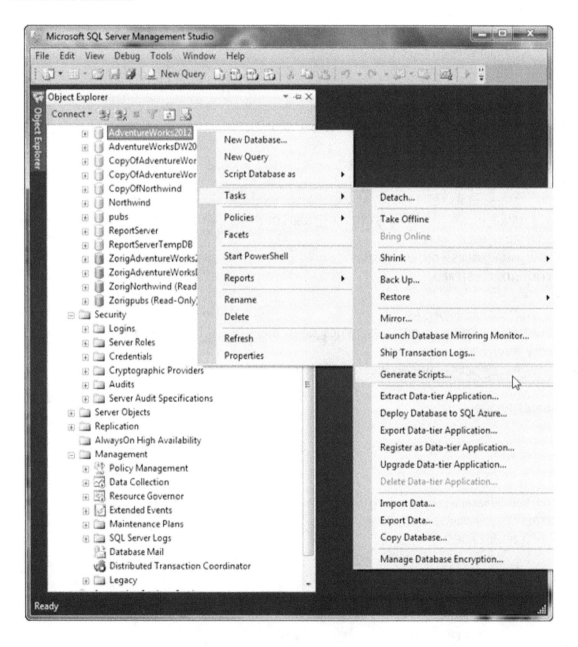

Script Wizard Optional Description Page

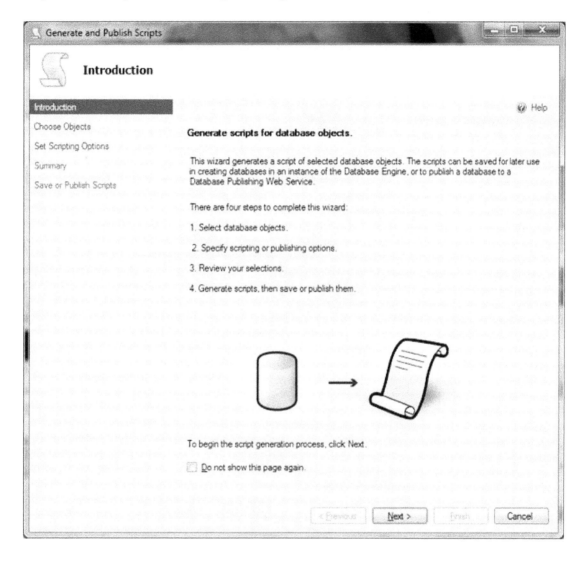

Object Selection Panel For Scripting

A number of options can be set for generation, including scripting of related objects.

The script generated by the Script Wizard for the Banking.Loan table and related objects

```
USE [AdventureWorks2012]
GO
SET ANSI_NULLS ON
GO
SET QUOTED_IDENTIFIER ON
GO
SET ANSI_PADDING ON
GO
CREATE TABLE [Banking].[Loan](
        [LoanID] [int] IDENTITY(1,1) NOT NULL,
        [BranchID] [int] NOT NULL,
        [LoanNumber] [char](20) NOT NULL,
        [LoanType] [varchar](30) NOT NULL,
        [Amount] [money] NOT NULL,
        [ModifiedDate] [datetime] NULL,
PRIMARY KEY CLUSTERED
(       [LoanID] ASC
)WITH (PAD_INDEX = OFF, STATISTICS_NORECOMPUTE = OFF, IGNORE_DUP_KEY = OFF,
ALLOW_ROW_LOCKS = ON, ALLOW_PAGE_LOCKS = ON) ON [PRIMARY],
UNIQUE NONCLUSTERED
(
        [LoanID] ASC
)WITH (PAD_INDEX = OFF, STATISTICS_NORECOMPUTE = OFF, IGNORE_DUP_KEY = OFF,
ALLOW_ROW_LOCKS = ON, ALLOW_PAGE_LOCKS = ON) ON [PRIMARY],
UNIQUE NONCLUSTERED
(
        [LoanNumber] ASC
)WITH (PAD_INDEX = OFF, STATISTICS_NORECOMPUTE = OFF, IGNORE_DUP_KEY = OFF,
ALLOW_ROW_LOCKS = ON, ALLOW_PAGE_LOCKS = ON) ON [PRIMARY]
) ON [PRIMARY]

GO
SET ANSI_PADDING ON
GO
ALTER TABLE [Banking].[Loan] ADD  DEFAULT (getdate()) FOR [ModifiedDate]
GO
ALTER TABLE [Banking].[Loan]  WITH CHECK ADD FOREIGN KEY([BranchID])
REFERENCES [Banking].[Branch] ([BranchID])
ON DELETE CASCADE
GO
```

SEQUENCE Objects

Sequence objects are new in SQL Server 2012. They are similar to the INT IDENTITY(1,1) sequence, however, there is a big difference: they don't "live" inside a table. They are table independent database objects. T-SQL demonstration script displays the flexibility of the new method for sequence number management.

```
-- Create a sequence object similar to INT IDENTITY(1,1)
CREATE SEQUENCE seqPurchaseOrder
AS INT
START WITH 1   INCREMENT BY 1;
GO


SELECT NEXT VALUE FOR seqPurchaseOrder;
GO 50
/* 1  2  3  .... 50 */


SELECT NEXT VALUE FOR seqPurchaseOrder;
GO
-- 51


SELECT NextOrderNo = NEXT VALUE FOR seqPurchaseOrder;
-- 52


SELECT NEXT VALUE FOR seqPurchaseOrder as NextOrderNo;
-- 54


EXEC sp_help seqPurchaseOrder;
```

Name	Owner	Type	Created_datetime
seqPurchaseOrder	dbo	sequence object	2016-06-27 09:14:32.940

```
DECLARE @List TABLE (id int identity(1,1) primary key, i int);
INSERT @List(i) SELECT NEXT VALUE FOR seqPurchaseOrder;
INSERT @List(i) SELECT NEXT VALUE FOR seqPurchaseOrder;
INSERT @List(i) SELECT NEXT VALUE FOR seqPurchaseOrder;
INSERT @List(i) SELECT NEXT VALUE FOR seqPurchaseOrder;
INSERT @List(i) VALUES (NEXT VALUE FOR seqPurchaseOrder);
SELECT * FROM @List
```

id	i
1	55
2	56
3	57
4	58
5	59

CHAPTER 4: Fundamentals of Relational Database Design

SEQUENCE Object Sharing

SEQUENCE is visible in other connections/session as well not only now but until it exists.

Create a new connection to test NEXT VALUE for seqPurchaseOrder.

```
-- Check current value
SELECT current_value
FROM sys.sequences
WHERE name = 'seqPurchaseOrder';
-- 58
```

```
-- Check metadata
SELECT name, object_id, schema_name(schema_id) as SchemaName, type
FROM sys.sequences;
```

name	object_id	SchemaName	type
seqPurchaseOrder	1338487847	dbo	SO

```
DECLARE @List TABLE (id int identity(1,1) primary key,
            i int default (NEXT VALUE FOR seqPurchaseOrder));
INSERT @List(i) DEFAULT VALUES;
INSERT @List(i) DEFAULT VALUES;
INSERT @List(i) DEFAULT VALUES;
INSERT @List(i) DEFAULT VALUES;
INSERT @List(i)DEFAULT VALUES;
SELECT * FROM @List
```

id	i
1	59
2	60
3	61
4	62
5	63

```
DROP SEQUENCE seqPurchaseOrder;
GO
```

```
SELECT NEXT VALUE FOR seqPurchaseOrder;
```

```
/* Error Message:  Msg 208, Level 16, State 1, Line 2

Invalid object name 'seqPurchaseOrder'.  */
```

Cyclical Sequence Objects

We can create cyclical sequence objects as well for enumerating cyclical temporal objects such as weekdays or months.

```
CREATE SEQUENCE seqCycleSeven
AS TINYINT
START WITH 1  INCREMENT BY 1  MINVALUE  1   MAXVALUE  7  CYCLE
GO


CREATE TABLE #Weekdays ( ID INT IDENTITY(1,1) PRIMARY KEY, Weekday nchar(20));
GO

-- Populate table with days progressing by addition of cycle number to current day
INSERT INTO #Weekdays
SELECT DATENAME(dw, dateadd(dd,NEXT VALUE for seqCycleSeven,CURRENT_TIMESTAMP));
GO 20


SELECT * FROM #Weekdays ORDER BY ID;
GO
```

ID	Weekday
1	Tuesday
2	Wednesday
3	Thursday
4	Friday
5	Saturday
6	Sunday
7	Monday
8	Tuesday
9	Wednesday
10	Thursday
11	Friday
12	Saturday
13	Sunday
14	Monday
15	Tuesday
16	Wednesday
17	Thursday
18	Friday
19	Saturday
20	Sunday

```
DROP SEQUENCE seqCycleSeven;  DROP TABLE #Weekdays;
```

CHAPTER 4: Fundamentals of Relational Database Design

Getting the Source Code with sp_helptext

The sp_helptext system procedure can be applied to get the source code for some objects, but not all. **Table source code can only be obtained with GUI scripting in Object Explorer.**

```
EXEC sp_helptext 'sp_who'
GO
-- Command(s) completed successfully. - 94 rows - Partial results.


CREATE PROCEDURE sys.Sp_who --- 1995/11/28 15:48
 @loginame SYSNAME = NULL --or 'active'
AS
  DECLARE @spidlow  INT,
       @spidhigh INT,
       @spid    INT,
       @sid    VARBINARY(85)

  SELECT @spidlow = 0,
     @spidhigh = 32767

  IF ( @loginame IS NOT NULL
     AND Upper(@loginame COLLATE latin1_general_ci_as) = 'ACTIVE' )
   BEGIN
    SELECT spid,
        ecid,
        status,
        loginame=Rtrim(loginame),
        hostname,
        blk=CONVERT(CHAR(5), blocked),
        dbname = CASE
              WHEN dbid = 0 THEN NULL
              WHEN dbid <> 0 THEN Db_name(dbid)
             END,
        cmd,
        request_id
     FROM   sys.sysprocesses_ex
     WHERE  spid >= @spidlow
        AND spid <= @spidhigh
        AND Upper(cmd) <> 'AWAITING COMMAND'

     RETURN ( 0 )
   END
```

CHAPTER 5: JOINing Tables with INNER & OUTER JOINs

SELECT with INNER JOIN

The SELECT statement is used to retrieve data from table(s). An INNER JOIN is a join in which the values   in the columns being joined are compared   using a comparison operator. Inner join also known as equi-join when equality condition is applied. Equi-join: PRIMARY KEY (table a) = FOREIGN KEY (table b).

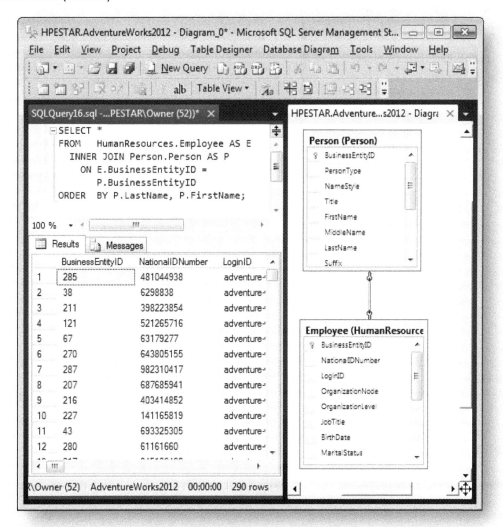

FOREIGN KEY Constraint as Base for INNER JOIN

The INNER JOIN is based on HumanResources.Employee.BusinessEntityID (PRIMARY KEY) is a FOREIGN KEY to Person.Person.BusinessEntityID. The Employee table is in one-to-one relationship with a subset of the Person table.

Diagram of Person.Person and Related Tables

The population of Person.Person includes all employees, contacts, and customers, therefore a key table in the database.

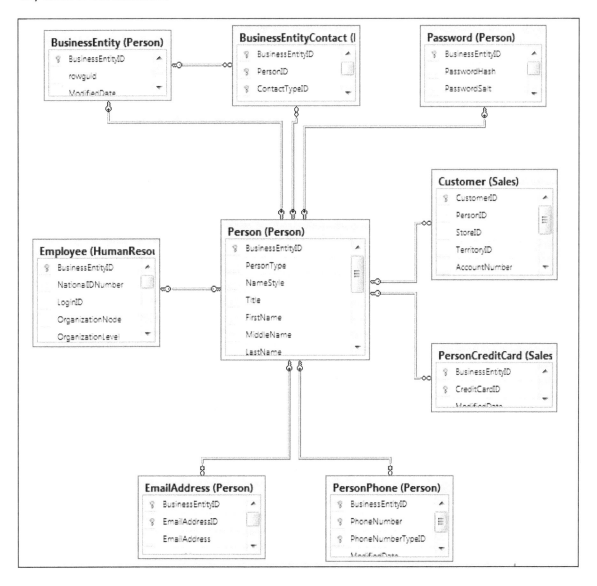

```
-- INNER JOIN ON PRIMARY KEY & FOREIGN KEY
SELECT * FROM Person.Person AS P
        INNER JOIN Person.PersonPhone AS PH
            ON P.BusinessEntityID = PH.BusinessEntityID;
-- (19972 row(s) affected)
```

EQUI-JOIN BETWEEN FOREIGN KEY & PRIMARY KEY

EQUI JOIN means the equality operator is used to match the left and right keys. The reason for the popularity: the goal of most query is to gather information from related tables records (rows). Query to demonstrate why are 3 tables necessary to get a meaningful business report with just a few columns.

```
USE AdventureWorks;
GO


SELECT          CONCAT(LastName, ', ', FirstName)          AS Consumer,
                EmailAddress,
                Phone,
                CU.AccountNumber,
                C.ContactID,
                I.CustomerID
FROM Person.Contact AS C
   INNER JOIN Sales.Individual AS I
      ON C.ContactID = I.ContactID
   INNER JOIN Sales.Customer AS CU
      ON I.CustomerID = CU.CustomerID
WHERE CU.CustomerType = 'I'
ORDER BY LastName, FirstName ;
GO
-- (18484 row(s) affected) - Partial results.
```

Consumer	EmailAddress	Phone	AccountNumber	ContactID	CustomerID
Pal, Yolanda	yolanda11@adventure-works.com	1 (11) 500 555-0110	AW00023748	2837	23748
Palit, Punya	punya0@adventure-works.com	164-555-0118	AW00017574	14759	17574
Parker, Adam	adam29@adventure-works.com	808-555-0157	AW00018228	14771	18228
Parker, Alex	alex26@adventure-works.com	613-555-0123	AW00029252	14783	29252
Parker, Alexandra	alexandra50@adventure-works.com	974-555-0142	AW00016866	8977	16866
Parker, Allison	allison30@adventure-works.com	750-555-0124	AW00026501	9021	26501
Parker, Amanda	amanda51@adventure-works.com	978-555-0167	AW00018081	8985	18081
Parker, Amber	amber7@adventure-works.com	1 (11) 500 555-0198	AW00023959	8999	23959
Parker, Andrea	andrea23@adventure-works.com	612-555-0113	AW00020091	8461	20091
Parker, Angel	angel21@adventure-works.com	815-555-0120	AW00014273	14779	14273
Parker, Bailey	bailey28@adventure-works.com	604-555-0112	AW00019529	9007	19529
Parker, Blake	blake44@adventure-works.com	432-555-0151	AW00015008	3413	15008
Parker, Caleb	caleb28@adventure-works.com	593-555-0116	AW00026318	14760	26318
Parker, Carlos	carlos25@adventure-works.com	937-555-0143	AW00020676	14778	20676
Parker, Charles	charles43@adventure-works.com	266-555-0118	AW00021267	4105	21267
Parker, Chloe	chloe5@adventure-works.com	360-555-0121	AW00027480	8965	27480
Parker, Connor	connor28@adventure-works.com	936-555-0177	AW00028839	14763	28839
Parker, Courtney	courtney5@adventure-works.com	266-555-0176	AW00017612	9002	17612
Parker, Dalton	dalton42@adventure-works.com	535-555-0190	AW00013064	3722	13064
Parker, Devin	devin40@adventure-works.com	897-555-0155	AW00011684	4192	11684
Parker, Eduardo	eduardo41@adventure-works.com	131-555-0192	AW00012939	4269	12939

Diagram of Sales.Customer and Related Tables

Customer is the source of revenue for any business. Therefore, proper table design is paramount.

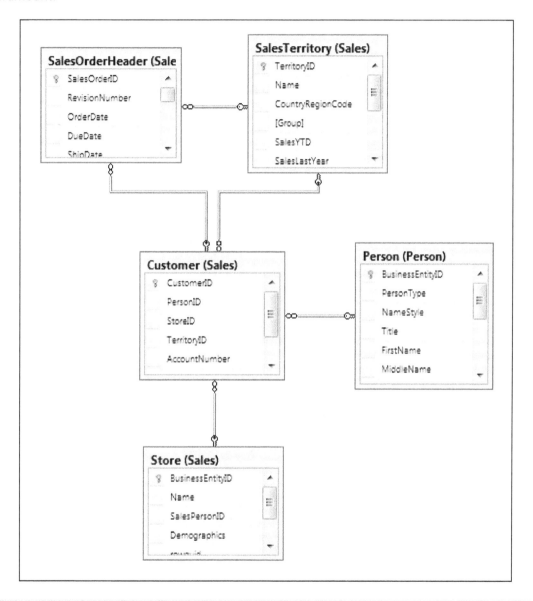

```
-- INNER JOIN ON PRIMARY KEY & FOREIGN KEY - NOTE: PK & FK named differently
SELECT * FROM Sales.Store AS S
          INNER JOIN Sales.Customer AS C   ON S.BusinessEntityID = C.StoreID;
-- (1336 row(s) affected)
```

CHAPTER 5: JOINing Tables with INNER & OUTER JOINs

Extracting All or Partial Data from JOINed Tables

T-SQL scripts to demonstrate how to JOIN two tables and extract all or subset of the information.

USE AdventureWorks2012;

```
-- SELECT all columns from the JOINed tables
SELECT *
FROM   HumanResources.Employee              AS E      -- E is a table alias
    INNER JOIN Person.Person                AS P      -- P is a table alias
        ON E.BusinessEntityID = P.BusinessEntityID
ORDER  BY P.LastName;
-- (290 row(s) affected) - Partial results.
```

FirstName	MiddleName	LastName
Syed	E	Abbas
Kim	B	Abercrombie
Hazem	E	Abolrous
Pilar	G	Ackerman
Jay	G	Adams

```
SELECT E.*                      -- SELECT Employee columns from the JOINed tables
FROM   HumanResources.Employee AS E
    INNER JOIN Person.Person AS P   ON E.BusinessEntityID = P.BusinessEntityID
ORDER  BY P.LastName;
-- Partial results.
```

JobTitle	BirthDate	MaritalStatus	Gender
Pacific Sales Manager	1969-02-11	M	M
Production Technician - WC60	1961-01-14	M	F
Quality Assurance Manager	1971-11-27	S	M
Shipping and Receiving Supervisor	1966-10-11	S	M

```
-- SELECT Person columns from the JOINed tables
SELECT P.* FROM   HumanResources.Employee AS E
            INNER JOIN Person.Person AS P      ON E.BusinessEntityID = P.BusinessEntityID
ORDER  BY P.LastName;
-- Partial results.
```

BusinessEntityID	PersonType
285	SP
38	EM
211	EM

CHAPTER 5: JOINing Tables with INNER & OUTER JOINs

SELECT All Columns From The Joined Tables Using Table Alias And Wildcard

```
SELECT E.*, P.*
FROM   HumanResources.Employee          AS E      -- E is a table alias
    INNER JOIN Person.Person            AS P      -- P is a table alias
        ON E.BusinessEntityID = P.BusinessEntityID
ORDER  BY P.LastName;
-- Same results as SELECT * FROM


-- Count JOINed rows
SELECT count(*)
FROM   HumanResources.Employee AS E
    INNER JOIN Person.Person AS P
        ON E.BusinessEntityID = P.BusinessEntityID
-- 290


-- Vertically output reduction: eliminate columns from the available pool
SELECT   E.BusinessEntityID              AS EmployeeID,    -- column alias
         E.JobTitle,
         P.FirstName,
         P.LastName
FROM   HumanResources.Employee AS E
    INNER JOIN Person.Person AS P    ON E.BusinessEntityID = P.BusinessEntityID
ORDER  BY P.LastName;
-- (290 row(s) affected) - Partial results.
```

EmployeeID	JobTitle	FirstName	LastName
285	Pacific Sales Manager	Syed	Abbas
38	Production Technician - WC60	Kim	Abercrombie
211	Quality Assurance Manager	Hazem	Abolrous
121	Shipping and Receiving Supervisor	Pilar	Ackerman

```
-- Create a new output column from the available pool of columns
SELECT   E.BusinessEntityID              AS EmployeeID,
         E.JobTitle,
         CONCAT(P.FirstName, ' ', P.LastName)     AS NAME
FROM   HumanResources.Employee AS E
    INNER JOIN Person.Person AS P     ON E.BusinessEntityID = P.BusinessEntityID
ORDER  BY P.LastName;
-- (290 row(s) affected) - Partial results.
```

EmployeeID	JobTitle	NAME
285	Pacific Sales Manager	Syed Abbas
38	Production Technician - WC60	Kim Abercrombie
211	Quality Assurance Manager	Hazem Abolrous
121	Shipping and Receiving Supervisor	Pilar Ackerman

CHAPTER 5: JOINing Tables with INNER & OUTER JOINs

Table Aliases for Readability

The table alias serves as shorthand for table name to improve the **readability of queries**. It should be as short as possible and as meaningful as possible when we have to use a few letters. The next T-SQL query applies four table aliases: c, soh, sod, p.

```
USE AdventureWorks;
SELECT DISTINCT SalesPerson = CONCAT(c.FirstName,SPACE(1), c.LastName)
FROM   Person.Contact c
    INNER JOIN Sales.SalesOrderHeader soh
     ON soh.SalesPersonId = c.ContactID
    INNER JOIN Sales.SalesOrderDetail sod
     ON soh.SalesOrderId = sod.SalesOrderId
    INNER JOIN Production.Product p
     ON sod.ProductID = p.ProductID    AND p.Name LIKE ('%Touring Frame%');
GO /*    SalesPerson
         Carla Eldridge
         Carol Elliott
         Gail Erickson  ....*/
```

Column Aliases for Readability & Presentation

The column alias serves as a meaningful column name either replacing a column name or filling in when there is no column name. In the previous example the = sign was used to establish the column alias. Alternate setting follows applying "AS" (it can be skipped) after the column. If the alias has spaces it has to be included in square brackets like [Bond Sales] or double quotes.

```
USE AdventureWorks;
SELECT DISTINCT  CONCAT(c.FirstName,' ', c.LastName)                  AS SalesPerson
FROM   Person.Contact c
    INNER JOIN Sales.SalesOrderHeader soh
     ON soh.SalesPersonId = c.ContactID
    INNER JOIN Sales.SalesOrderDetail sod
     ON soh.SalesOrderId = sod.SalesOrderId
    INNER JOIN Production.Product p
     ON sod.ProductID = p.ProductID   AND p.Name LIKE ('%Touring Frame%');
-- (17 row(s) affected) - Partial results.
```

SalesPerson
Carla Eldridge
Carol Elliott
Gail Erickson
Gary Drury
Janeth Esteves
Jauna Elson
John Emory

Derived Table Alias with a List of Column Aliases

Optionally column alias list can be specified for derived tables just like in CTE definition. T-SQL query demonstrates nested derived tables with table-column aliases (P & J).

```
SELECT DISTINCT ProdID, ProdName, ProdPrice, OrderQuantity
FROM    (
                SELECT   ID, ProductName, Price,          -- Derived table columns
                         OrderQty                         -- SOD column
                FROM AdventureWorks2012.Sales.SalesOrderDetail SOD
                 INNER JOIN
                    (SELECT ProductID, Name, ListPrice
                     FROM AdventureWorks2012.Production.Product
                    ) P(ID, ProductName, Price)           -- inner derived table
                 ON SOD.ProductID = P.ID
        ) J (ProdID, ProdName, ProdPrice, OrderQuantity)  -- outer derived table
ORDER BY ProdPrice DESC, ProdName;
-- (2667 row(s) affected) - Partial results.
```

ProdID	ProdName	ProdPrice	OrderQuantity
750	Road-150 Red, 44	3578.27	3
750	Road-150 Red, 44	3578.27	6
750	Road-150 Red, 44	3578.27	1
750	Road-150 Red, 44	3578.27	4
750	Road-150 Red, 44	3578.27	2
750	Road-150 Red, 44	3578.27	5
751	Road-150 Red, 48	3578.27	6
751	Road-150 Red, 48	3578.27	3
751	Road-150 Red, 48	3578.27	2
751	Road-150 Red, 48	3578.27	5
751	Road-150 Red, 48	3578.27	4
751	Road-150 Red, 48	3578.27	1
752	Road-150 Red, 52	3578.27	5
752	Road-150 Red, 52	3578.27	3
752	Road-150 Red, 52	3578.27	6
752	Road-150 Red, 52	3578.27	1
752	Road-150 Red, 52	3578.27	4
752	Road-150 Red, 52	3578.27	2
753	Road-150 Red, 56	3578.27	6
753	Road-150 Red, 56	3578.27	3

INNER JOIN with Additional Conditions

The ON clause of a JOIN can include additional conditions as the following demonstration shows. The INNER JOIN is still based on FOREIGN KEY relationship, but only a subset of records (rows) returned due to the additional conditions, or JOIN predicates. The first query returns the distinct set of cases where the Selling Price was below the ListPrice for ProductID 800 which is a yellow road bike. The second query covers the remaining range where the Selling Price was equal or above the ListPrice.

```
USE AdventureWorks2012;
SELECT DISTINCT( P.ProductID ),
        ProductName = P.Name,              -- column alias
        P.ListPrice,
        SOD.UnitPrice AS 'Selling Price'   -- column alias
FROM   Sales.SalesOrderDetail AS SOD       -- table alias
    INNER JOIN  Production.Product AS P     -- table alias
    ON SOD.ProductID = P.ProductID
        AND SOD.UnitPrice < P.ListPrice              -- JOIN predicate
        AND  P.ProductID = 800;                      -- JOIN predicate
```

ProductID	ProductName	ListPrice	Selling Price
800	Road-550-W Yellow, 44	1120.49	600.2625
800	Road-550-W Yellow, 44	1120.49	672.294
800	Road-550-W Yellow, 44	1120.49	1000.4375

```
SELECT DISTINCT( P.ProductID ),
        ProductName = P.Name,
        P.ListPrice,
        SOD.UnitPrice AS 'Selling Price'
FROM   Sales.SalesOrderDetail AS SOD
    INNER JOIN  Production.Product AS P
    ON SOD.ProductID = P.ProductID
        AND SOD.UnitPrice >= P.ListPrice
        AND  P.ProductID BETWEEN 800 AND 900
ORDER BY ProductName;
-- (26 row(s) affected) - Partial results.
```

ProductID	ProductName	ListPrice	Selling Price
879	All-Purpose Bike Stand	159.00	159.00
877	Bike Wash - Dissolver	7.95	7.95
866	Classic Vest, L	63.50	63.50
865	Classic Vest, M	63.50	63.50
864	Classic Vest, S	63.50	63.50
878	Fender Set - Mountain	21.98	21.98
860	Half-Finger Gloves, L	24.49	24.49
859	Half-Finger Gloves, M	24.49	24.49
858	Half-Finger Gloves, S	24.49	24.49
876	Hitch Rack - 4-Bike	120.00	120.00

Counting Rows in JOINs

As the T-SQL script following shows, the basic FOREIGN KEY based JOIN returns 121,317 rows which is all the rows in Sales.SalesOrderDetail table. The additional condition P.ProductID = 800 selects a subset of 495 rows which is then divided between the < and >= conditions.

```
USE AdventureWorks2012;
SELECT Rows = count(*)
FROM   Sales.SalesOrderDetail AS SOD
     INNER JOIN  Production.Product AS P    ON SOD.ProductID = P.ProductID
-- 121317

SELECT Rows = count(*)
FROM   Sales.SalesOrderDetail AS SOD
     INNER JOIN  Production.Product AS P   ON SOD.ProductID = P.ProductID   AND P.ProductID = 800;
-- 495

SELECT Rows = count(*)
FROM   Sales.SalesOrderDetail AS SOD
     INNER JOIN  Production.Product AS P
     ON SOD.ProductID = P.ProductID
       AND SOD.UnitPrice < P.ListPrice
       AND P.ProductID = 800;
-- 285

SELECT Rows = count(*)
FROM   Sales.SalesOrderDetail AS SOD
     INNER JOIN  Production.Product AS P
     ON SOD.ProductID = P.ProductID
       AND SOD.UnitPrice >= P.ListPrice
       AND P.ProductID = 800;
-- 210

SELECT COUNT(P.ProductID)
FROM   Sales.SalesOrderDetail AS SOD
     INNER JOIN  Production.Product AS P
     ON SOD.ProductID = P.ProductID
       AND SOD.UnitPrice >= P.ListPrice
       AND  P.ProductID BETWEEN 800 AND 900;
-- 21085

SELECT COUNT(DISTINCT P.ProductID)
FROM   Sales.SalesOrderDetail AS SOD
     INNER JOIN  Production.Product AS P
     ON SOD.ProductID = P.ProductID   AND SOD.UnitPrice >= P.ListPrice
         AND  P.ProductID BETWEEN 800 AND 900;
```

CHAPTER 5: JOINing Tables with INNER & OUTER JOINs

INNER JOIN with 3 Tables

T-SQL query to demonstrate JOINing three tables. Due to the application of the FORMAT function, column name is lost. Therefore we have to alias the formatted column with the original column name or something else. Both INNER JOINs are based on FOREIGN KEY relationships. PV.ProductID is an FK to the Production.Product table, and the PV.VendorID is an FK to the Purchasing.Vendor table. The Purchasing.ProductVendor table is a junction table representing many-to-many relationships between products and vendors: a vendor may supply many products (see Beaumont Bikes in results) and a product may be supplied by many vendors (see Chainring in results).

```
USE AdventureWorks;
GO
SELECT          P.ProductNumber,
                P.Name                                  AS Product,
                V.Name                                  AS Vendor,
                FORMAT (PV.LastReceiptCost, 'c', 'en-US')   AS LastReceiptCost
FROM Production.Product AS P
  INNER JOIN Purchasing.ProductVendor AS PV
        ON P.ProductID = PV.ProductID
  INNER JOIN Purchasing.Vendor AS V
        ON V.VendorID = PV.VendorID
ORDER BY Product;
GO
-- (406 row(s) affected) - Partial results.
```

ProductNumber	Product	Vendor	LastReceiptCost
AR-5381	Adjustable Race	Litware, Inc.	$50.26
BA-8327	Bearing Ball	Wood Fitness	$41.92
CH-0234	Chain	Varsity Sport Co.	$15.74
CR-7833	Chainring	Beaumont Bikes	$25.42
CR-7833	Chainring	Bike Satellite Inc.	$26.37
CR-7833	Chainring	Training Systems	$28.70
CB-2903	Chainring Bolts	Beaumont Bikes	$47.47
CB-2903	Chainring Bolts	Bike Satellite Inc.	$45.37
CB-2903	Chainring Bolts	Training Systems	$49.64
CN-6137	Chainring Nut	Beaumont Bikes	$42.80
CN-6137	Chainring Nut	Bike Satellite Inc.	$40.49
CN-6137	Chainring Nut	Training Systems	$44.32
RA-7490	Cone-Shaped Race	Midwest Sport, Inc.	$44.22
CR-9981	Crown Race	Business Equipment Center	$50.26
RA-2345	Cup-Shaped Race	Bloomington Multisport	$48.76
DC-8732	Decal 1	SUPERSALES INC.	$0.21
DC-9824	Decal 2	SUPERSALES INC.	$0.21
LE-6000	External Lock Washer 1	Pro Sport Industries	$41.24
LE-6000	External Lock Washer 1	Aurora Bike Center	$43.27
LE-6000	External Lock Washer 1	Expert Bike Co	$41.17

T-SQL Query To Return All Road Frames Offered For Sale By AdventureWorks Cycles

```
USE AdventureWorks2012;
SELECT        UPPER(PC.Name)          AS Category,  PSC.Name              AS Subcategory,
              P.Name          AS Product,  FORMAT(ListPrice, 'c', 'en-US')     AS ListPrice,
              FORMAT(StandardCost, 'c', 'en-US')                         AS StandardCost
FROM Production.Product AS P
  INNER JOIN Production.ProductSubcategory AS PSC
            ON PSC.ProductSubcategoryID = P.ProductSubcategoryID
  INNER JOIN Production.ProductCategory AS PC
            ON PC.ProductCategoryID = PSC.ProductCategoryID
WHERE PSC.Name like 'Road Frames' ORDER BY Category, Subcategory, Product;
```

Category	Subcategory	Product	ListPrice	StandardCost
COMPONENTS	Road Frames	HL Road Frame - Black, 44	$1,431.50	$868.63
COMPONENTS	Road Frames	HL Road Frame - Black, 48	$1,431.50	$868.63
COMPONENTS	Road Frames	HL Road Frame - Black, 52	$1,431.50	$868.63
COMPONENTS	Road Frames	HL Road Frame - Black, 58	$1,431.50	$1,059.31
COMPONENTS	Road Frames	HL Road Frame - Black, 62	$1,431.50	$868.63
COMPONENTS	Road Frames	HL Road Frame - Red, 44	$1,431.50	$868.63
COMPONENTS	Road Frames	HL Road Frame - Red, 48	$1,431.50	$868.63
COMPONENTS	Road Frames	HL Road Frame - Red, 52	$1,431.50	$868.63
COMPONENTS	Road Frames	HL Road Frame - Red, 56	$1,431.50	$868.63
COMPONENTS	Road Frames	HL Road Frame - Red, 58	$1,431.50	$1,059.31
COMPONENTS	Road Frames	HL Road Frame - Red, 62	$1,431.50	$868.63
COMPONENTS	Road Frames	LL Road Frame - Black, 44	$337.22	$204.63
COMPONENTS	Road Frames	LL Road Frame - Black, 48	$337.22	$204.63
COMPONENTS	Road Frames	LL Road Frame - Black, 52	$337.22	$204.63
COMPONENTS	Road Frames	LL Road Frame - Black, 58	$337.22	$204.63
COMPONENTS	Road Frames	LL Road Frame - Black, 60	$337.22	$204.63
COMPONENTS	Road Frames	LL Road Frame - Black, 62	$337.22	$204.63
COMPONENTS	Road Frames	LL Road Frame - Red, 44	$337.22	$187.16
COMPONENTS	Road Frames	LL Road Frame - Red, 48	$337.22	$187.16
COMPONENTS	Road Frames	LL Road Frame - Red, 52	$337.22	$187.16
COMPONENTS	Road Frames	LL Road Frame - Red, 58	$337.22	$187.16
COMPONENTS	Road Frames	LL Road Frame - Red, 60	$337.22	$187.16
COMPONENTS	Road Frames	LL Road Frame - Red, 62	$337.22	$187.16
COMPONENTS	Road Frames	ML Road Frame - Red, 44	$594.83	$352.14
COMPONENTS	Road Frames	ML Road Frame - Red, 48	$594.83	$352.14
COMPONENTS	Road Frames	ML Road Frame - Red, 52	$594.83	$352.14
COMPONENTS	Road Frames	ML Road Frame - Red, 58	$594.83	$352.14
COMPONENTS	Road Frames	ML Road Frame - Red, 60	$594.83	$352.14
COMPONENTS	Road Frames	ML Road Frame-W - Yellow, 38	$594.83	$360.94
COMPONENTS	Road Frames	ML Road Frame-W - Yellow, 40	$594.83	$360.94
COMPONENTS	Road Frames	ML Road Frame-W - Yellow, 42	$594.83	$360.94
COMPONENTS	Road Frames	ML Road Frame-W - Yellow, 44	$594.83	$360.94
COMPONENTS	Road Frames	ML Road Frame-W - Yellow, 48	$594.83	$360.94

CHAPTER 5: JOINing Tables with INNER & OUTER JOINs

INNER JOIN with Junction Table

Three tables INNER JOIN includes the titleauthor junction table which represent many-to-many relationship. All JOINs are EQUI-JOINs with FOREIGN KEYs and PRIMARY KEYs.

```
USE pubs;

SELECT          FORMAT(ytd_sales, 'c', 'en-US')                        AS YTDSales,
                CONCAT(au.au_fname, ' ', au.au_lname)                  AS Author,
                FORMAT((ytd_sales * royalty) / 100,'c','en-US')        AS AuthorRev,
                FORMAT((ytd_sales - (ytd_sales * royalty) / 100),'c','en-US')  AS PublisherRev
FROM titles t
        INNER JOIN titleauthor ta
            ON t.title_id = ta.title_id
        INNER JOIN authors au
            ON ta.au_id = au.au_id
ORDER BY        YTDSales DESC,          -- Major sort key
                Author ASC;             -- Minor sort key
GO
```

YTDSales	Author	AuthorRev	PublisherRev
$8,780.00	Cheryl Carson	$1,404.00	$7,376.00
$4,095.00	Abraham Bennet	$409.00	$3,686.00
$4,095.00	Akiko Yokomoto	$409.00	$3,686.00
$4,095.00	Ann Dull	$409.00	$3,686.00
$4,095.00	Burt Gringlesby	$409.00	$3,686.00
$4,095.00	Dean Straight	$409.00	$3,686.00
$4,095.00	Marjorie Green	$409.00	$3,686.00
$4,095.00	Michael O'Leary	$409.00	$3,686.00
$4,095.00	Sheryl Hunter	$409.00	$3,686.00
$4,072.00	Johnson White	$407.00	$3,665.00
$375.00	Livia Karsen	$37.00	$338.00
$375.00	Stearns MacFeather	$37.00	$338.00
$375.00	Sylvia Panteley	$37.00	$338.00
$3,876.00	Michael O'Leary	$387.00	$3,489.00
$3,876.00	Stearns MacFeather	$387.00	$3,489.00
$3,336.00	Charlene Locksley	$333.00	$3,003.00
$22,246.00	Anne Ringer	$5,339.00	$16,907.00
$22,246.00	Michel DeFrance	$5,339.00	$16,907.00
$2,045.00	Albert Ringer	$245.00	$1,800.00
$2,045.00	Anne Ringer	$245.00	$1,800.00
$2,032.00	Innes del Castillo	$243.00	$1,789.00
$18,722.00	Marjorie Green	$4,493.00	$14,229.00
$15,096.00	Reginald Blotchet-Halls	$2,113.00	$12,983.00
$111.00	Albert Ringer	$11.00	$100.00
NULL	Charlene Locksley	NULL	NULL

NON-EQUI JOINs for Data Analytics

We can use not equal operators in JOIN predicates as demonstrated in the next query. The second predicate in the JOIN is less than JOIN.

```
USE AdventureWorks2012;
GO
-- List of "red" products sold at a discount
SELECT DISTINCT       p.ProductNumber,
                      p.Name                              AS ProductName,
                      FORMAT(p.ListPrice,'c','en-US')     AS ListPrice,
                      FORMAT(sod.UnitPrice,'c','en-US')   AS SellPrice
FROM Sales.SalesOrderDetail AS sod
  INNER JOIN Production.Product AS p
        ON sod.ProductID = p.ProductID
        AND sod.UnitPrice < p.ListPrice
WHERE Color = 'Red'
ORDER BY p.ProductNumber;
--(86 row(s) affected) - Partial results.
```

ProductNumber	ProductName	ListPrice	SellPrice
BK-R50R-44	Road-650 Red, 44	$782.99	$234.90
BK-R50R-44	Road-650 Red, 44	$782.99	$419.46
BK-R50R-44	Road-650 Red, 44	$782.99	$430.64
BK-R50R-44	Road-650 Red, 44	$782.99	$454.13
BK-R50R-44	Road-650 Red, 44	$782.99	$469.79
BK-R50R-44	Road-650 Red, 44	$782.99	$563.75
BK-R50R-44	Road-650 Red, 44	$782.99	$699.10
BK-R50R-48	Road-650 Red, 48	$782.99	$419.46
BK-R50R-48	Road-650 Red, 48	$782.99	$430.64
BK-R50R-48	Road-650 Red, 48	$782.99	$454.13
BK-R50R-48	Road-650 Red, 48	$782.99	$469.79
BK-R50R-48	Road-650 Red, 48	$782.99	$563.75

To resolve the duplicate issue which makes DISTINCT usage necessary, we have to include the SalesOrderID column.

```
SELECT                        p.ProductNumber,
                              p.Name                              AS ProductName,
                              FORMAT(p.ListPrice,'c','en-US')     AS ListPrice,
                              FORMAT(sod.UnitPrice,'c','en-US')   AS SellPrice,
                              sod.SalesOrderID
FROM Sales.SalesOrderDetail AS sod
  INNER JOIN Production.Product AS p
        ON sod.ProductID = p.ProductID
        AND sod.UnitPrice < p.ListPrice
WHERE Color = 'Red'   ORDER BY p.ProductNumber;
-- (8408 row(s) affected)
```

CHAPTER 5: JOINing Tables with INNER & OUTER JOINs

Interchangeability of ON & WHERE Predicates in INNER JOINs

We can freely place the predicates to either the ON clause or the WHERE clause in an INNER JOIN. This is not true for OUTER JOINs such as LEFT JOINs.

```
USE AdventureWorks2012;
-- List of "blue" products sold at a discount
SELECT DISTINCT  p.ProductNumber, p.Name                    AS ProductName,
                 FORMAT(p.ListPrice,'c','en-US')            AS ListPrice,
                 FORMAT(sod.UnitPrice,'c','en-US')          AS SellPrice
FROM Sales.SalesOrderDetail AS sod
   INNER JOIN Production.Product AS p
        ON sod.ProductID = p.ProductID
        AND sod.UnitPrice < p.ListPrice
WHERE Color = 'Blue'  ORDER BY p.ProductNumber;
--(57 row(s) affected)
```

```
SELECT DISTINCT  p.ProductNumber, p.Name                    AS ProductName,
                 FORMAT(p.ListPrice,'c','en-US')            AS ListPrice,
                 FORMAT(sod.UnitPrice,'c','en-US')          AS SellPrice
FROM Sales.SalesOrderDetail AS sod
   INNER JOIN Production.Product AS p
        ON sod.ProductID = p.ProductID
        AND sod.UnitPrice < p.ListPrice
        AND Color = 'Blue'
ORDER BY p.ProductNumber;
--(57 row(s) affected)
```

```
SELECT DISTINCT  p.ProductNumber, p.Name                    AS ProductName,
                 FORMAT(p.ListPrice,'c','en-US')            AS ListPrice,
                 FORMAT(sod.UnitPrice,'c','en-US')          AS SellPrice
FROM Sales.SalesOrderDetail AS sod
   INNER JOIN Production.Product AS p
   ON sod.ProductID = p.ProductID
WHERE sod.UnitPrice < p.ListPrice    AND Color = 'Blue'  ORDER BY p.ProductNumber;
--(57 row(s) affected)
```

```
-- Old-style INNER JOIN with table list and WHERE clause
SELECT DISTINCT  p.ProductNumber, p.Name                    AS ProductName,
                 FORMAT(p.ListPrice,'c','en-US')            AS ListPrice,
                 FORMAT(sod.UnitPrice,'c','en-US')          AS SellPrice
FROM Sales.SalesOrderDetail AS sod,  Production.Product AS p
WHERE sod.ProductID = p.ProductID
        AND sod.UnitPrice < p.ListPrice
        AND Color = 'Blue'
ORDER BY p.ProductNumber;          --(57 row(s) affected)
```

SELF-JOIN for Analytics Within a Table

When a table is JOINed to itself, it is a called a self-join. The purpose of such a JOIN is to examine data relations within the table. The Production.Product table is self-joined to itself on the ProductSubcategoryID FOREIGN KEY(not on a PRIMARY KEY), a many-to-many JOIN. Subsequently, we made the query "friendlier" by using subcategory names as opposed to ID-s.

```
SELECT DISTINCT  P1.ProductSubcategoryID,
                 P1.ListPrice                    AS ListPrice1,
                 P2.ListPrice                    AS ListPrice2
FROM   Production.Product P1
 INNER JOIN Production.Product P2
  ON P1.ProductSubcategoryID = P2.ProductSubcategoryID
  AND P1.ListPrice < P2.ListPrice
  AND P1.ListPrice < $15
  AND P2.ListPrice < $15;
```

ProductSubcategoryID	ListPrice1	ListPrice2
23	8.99	9.50
28	4.99	8.99
28	4.99	9.99
28	8.99	9.99
37	2.29	3.99
37	2.29	4.99
37	3.99	4.99

```
SELECT DISTINCT  PS.Name AS Subcategory,
                 P1.ListPrice     AS ListPrice1,
                 P2.ListPrice     AS ListPrice2
FROM   Production.ProductSubcategory PS
    INNER JOIN Production.Product P1
        ON PS.ProductSubcategoryID = P1.ProductSubcategoryID
    INNER JOIN Production.Product P2
        ON P1.ProductSubcategoryID = P2.ProductSubcategoryID
        AND P1.ListPrice < P2.ListPrice                    -- To prevent duplicate processing
        AND P1.ListPrice < $15
        AND P2.ListPrice < $15;
```

Subcategory	ListPrice1	ListPrice2
Bottles and Cages	4.99	8.99
Bottles and Cages	4.99	9.99
Bottles and Cages	8.99	9.99
Socks	8.99	9.50
Tires and Tubes	2.29	3.99
Tires and Tubes	2.29	4.99
Tires and Tubes	3.99	4.99

CHAPTER 5: JOINing Tables with INNER & OUTER JOINs

T-SQL SELF-JOIN Query Lists The Competing Suppliers For Each Product Purchased From Vendor

Since the ProductID in the ProductVendor table is part of a composite PRIMARY KEY, we can conclude that it is a many-to-many JOIN.

```
SELECT DISTINCT
            Vendor = V.[Name],
            P1.BusinessEntityID,
            Product = P.[Name],
            P1.ProductID
FROM   Production.Product P
    INNER JOIN Purchasing.ProductVendor P1
        ON P.ProductID = P1.ProductID
    INNER JOIN Purchasing.Vendor V
        ON P1.BusinessEntityID = V.BusinessEntityID
    INNER JOIN Purchasing.ProductVendor P2
        ON P1.ProductID = P2.ProductID
WHERE  P1.BusinessEntityID <> P2.BusinessEntityID
ORDER  BY Product, Vendor
-- (347 row(s) affected) - Partial results.
```

Vendor	BusinessEntityID	Product	ProductID
Beaumont Bikes	1602	Chainring	322
Bike Satellite Inc.	1604	Chainring	322
Training Systems	1514	Chainring	322
Beaumont Bikes	1602	Chainring Bolts	320
Bike Satellite Inc.	1604	Chainring Bolts	320
Training Systems	1514	Chainring Bolts	320
Beaumont Bikes	1602	Chainring Nut	321
Bike Satellite Inc.	1604	Chainring Nut	321
Training Systems	1514	Chainring Nut	321
Aurora Bike Center	1616	External Lock Washer 1	409
Expert Bike Co	1672	External Lock Washer 1	409
Pro Sport Industries	1686	External Lock Washer 1	409
Aurora Bike Center	1616	External Lock Washer 2	411
Pro Sport Industries	1686	External Lock Washer 2	411
Aurora Bike Center	1616	External Lock Washer 3	403
Expert Bike Co	1672	External Lock Washer 3	403
Pro Sport Industries	1686	External Lock Washer 3	403
Aurora Bike Center	1616	External Lock Washer 4	404
Expert Bike Co	1672	External Lock Washer 4	404
Pro Sport Industries	1686	External Lock Washer 4	404
Aurora Bike Center	1616	External Lock Washer 5	406
Expert Bike Co	1672	External Lock Washer 5	406
Pro Sport Industries	1686	External Lock Washer 5	406
Aurora Bike Center	1616	External Lock Washer 6	408
Expert Bike Co	1672	External Lock Washer 6	408

Applying SELF-JOIN for Numbering Result Lines

T-SQL script to demonstrate how SELF-JOIN can be used for numbering lines in query results. Note that in these days we would use **ROW_NUMBER()** function which has been introduced with SQL Server 2005.

```
USE Northwind ;
GO


SELECT  OD.OrderID,
            SeqNo                               AS LineItem,
            OD.ProductID,
            FORMAT(UnitPrice,'c','en-US')       AS UnitPrice,
            Quantity,
            FORMAT(Discount, 'p')               AS Discount
FROM    [Order Details] OD
  INNER JOIN (SELECT  count(* ) AS SeqNo,
            a.OrderID,
            a.ProductID
        FROM    [Order Details] A
            INNER JOIN [Order Details] B
            ON A.ProductID >= B.ProductID            -- Prevent duplicates
            AND A.OrderID = B.OrderID
        GROUP BY A.OrderID,   A.ProductID) a
    ON OD.OrderID = a.OrderID
        AND OD.ProductID = a.ProductID
WHERE   OD.OrderID < 10400
ORDER BY        OD.OrderID,
            LineItem
-- (405 row(s) affected) - Partial results.
```

Vendor	AddressLine1	AddressLine2	City	State	Country
A. Datum Corporation	2596 Big Canyon Road		New York	New York	United States
Advanced Bicycles	7995 Edwards Ave.		Lynnwood	Washington	United States
Allenson Cycles	4659 Montoya		Altadena	California	United States
American Bicycles and Wheels	1667 Warren Street		West Covina	California	United States
American Bikes	7179 Montana		Torrance	California	United States
Anderson's Custom Bikes	9 Guadalupe Dr.		Burbank	California	United States
Aurora Bike Center	65 Park Glen Court		Port Orchard	Washington	United States
Australia Bike Retailer	28 San Marino Ct.		Bellingham	Washington	United States
Beaumont Bikes	2472 Alexander Place		West Covina	Idaho	United States
Bergeron Off-Roads	9830 May Way		Mill Valley	Montana	United States
Bicycle Specialists	1286 Cincerto Circle		Lake Oswego	Oregon	United States
Bike Satellite Inc.	2141 Delaware Ct.		Downey	Tennessee	United States
Bloomington Multisport	218 Fall Creek Road		West Covina	California	United States
Burnett Road Warriors	5807 Churchill Dr.		Corvallis	Oregon	United States
Business Equipment Center	6061 St. Paul Way		Everett	Montana	United States
Capital Road Cycles	628 Muir Road		Los Angeles	California	United States
Carlson Specialties	2313 B Southampton Rd		Missoula	Montana	United States
Chicago City Saddles	3 Gehringer Drive		Daly City	California	United States
Chicago Rent-All	15 Pear Dr.		Newport Beach	California	United States
Circuit Cycles	1 Mt. Dell Drive		Portland	Oregon	United States

CHAPTER 5: JOINing Tables with INNER & OUTER JOINs

INNER JOIN with 5 Tables

It takes accessing five tables to get the vendor name & address information in AdventureWorks. In fact this is the main complaint against 3NF relational database design: too many JOINs required to extract data. True, but the benefits of 3NF design are overwhelming. A way to overcome the "too many JOINs" issue is creating views which are pre-canned SELECT queries.

```
USE AdventureWorks;
GO
```

```
SELECT V.Name               AS Vendor,
    A.AddressLine1,
    isnull(A.AddressLine2, '')        AS AddressLine2,
    A.City,
    SP.Name                 AS State,
    CR.Name           AS Country
FROM   Purchasing.Vendor AS V
    INNER JOIN Purchasing.VendorAddress AS VA
        ON VA.VendorID = V.VendorID
    INNER JOIN Person.Address AS A
        ON A.AddressID = VA.AddressID
    INNER JOIN Person.StateProvince AS SP
        ON SP.StateProvinceID = A.StateProvinceID
    INNER JOIN Person.CountryRegion AS CR
        ON CR.CountryRegionCode = SP.CountryRegionCode
ORDER  BY Vendor;
GO
-- (104 row(s) affected) - Partial results.
```

Vendor	AddressLine1	AddressLine2	City	State	Country
A. Datum Corporation	2596 Big Canyon Road		New York	New York	United States
Advanced Bicycles	7995 Edwards Ave.		Lynnwood	Washington	United States
Allenson Cycles	4659 Montoya		Altadena	California	United States
American Bicycles and Wheels	1667 Warren Street		West Covina	California	United States
American Bikes	7179 Montana		Torrance	California	United States
Anderson's Custom Bikes	9 Guadalupe Dr.		Burbank	California	United States
Aurora Bike Center	65 Park Glen Court		Port Orchard	Washington	United States
Australia Bike Retailer	28 San Marino Ct.		Bellingham	Washington	United States
Beaumont Bikes	2472 Alexander Place		West Covina	Idaho	United States
Bergeron Off-Roads	9830 May Way		Mill Valley	Montana	United States
Bicycle Specialists	1286 Cincerto Circle		Lake Oswego	Oregon	United States
Bike Satellite Inc.	2141 Delaware Ct.		Downey	Tennessee	United States
Bloomington Multisport	218 Fall Creek Road		West Covina	California	United States
Burnett Road Warriors	5807 Churchill Dr.		Corvallis	Oregon	United States
Business Equipment Center	6061 St. Paul Way		Everett	Montana	United States
Capital Road Cycles	628 Muir Road		Los Angeles	California	United States

Creating View as Workaround for "Too Many JOINs"

It is so simple to create a view, that counterproductive if not done for queries which are used again and again. Given that large database systems may have a great number of views, meaningful long names are paremount.

```
-- No implicit ORDER BY can be included in a view - no trick around it either
CREATE VIEW vVendorAddress  AS
SELECT V.Name                 AS Vendor,
    A.AddressLine1,
    isnull(A.AddressLine2, '')        AS AddressLine2,
    A.City,
    SP.Name                 AS State,
    CR.Name           AS Country
FROM   Purchasing.Vendor AS V
    INNER JOIN Purchasing.VendorAddress AS VA       ON VA.VendorID = V.VendorID
    INNER JOIN Person.Address AS A          ON A.AddressID = VA.AddressID
    INNER JOIN Person.StateProvince AS SP        ON SP.StateProvinceID = A.StateProvinceID
    INNER JOIN Person.CountryRegion AS CR      ON CR.CountryRegionCode = SP.CountryRegionCode
ORDER  BY Vendor;
GO  /* Msg 1033, Level 15, State 1, Procedure vVendorAddress, Line 18
The ORDER BY clause is invalid in views, inline functions, derived tables, subqueries, and common table
expressions, unless TOP, OFFSET or FOR XML is also specified.  */
```

```
CREATE VIEW vVendorAddress  AS
SELECT V.Name                 AS Vendor,
    A.AddressLine1,
    isnull(A.AddressLine2, '')        AS AddressLine2,
    A.City,
    SP.Name                 AS State,
    CR.Name           AS Country
FROM   Purchasing.Vendor AS V
    INNER JOIN Purchasing.VendorAddress AS VA       ON VA.VendorID = V.VendorID
    INNER JOIN Person.Address AS A          ON A.AddressID = VA.AddressID
    INNER JOIN Person.StateProvince AS SP        ON SP.StateProvinceID = A.StateProvinceID
    INNER JOIN Person.CountryRegion AS CR      ON CR.CountryRegionCode = SP.CountryRegionCode
GO
```

```
SELECT TOP 5 * FROM vVendorAddress ORDER BY Vendor;
```

Vendor	AddressLine1	AddressLine2	City	State	Country
A. Datum Corporation	2596 Big Canyon Road		New York	New York	United States
Advanced Bicycles	7995 Edwards Ave.		Lynnwood	Washington	United States
Allenson Cycles	4659 Montoya		Altadena	California	United States
American Bicycles and Wheels	1667 Warren Street		West Covina	California	United States
American Bikes	7179 Montana		Torrance	California	United States

CHAPTER 5: JOINing Tables with INNER & OUTER JOINs

Non-Key INNER JOIN for Analytics

So far we have seen INNER JOINs based on FOREIGN KEY to PRIMARY equality relationships. The next INNER JOIN is based on the equality of the first 5 letters of last names. It is also a SELF-JOIN. In addition to the last name part equality, two more conditions are reducing the result set. The < condition is intended to reduce duplicates and the first letter of last name is 'S' limits the query results further. This is a many-to-many JOIN.

```
USE AdventureWorks2012;

SELECT  DISTINCT
    CONCAT( A.FirstName, space(1), A.LastName)      AS Person,
    CONCAT( B.FirstName, space(1), B.LastName)      AS LastNameNeighbor
FROM   Person.Person A
    INNER JOIN  Person.Person B
     ON LEFT(A.LastName, 5) = LEFT(B.LastName, 5)
       AND A.LastName < B.LastName
       AND LEFT(A.LastName, 1) = 'S'
ORDER  BY         Person,
                  LastNameNeighbor;
-- (169 row(s) affected) - Partial results.
```

Person	LastNameNeighbor
Abigail Smith	Lorrin Smith-Bates
Adriana Smith	Lorrin Smith-Bates
Alexander Smith	Lorrin Smith-Bates
Alexandra Smith	Lorrin Smith-Bates
Alexis Smith	Lorrin Smith-Bates
Allen Smith	Lorrin Smith-Bates
Alyssa Smith	Lorrin Smith-Bates
Andre Smith	Lorrin Smith-Bates
Andrew Smith	Lorrin Smith-Bates
Arthur Smith	Lorrin Smith-Bates
Ashley Smith	Lorrin Smith-Bates
Austin Smith	Lorrin Smith-Bates
Barry Srini	Sethu Srinivasan
Ben Smith	Lorrin Smith-Bates
Benjamin Smith	Lorrin Smith-Bates
Beth Srini	Sethu Srinivasan
Brandon Smith	Lorrin Smith-Bates
Brandy Srini	Sethu Srinivasan
Brett Srini	Sethu Srinivasan
Brianna Smith	Lorrin Smith-Bates

JOINing Tables without Relationship for Combinatorics

SQL Server will execute such a JOIN on any pair of compatible columns as demonstrated by the next T-SQL query. Note this is only a demo, there is no business meaning to it unless the combinatorial results are useful for some application. A more practical example in the pubs database matching author city with publisher city using a JOIN.

```
USE Northwind;   -- Cross database JOIN query
SELECT   P.ProductID,
         P.ProductName          AS NorthwindProduct,
         PP.Name                AS AWProduct
FROM dbo.Products P
         INNER JOIN AdventureWorks2008.Production.Product PP      ON P.ProductID = PP.ProductID
ORDER BY P.ProductID;
```

ProductID	NorthwindProduct	AWProduct
1	Chai	Adjustable Race
2	Chang	Bearing Ball
3	Aniseed Syrup	BB Ball Bearing
4	Chef Anton's Cajun Seasoning	Headset Ball Bearings

Cartesian Product

When all rows in one table combined with all rows of another table it is called a Cartesian product. The cardinality of such a JOIN is (Table 1 Rows) x (Table 2 Rows).

```
-- Old-fashioned no JOIN predicate 2-table query - Cardinality 4x4 = 16
SELECT Category1 = A.Name, Category2 = B.Name
FROM Production.ProductCategory A, Production.ProductCategory B ORDER BY Category1, Category2;
```

```
-- Equivalent CROSS JOIN
SELECT Category1 = A.Name, Category2 = B.Name
FROM Production.ProductCategory A  CROSS JOIN Production.ProductCategory B
ORDER BY Category1, Category2;
```

Category1	Category2
Accessories	Accessories
Accessories	Bikes
Accessories	Clothing
Accessories	Components
Bikes	Accessories
Bikes	Bikes
Bikes	Clothing
Bikes	Components
Clothing	Accessories
Clothing	Bikes
Clothing	Clothing
Clothing	Components
Components	Accessories
Components	Bikes
Components	Clothing
Components	Components

CHAPTER 5: JOINing Tables with INNER & OUTER JOINs

SQL OUTER JOIN for Inclusion of Unmatched Rows

We have seen that INNER JOINs return rows only when there is at least one row from both tables that satisfies the join condition or conditions such as FOREIGN KEY matching the referenced PRIMARY KEY. Inner join queries do not return the rows that do not meet the ON condition with a row from the other table.

OUTER JOINs, however, return all rows from one or both tables in the JOIN. All rows are returned from the left table in a LEFT OUTER JOIN (including non-matching rows), and all rows are returned from the right table in a RIGHT OUTER JOIN. All rows from both tables are returned in a FULL OUTER JOIN. LEFT OUTER JOIN is totally equivalent to RIGHT OUTER JOIN. LEFT OUTER JOIN is mostly used by programmers in countries where the writing is left to right. **RIGHT OUTER JOIN is typically used by developers in countries where the writing is right to left. The non-matching rows in an OUTER JOIN are returned with NULL value fields**, therefore, they can be distinquished from the matching rows with a null test.

The following are synonyms:

LEFT JOIN - LEFT OUTER JOIN

RIGHT JOIN - RIGHT OUTER JOIN

FULL JOIN - FULL OUTER JOIN

The legacy syntax for outer joins *= (left join) or =* (right join) is not supported anymore. T-SQL example script lists products (left table) even if they are not being sold such as assembly parts.

```
USE AdventureWorks2012;
SELECT          P.Name,          SOD.SalesOrderID,
          CASE     WHEN SalesOrderID is null THEN 'Non-matching'
                   ELSE 'Matching' END                AS JoinInfo
FROM   Production.Product P
   LEFT OUTER JOIN Sales.SalesOrderDetail SOD     ON P.ProductID = SOD.ProductID
ORDER  BY P.Name;  -- (121555 row(s) affected) - Partial results.
```

Name	SalesOrderID	JoinInfo
Adjustable Race	NULL	Non-matching
All-Purpose Bike Stand	51179	Matching
All-Purpose Bike Stand	51488	Matching
All-Purpose Bike Stand	51520	Matching
All-Purpose Bike Stand	51558	Matching
All-Purpose Bike Stand	51882	Matching
All-Purpose Bike Stand	51903	Matching
All-Purpose Bike Stand	51970	Matching
All-Purpose Bike Stand	52010	Matching
All-Purpose Bike Stand	52032	Matching

LEFT JOIN: Include Unmatched Rows from Left Table

In the LEFT JOIN example, the Vendor table is LEFT JOINed to the PurchaseOrderHeader table to find out which vendors did not supply anything. The LEFT JOIN is based on FOREIGN KEY relationship.

```
USE AdventureWorks2012;

SELECT Vendor = V.Name
FROM   Purchasing.Vendor V
    LEFT JOIN Purchasing.PurchaseOrderHeader POH
        ON V.BusinessEntityID = POH.VendorID
WHERE  POH.VendorID IS NULL            -- Test if POH columns are null
ORDER by Vendor;   -- (18 row(s) affected) - Partial results.
```

Vendor
A. Datum Corporation
Cycling Master
Electronic Bike Co.
GMA Ski & Bike
Holiday Skate & Cycle
Illinois Trek & Clothing

T-SQL query to check which pedal products for sale were reviewed and which ones not.

```
SELECT  p.Name            AS ProductName,
        ProductNumber,
        pr.ProductReviewID,
        pr.ReviewerName,
        pr.Rating
FROM Production.Product p
   LEFT JOIN Production.ProductReview pr
        ON p.ProductID = pr.ProductID
WHERE p.ProductSubcategoryID is not null   AND p.Name like '%pedal%' ORDER BY ProductNumber;
-- (8 row(s) affected)
```

ProductName	ProductNumber	ProductReviewID	ReviewerName	Rating
LL Mountain Pedal	PD-M282	NULL	NULL	NULL
ML Mountain Pedal	PD-M340	NULL	NULL	NULL
HL Mountain Pedal	PD-M562	2	David	4
HL Mountain Pedal	PD-M562	3	Jill	2
LL Road Pedal	PD-R347	NULL	NULL	NULL
ML Road Pedal	PD-R563	NULL	NULL	NULL
HL Road Pedal	PD-R853	NULL	NULL	NULL
Touring Pedal	PD-T852	NULL	NULL	NULL

CHAPTER 5: JOINing Tables with INNER & OUTER JOINs

RIGHT JOIN - Same as LEFT with Tables Switched

The RIGHT JOIN is totally equivalent, including performance, to the corresponding LEFT JOIN. RIGHT JOIN is more frequently used in countries where they write right to left.

```
USE AdventureWorks2012;

SELECT Vendor = V.Name
FROM   Purchasing.PurchaseOrderHeader POH
    RIGHT JOIN Purchasing.Vendor V
     ON V.BusinessEntityID = POH.VendorID
WHERE  POH.VendorID IS NULL
ORDER by Vendor;
-- (18 row(s) affected) - Partial results.
```

Vendor
A. Datum Corporation
Cycling Master
Electronic Bike Co.
GMA Ski & Bike
Holiday Skate & Cycle

T-SQL RIGHT JOIN examples progress toward a query to provide users with a good report.

```
USE AdventureWorks2012;

SELECT ST.Name AS  Territory,
    SP.BusinessEntityID
FROM   Sales.SalesTerritory ST
    RIGHT OUTER JOIN Sales.SalesPerson SP
     ON ST.TerritoryID = SP.TerritoryID;
-- (17 row(s) affected)
```

```
SELECT   isnull(ST.Name, ' ')                        AS Territory,
       SP.BusinessEntityID,
       CONCAT (C.FirstName, ' ', C.LastName)     AS Name
FROM   Sales.SalesTerritory ST
    RIGHT OUTER JOIN Sales.SalesPerson SP
     ON ST.TerritoryID = SP.TerritoryID
    INNER JOIN Person.Person C
     ON SP.BusinessEntityID = C.BusinessEntityID;
-- (17 row(s) affected)
```

Add a WHERE condition filter on Sales.SalesPerson SalesYTD column

The NULLs indicate the no match rows in the RIGHT OUTER JOIN.

```
SELECT  ST.CountryRegionCode,
        ST.Name                                    AS Territory,
        SP.BusinessEntityID                        AS EmployeeID,
        CONCAT(C.FirstName, ' ', C.LastName )      AS Name
FROM  Sales.SalesTerritory ST
    RIGHT OUTER JOIN Sales.SalesPerson SP
     ON ST.TerritoryID = SP.TerritoryID
    INNER JOIN Person.Person C
     ON SP.BusinessEntityID = C.BusinessEntityID
WHERE SP.SalesYTD > 1000.0
ORDER BY        CountryRegionCode,
                Territory;
GO
-- (17 row(s) affected)
```

CountryRegionCode	Territory	EmployeeID	Name
NULL	NULL	274	Stephen Jiang
NULL	NULL	285	Syed Abbas
NULL	NULL	287	Amy Alberts
AU	Australia	286	Lynn Tsoflias
CA	Canada	278	Garrett Vargas
CA	Canada	282	José Saraiva
DE	Germany	288	Rachel Valdez
FR	France	290	Ranjit Varkey Chudukatil
GB	United Kingdom	289	Jae Pak
US	Central	277	Jillian Carson
US	Northeast	275	Michael Blythe
US	Northwest	283	David Campbell
US	Northwest	284	Tete Mensa-Annan
US	Northwest	280	Pamela Ansman-Wolfe
US	Southeast	279	Tsvi Reiter
US	Southwest	276	Linda Mitchell
US	Southwest	281	Shu Ito

```
-- Counting the RIGHT JOIN  match rows using a ProductSubcategory column
SELECT COUNT( S.Name)
FROM Production.ProductSubcategory S RIGHT JOIN Production.Product P
   ON S.ProductSubcategoryID = P.ProductSubcategoryID;
-- 295
```

CHAPTER 5: JOINing Tables with INNER & OUTER JOINs

Cardinality of OUTER JOINs

The number of rows returned in an OUTER JOIN is equal to the matching rows plus the non-matching rows from either or both tables. **To identify the non-matching rows (the ones with the NULLs) in an outer join we have to choose a not-nullable column like the PRIMARY KEY column.** T-SQL script demonstrates the cardinality involved with a LEFT JOIN.

```
USE AdventureWorks2012;

-- Rows in LEFT JOIN
SELECT Rows = count(*)
FROM   Production.Product P
    LEFT OUTER JOIN Sales.SalesOrderDetail SOD
         ON P.ProductID = SOD.ProductID
-- 121555
```

```
-- Rows in right table
SELECT Rows = count(*)
FROM Sales.SalesOrderDetail
-- 121317
```

```
-- Non-matching rows in left table
SELECT Rows = count(*)
FROM   Production.Product P
    LEFT OUTER JOIN Sales.SalesOrderDetail SOD
         ON P.ProductID = SOD.ProductID
WHERE SalesOrderID is NULL
-- 238
```

```
-- Right table rows + non-matching left table rows = rows returned by left join
SELECT 121317 + 238
-- 121555
```

Since the count queries are single valued, we can do the following summation.

```
SELECT (SELECT Rows = count(*)  FROM Sales.SalesOrderDetail )
+
(SELECT Rows = count(*)
FROM   Production.Product P
    LEFT OUTER JOIN Sales.SalesOrderDetail SOD
         ON P.ProductID = SOD.ProductID
WHERE SalesOrderID is NULL);
GO  -- 121555
```

LEFT JOIN & RIGHT JOIN on the Same Table

LEFT JOIN & RIGHT JOIN can be combined on the same table to keep all rows from that table even if they don't match the other two tables. The Production.Product table has a FOREIGN KEY referencing the ProductSubcategory table and another FOREIGN KEY referencing the UnitMeasure table.

FULL JOIN to Include All Unmatched Rows

The operation FULL JOIN combines LEFT JOIN and RIGHT JOIN, therefore it does not matter which is the left table or right table, it is a fully symmetrical set operation. T-SQL script demonstrates FULL OUTER JOIN.

```
USE tempdb;
-- Create tables for demo
SELECT distinct Color INTO Color
FROM AdventureWorks2012.Production.Product
WHERE Color is not null;
GO
```

```
SELECT ID=IDENTITY(int, 1, 1), * INTO NormalColor
FROM Color;
SELECT ID=IDENTITY(int, 1, 1), Color=CONCAT('Light', Color)  INTO LightColor
FROM Color;
```

```
DELETE NormalColor WHERE Color = 'Red';
```

```
DELETE LightColor WHERE Color = 'LightBlue';
```

```
-- Demo tables ready - full join query
SELECT   NormalColor      = n.Color,
         LightColor       = l.Color
FROM   NormalColor n      FULL OUTER JOIN LightColor l    ON n.ID = l.ID
ORDER BY NormalColor;
```

NormalColor	LightColor
NULL	LightRed
Black	LightBlack
Blue	NULL
Grey	LightGrey
Multi	LightMulti
Silver	LightSilver
Silver/Black	LightSilver/Black
White	LightWhite
Yellow	LightYellow

```
DROP TABLE  tempdb.dbo.Color;  DROP TABLE tempdb.dbo.NormalColor;
DROP TABLE tempdb.dbo.LightColor;
GO
```

CROSS JOIN for Cartesian Product

A CROSS JOIN with no connecting columns for joining produces a Cartesian product: combines all rows of the left table with all rows of the right tables. If the left table has x rows and the right table y rows, the CROSS JOIN is going to have x*y rows. That is called Cartesian explosion as it happens sometimes unintentionally in database development. In fact, a huge CROSS JOIN can bring SQL Server "to its knees", overwhelming CPU and disk resources. On the same note, no matter how powerful is the hardware platform, a bad runaway query can make SQL Server unresponsive to normal queries from other connections. T-SQL script to demonstrate CROSS JOIN.

```
USE AdventureWorks2012;

-- Cardinality of CROSS JOIN
SELECT count(*) from HumanResources.Employee;          -- 290
SELECT count(*) from HumanResources.Department;        -- 16
SELECT 16 * 290;                                       -- 4640

SELECT          E.BusinessEntityID          AS EMPLOYEEID,
                D.Name                       AS DEPARTMENT
FROM   HumanResources.Employee E   CROSS JOIN HumanResources.Department D
ORDER  BY       EMPLOYEEID,       DEPARTMENT;
-- (4640 row(s) affected) - Partial results.
```

EMPLOYEEID	DEPARTMENT
1	Production Control
1	Purchasing
1	Quality Assurance
1	Research and Development
1	Sales
1	Shipping and Receiving
1	Tool Design
2	Document Control
2	Engineering
2	Executive
2	Facilities and Maintenance
2	Finance
2	Human Resources
2	Information Services
2	Marketing
2	Production

CROSS JOIN Generated Multiplication Table

A CROSS JOIN can be used to create combinatorical results. In the next example, a multiplication table is created using a CROSS JOIN which is also a SELF-JOIN. CTE stands for Common Table Expression, which can be used as a table in SELECT and other queries. The master database spt_values table is used to get a sequence of numbers. The ".." in the table reference means: use the default schema which is "dbo".

```
; WITH cteNumber                          -- cte for numbers 1 to 10
    AS (SELECT NUMBER
      FROM   master..spt_values
      WHERE  TYPE = 'P'
          AND NUMBER BETWEEN 1 AND 10)
SELECT MULTIPLICATION=CONCAT( ltrim(str(B.NUMBER)) , ' * '
          , ltrim(str(A.NUMBER)) , ' = '
          , ltrim(str(A.NUMBER * B.NUMBER)) )
FROM   cteNumber A   CROSS JOIN cteNumber B;
-- (100 row(s) affected) - Partial results.
```

MULTIPLICATION
1 * 1 = 1
1 * 2 = 2
1 * 3 = 3
1 * 4 = 4
1 * 5 = 5
1 * 6 = 6
1 * 7 = 7
1 * 8 = 8
1 * 9 = 9
1 * 10 = 10
2 * 1 = 2
2 * 2 = 4
2 * 3 = 6
2 * 4 = 8
2 * 5 = 10
2 * 6 = 12
2 * 7 = 14
2 * 8 = 16
2 * 9 = 18
2 * 10 = 20
3 * 1 = 3
3 * 2 = 6
3 * 3 = 9
3 * 4 = 12
3 * 5 = 15

INNER JOIN with 7 Tables

 T-SQL query lists AdventureWorks Cycles retail (web) customers with total purchase amount and order dates. The name & address displays multiple times if a customer did multiple purchases. Generally, that is undesirable, and requires end-user report design considerations how to resolve it. The sorting uses Sales.SalesOrderHeader OrderDate which is datetime data type, instead of the mdy format string report date. mdy string format dates do not sort in chronological order.

```
USE AdventureWorks;
GO

SELECT CONCAT(C.LastName, ', ', C.FirstName)          AS CustomerName,
       A.City,
       SP.Name                                        AS State,
       CR.Name                                        AS Country,
       A.PostalCode,
       FORMAT(SOH.TotalDue, 'c','en-US')              AS SalesAmount,
       FORMAT(SOH.OrderDate,'d')                      AS OrderDate
FROM Person.Contact AS C
  INNER JOIN Sales.Individual AS I
        ON C.ContactID = I.ContactID
  INNER JOIN Sales.CustomerAddress AS CA
        ON CA.CustomerID = I.CustomerID
  INNER JOIN Person.Address AS A
        ON A.AddressID = CA.AddressID
  INNER JOIN Person.StateProvince SP
        ON SP.StateProvinceID = A.StateProvinceID
  INNER JOIN Person.CountryRegion CR
        ON CR.CountryRegionCode = SP.CountryRegionCode
  INNER JOIN Sales.SalesOrderHeader SOH
        ON C.ContactID = SOH.CustomerID
ORDER BY CustomerName, soh.OrderDate ;
-- (16493 row(s) affected)  - Partial results.
```

CustomerName	City	State	Country	PostalCode	SalesAmount	OrderDate
Adams, Aaron	Downey	California	United States	90241	$734.70	3/4/2004
Adams, Adam	Newport Beach	California	United States	92625	$2,566.12	4/16/2004
Adams, Alex	Lake Oswego	Oregon	United States	97034	$2,410.63	3/18/2003
Adams, Alex	Lake Oswego	Oregon	United States	97034	$1,293.38	12/9/2003
Adams, Alex	Lake Oswego	Oregon	United States	97034	$2,643.12	2/1/2004
Adams, Angel	Burlingame	California	United States	94010	$865.20	5/24/2003
Adams, Angel	Burlingame	California	United States	94010	$2,597.81	3/1/2004
Adams, Carlos	Langford	British Columbia	Canada	V9	$44.18	6/28/2004
Adams, Connor	Westminster	British Columbia	Canada	V3L 1H4	$183.74	4/14/2004
Adams, Elijah	Seattle	Washington	United States	98104	$8.04	11/2/2003

CHAPTER 5: JOINing Tables with INNER & OUTER JOINs

INNER JOIN with GROUP BY Subquery

We have to make the GROUP BY subquery into a derived table first. Subsequently, we can apply it just like any other table in a query.

```
USE AdventureWorks2012;
GO

SELECT  Subcategory = Name,
        Color,
        ColorCount,
        AvgListPrice
FROM  (
        SELECT ProductSubcategoryID,              -- grouping column
        Color = COALESCE(Color, 'N/A'),           -- grouping column with transformation
        ColorCount = COUNT(*),                     -- aggregate function
        AvgListPrice = AVG(COALESCE(ListPrice, 0.0))  -- aggregate function
        FROM   AdventureWorks2008.Production.Product
        GROUP  BY      ProductSubcategoryID,
                       Color) x                    -- derived table (subquery)
    INNER JOIN Production.ProductSubcategory psc
        ON psc.ProductSubcategoryID = x.ProductSubcategoryID
ORDER  BY Subcategory,
        Color;
GO
-- (48 row(s) affected) - Partial results.
```

Subcategory	Color	ColorCount	AvgListPrice
Bib-Shorts	Multi	3	89.990000
Bike Racks	N/A	1	120.000000
Bike Stands	N/A	1	159.000000
Bottles and Cages	N/A	3	7.990000
Bottom Brackets	N/A	3	92.240000
Brakes	Silver	2	106.500000
Caps	Multi	1	8.990000
Chains	Silver	1	20.240000
Cleaners	N/A	1	7.950000
Cranksets	Black	3	278.990000
Derailleurs	Silver	2	106.475000
Fenders	N/A	1	21.980000

Making Queries Readable & Results Presentable

A database developer has to make a query readable for productivity gain in development and ease of maintenance. At the same time the results must be readable to the user. The next query with results demonstrates how to achieve both objectives.

```
USE AdventureWorks2012;
GO

SELECT  PC.Name                               AS Category,
        PSC.Name                              AS Subcategory,
        PM.Name                               AS Model,
        P.Name                                AS ProductName,
        FORMAT(ListPrice,'c','en-US')         AS Price
FROM Production.Product AS P
    INNER JOIN Production.ProductModel AS PM
        ON PM.ProductModelID = P.ProductModelID
    INNER JOIN Production.ProductSubcategory AS PSC
        ON PSC.ProductSubcategoryID = P.ProductSubcategoryID
    INNER JOIN Production.ProductCategory AS PC
        ON PC.ProductCategoryID = PSC.ProductCategoryID
ORDER BY Category, Subcategory, ProductName;
GO
-- (295 row(s) affected) - Partial results.
```

The confusing 4 "Name" columns are clarified by well-chosen column aliases. The meaningful column aliases are used in the ORDER BY clause even though not required. To help the user, the list price is currency formatted.

Category	Subcategory	Model	ProductName	Price
Accessories	Bike Racks	Hitch Rack - 4-Bike	Hitch Rack - 4-Bike	$120.00
Accessories	Bike Stands	All-Purpose Bike Stand	All-Purpose Bike Stand	$159.00
Accessories	Bottles and Cages	Mountain Bottle Cage	Mountain Bottle Cage	$9.99
Accessories	Bottles and Cages	Road Bottle Cage	Road Bottle Cage	$8.99
Accessories	Bottles and Cages	Water Bottle	Water Bottle - 30 oz.	$4.99
Accessories	Cleaners	Bike Wash	Bike Wash - Dissolver	$7.95
Accessories	Fenders	Fender Set - Mountain	Fender Set - Mountain	$21.98
Accessories	Helmets	Sport-100	Sport-100 Helmet, Black	$34.99
Accessories	Helmets	Sport-100	Sport-100 Helmet, Blue	$34.99
Accessories	Helmets	Sport-100	Sport-100 Helmet, Red	$34.99

CHAPTER 5: JOINing Tables with INNER & OUTER JOINs

A 12 Tables JOIN Query

The next query JOINs 11 tables, some of the tables occur more than once in the query.

```
USE AdventureWorks;

DECLARE        @Year  int,
               @Month int

SET @Year      = 2004;
SET @Month     = 1;

SELECT SOH.SalesOrderNumber                          AS SON,
    SOH.PurchaseOrderNumber                          AS PO,
    S.Name                                           AS Store,
    CONVERT(VARCHAR, SOH.OrderDate, 110)             AS OrderDate,
    CONVERT(VARCHAR, SOH.ShipDate, 110)              AS ShipDate,
    FORMAT(TotalDue,'c','en-US')                     AS [Total Due],
    CONCAT(C.FirstName,' ',C.LastName)               AS SalesStaff,
    SM.Name                                          AS ShpngMethod,
    BA.AddressLine1                                  AS BlngAddress1,
    Isnull(BA.AddressLine2, '')                      AS BlngAddress2,
    BA.City                                          AS BlngCity,
    BSP.Name                                         AS BlngStateProvince,
    BA.PostalCode                                    AS BlngPostalCode,
    BCR.Name                                         AS BlngCountryRegion,
    SA.AddressLine1                                  AS ShpngAddress1,
    Isnull(SA.AddressLine2, '')                      AS ShpngAddress2,
    SA.City                                          AS ShpngCity,
    SSP.Name                                         AS ShpngStateProvince,
    SA.PostalCode                                    AS ShpngPostalCode,
    SCR.Name                                         AS ShpngCountryRegion,
    CONCAT(CC.FirstName,' ',CC.LastName)             AS CustomerContact,
    CC.Phone                                         AS CustomerPhone,
    SOH.AccountNumber
FROM   Person.Address SA
    INNER JOIN Person.StateProvince SSP
       ON SA.StateProvinceID = SSP.StateProvinceID
    INNER JOIN Person.CountryRegion SCR
       ON SSP.CountryRegionCode = SCR.CountryRegionCode
    INNER JOIN Sales.SalesOrderHeader SOH
        INNER JOIN Person.Contact CC
           ON SOH.ContactID = CC.ContactID
        INNER JOIN Person.Address BA
            INNER JOIN Person.StateProvince BSP
               ON BA.StateProvinceID = BSP.StateProvinceID
            INNER JOIN Person.CountryRegion BCR
```

CHAPTER 5: JOINing Tables with INNER & OUTER JOINs

```
-- T-SQL query continued

                ON BSP.CountryRegionCode =
                  BCR.CountryRegionCode
              ON SOH.BillToAddressID = BA.AddressID
            ON SA.AddressID = SOH.ShipToAddressID
      INNER JOIN Person.Contact C
          INNER JOIN HumanResources.Employee E
              ON C.ContactID = E.ContactID
          ON SOH.SalesPersonID = E.EmployeeID
      INNER JOIN Purchasing.ShipMethod SM
          ON SOH.ShipMethodID = SM.ShipMethodID
      INNER JOIN Sales.Store S
          ON SOH.CustomerID = S.CustomerID
WHERE  SOH.OrderDate >= datefromparts(@Year, @month, 1)
    AND  SOH.OrderDate < dateadd(mm,1,datefromparts(@Year, @month, 1))
ORDER  BY Store,  OrderDate DESC;
GO
-- (96 row(s) affected) - Partial results.
```

SON	PO	Store	OrderDate	ShipDate	Total Due	SalesStaff	ShpngMethod	BlngAddress1
SO61257	PO3741176337	Activity Center	01-01-2004	01-08-2004	$12,764.08	Tsvi Reiter	CARGO TRANSPORT 5	Factory Stores Of America
SO61256	PO1421187796	All Cycle Shop	01-01-2004	01-08-2004	$201.08	Tete Mensa-Annan	CARGO TRANSPORT 5	25111 228th St Sw
SO61251	PO6380165323	All Seasons Sports Supply	01-01-2004	01-08-2004	$2,863.30	Michael Blythe	CARGO TRANSPORT 5	Ohms Road
SO61263	PO5452121402	Amalgamated Parts Shop	01-01-2004	01-08-2004	$39,103.04	Rachel Valdez	CARGO TRANSPORT 5	Brunnenstr 422
SO61227	PO10730172247	Area Bike Accessories	01-01-2004	01-08-2004	$75,916.89	Shu Ito	CARGO TRANSPORT 5	6900 Sisk Road
SO61187	PO13978135025	Basic Bike Company	01-01-2004	01-08-2004	$72.92	David Campbell	CARGO TRANSPORT 5	15 East Main
SO61190	PO12441157171	Best Cycle Store	01-01-2004	01-08-2004	$49,337.61	Rachel Valdez	CARGO TRANSPORT 5	Berliner Platz 45
SO61221	PO15399128383	Best o' Bikes	01-01-2004	01-08-2004	$5,872.73	Michael Blythe	CARGO TRANSPORT 5	250880 Baur Blvd
SO61173	PO522171689	Better Bike Shop	01-01-2004	01-08-2004	$38,511.29	Tsvi Reiter	CARGO TRANSPORT 5	42525 Austell Road
SO61254	PO4872176154	Bicycle Exporters	01-01-2004	01-08-2004	$10,665.06	Rachel Valdez	CARGO TRANSPORT 5	Hellweg 4934
SO61243	PO7859152962	Bike Dealers Association	01-01-2004	01-08-2004	$18,976.48	Shu Ito	CARGO TRANSPORT 5	9952 E. Lohman Ave.
SO61250	PO4930183869	Bikes for Kids and Adults	01-01-2004	01-08-2004	$3,852.87	Jae Pak	CARGO TRANSPORT 5	9900 Ronson Drive
SO61209	PO11484136165	Casual Bicycle Store	01-01-2004	01-08-2004	$37,314.33	Jillian Carson	CARGO TRANSPORT 5	Westside Plaza
SO61204	PO15312134209	Citywide Service and Repair	01-01-2004	01-08-2004	$29,797.18	Jae Pak	CARGO TRANSPORT 5	Box 99354 300 Union Street
SO61192	PO10092119585	Classic Cycle Store	01-01-2004	01-08-2004	$3,691.57	Jillian Carson	CARGO TRANSPORT 5	630 Oldgate Lane

CHAPTER 5: JOINing Tables with INNER & OUTER JOINs

Order of Tables or Predicates Does Not Matter

Frequent question: does the order of tables matter in a JOIN? Should I put BETWEEN predicate before LIKE predicate? Valid syntax variations do not matter. The database engine translates the query to an internal form prior to creating an execution plan. Thus the different variations get translated to the same internal form. The only way we have some control over the database engine if we rewrite a single statement complex query to a multi-statements script.

Nondeterministic CTE

CTE is evaluated for every reference, therefore it may return different results if certain functions are used such as newid(), thus yielding a nondeterministic CTE.

```
;WITH CTE AS (SELECT Random = NEWID()),
CTE1 AS (SELECT * FROM CTE),
CTE2 AS (SELECT * FROM CTE),
CTE3 AS (SELECT * FROM CTE),
CTE4 AS (SELECT * FROM CTE),
CTE5 AS (SELECT * FROM CTE)
SELECT * FROM CTE1
UNION ALL
SELECT * FROM CTE2
UNION ALL
SELECT * FROM CTE3
UNION ALL
SELECT * FROM CTE4
UNION ALL
SELECT * FROM CTE5
UNION ALL
SELECT * FROM CTE
UNION ALL
SELECT * FROM CTE
UNION ALL
SELECT * FROM CTE;
```

Random
08D45FE2-52C6-4E15-83A3-0B2F27837887
D6A094E6-0C8A-43E4-B6C4-8821F6EE8E73
281A5852-3D9A-4F2A-99FA-F60EE28FD2E0
C327ED19-5C03-4D9B-A8E8-6ACABAA08F1C
80DDE508-A6AA-4F2B-AB2F-CEEF7EC5E163
5F611B03-46F4-4EED-A8E0-76020527899D
FF8DAE17-65F6-4D80-8AF5-29EBAEBD2FEB
CF342DC9-4CF9-46FD-87F0-3213106C447D

The CROSS APPLY Operator

The APPLY (CROSS APPLY & OUTER APPLY) operators were introduced with SQL Server 2005. The CROSS APPLY operator merges rows from tables (or views) with rows from table-valued function, a form of JOIN.

```
USE AdventureWorks2012;
SELECT
        q.last_execution_time               AS LastRun,
        t.TEXT                              AS QueryText,
        q.sql_handle                        AS SQLHandle
FROM    sys.dm_exec_query_stats AS q                        -- system view
            CROSS APPLY
            sys.dm_exec_sql_text(q.sql_handle) AS t         -- table-valued system function
WHERE LEFT(t.TEXT,8)='SELECT *'  ORDER BY LastRun DESC;
```

LastRun	QueryText
2016-08-01 14:46:12.537	SELECT * FROM Sales.SalesOrderHeader
2016-08-01 14:44:54.257	SELECT * FROM Production.Product
2016-08-01 13:29:25.213	SELECT * FROM sys.dm_os_wait_stats
2016-08-01 09:36:57.980	select * from sys.sysforeignkeys s
2016-08-01 09:36:39.077	select * from sysforeignkeys s

```
-- Return the top N purchase order by amount - inline table-valued function
CREATE FUNCTION dbo.ufnGetTopNPurchases(@VendorID AS INT, @N AS INT)
RETURNS TABLE  AS
RETURN
 SELECT TOP ( @N ) *   FROM Purchasing.PurchaseOrderHeader
  WHERE VendorID = @VendorID    ORDER BY TotalDue DESC;
GO   -- Command(s) completed successfully.
```

```
-- List the top 5 highest purchases from vendors
SELECT V.VendorID,
        P.PurchaseOrderID,
        FORMAT(P.TotalDue, 'c','en-US')     AS TotalDue
FROM    Purchasing.Vendor AS V  CROSS APPLY  dbo.ufnGetTopNPurchases(V.VendorID, 5) AS P
ORDER BY  V.VendorID, TotalDue DESC
-- (395 row(s) affected) - Partial results.
```

VendorID	PurchaseOrderID	TotalDue
74	325	$1,654.75
74	1727	$855.22
74	2517	$855.22
74	3307	$855.22
74	167	$785.61

CHAPTER 5: JOINing Tables with INNER & OUTER JOINs

Using CROSS APPLY with Columns Specified Table Alias

A regular table alias would result in error in the following delimited string list query. Table alias with column(s) specifications "o(list)" works, the table alias is "o", it has one column "list".

CROSS APPLY: Most Popular Sales Products Info

```
CREATE FUNCTION ufnProductDetails (@ProductID INT) RETURNS TABLE  AS RETURN
(        SELECT ProductNumber, ListPrice, Color
        FROM Production.Product WHERE ProductID = @ProductID  );
GO
;WITH CTE AS (    SELECT ProductID FROM Sales.SalesOrderDetail
                            GROUP BY ProductID HAVING COUNT(*) > 1000 )
SELECT ProductNumber, ListPrice, Color
FROM CTE CROSS APPLY ufnProductDetails (ProductID)
WHERE Color is not null ORDER BY ProductNumber;  -- (15 row(s) affected);
```

CHAPTER 5: JOINing Tables with INNER & OUTER JOINs

CHAPTER 6: Basic SELECT Statement Syntax & Examples

Simple SELECT Statement Variations

SELECT is the most famous statement in the SQL language. It is used to query tables, and generate reports for users. Although SQL Server Reporting Services and other 3rd party packages available for reporting purposes, frequently reports are generated straight from the database with SELECT queries. The next query returns all rows, all columns sorted on DepartmentID.

```
USE AdventureWorks2012;

SELECT * FROM  HumanResources.Department  ORDER BY DepartmentID;
-- (16 row(s) affected)
```

DepartmentID	Name	GroupName	ModifiedDate
1	Engineering	Research and Development	1998-06-01 00:00:00.000
2	Tool Design	Research and Development	1998-06-01 00:00:00.000
3	Sales	Sales and Marketing	1998-06-01 00:00:00.000
4	Marketing	Sales and Marketing	1998-06-01 00:00:00.000
5	Purchasing	Inventory Management	1998-06-01 00:00:00.000
6	Research and Development	Research and Development	1998-06-01 00:00:00.000
7	Production	Manufacturing	1998-06-01 00:00:00.000
8	Production Control	Manufacturing	1998-06-01 00:00:00.000
9	Human Resources	Executive General and Administration	1998-06-01 00:00:00.000
10	Finance	Executive General and Administration	1998-06-01 00:00:00.000
11	Information Services	Executive General and Administration	1998-06-01 00:00:00.000
12	Document Control	Quality Assurance	1998-06-01 00:00:00.000
13	Quality Assurance	Quality Assurance	1998-06-01 00:00:00.000
14	Facilities and Maintenance	Executive General and Administration	1998-06-01 00:00:00.000
15	Shipping and Receiving	Inventory Management	1998-06-01 00:00:00.000
16	Executive	Executive General and Administration	1998-06-01 00:00:00.000

Since the time part of ModifiedDate is not being used, and that makes business sense, we can format it just as date.

```
SELECT TOP (3) DepartmentID, Name, GroupName, CONVERT(DATE, ModifiedDate) AS ModifiedDate
FROM  HumanResources.Department  ORDER BY DepartmentID;
-- (16 row(s) affected)
```

DepartmentID	Name	GroupName	ModifiedDate
1	Engineering	Research and Development	1998-06-01
2	Tool Design	Research and Development	1998-06-01
3	Sales	Sales and Marketing	1998-06-01

SELECT query with sort on EnglishProductName in DESCending order
ASCending sort is the default.

```
USE AdventureWorksDW2012
GO
```

```
SELECT  *
FROM    DimProduct
ORDER BY EnglishProductName DESC
GO
-- (606 row(s) affected) - Partial results.
```

EnglishProductName	SpanishProductName	FrenchProductName	StandardCost
Women's Tights, S	Mallas para mujer, P	Collants pour femmes, taille S	30.9334
Women's Tights, M	Mallas para mujer, M	Collants pour femmes, taille M	30.9334
Women's Tights, L	Mallas para mujer, G	Collants pour femmes, taille L	30.9334
Women's Mountain Shorts, S			26.1763
Women's Mountain Shorts, M			26.1763
Women's Mountain Shorts, L			26.1763
Water Bottle - 30 oz.			1.8663
Touring-Panniers, Large	Cesta de paseo, grande	Sacoches de vélo de randonnée, grande capacité	51.5625
Touring-3000 Yellow, 62	Paseo: 3000, amarilla, 62	Vélo de randonnée 3000 jaune, 62	461.4448
Touring-3000 Yellow, 58	Paseo: 3000, amarilla, 58	Vélo de randonnée 3000 jaune, 58	461.4448

The next query sorts on the SpanishProductName column in ascending order.

```
SELECT  *
FROM    DimProduct
ORDER BY SpanishProductName ASC
GO
-- (606 row(s) affected) - Partial results.
```

EnglishProductName	SpanishProductName
HL Crankset	Bielas GA
LL Crankset	Bielas GB
ML Crankset	Bielas GM
Mountain Pump	Bomba de montaña
Cable Lock	Cable antirrobo
Chain	Cadena
Mountain Bike Socks,	Calcetines para bicicleta de montaña, G

Sorting on FrenchProductName, if empty, use EnglishProductName.

```
SELECT  * FROM    DimProduct ORDER BY FrenchProductName, EnglishProductName;
GO
```

CHAPTER 6: Basic SELECT Statement Syntax & Examples

Using the TOP Clause in SELECT Queries

The TOP clause limits the number of rows returned as specified in the TOP expression according the sorted order if any. In the following query, the sorting is based on a major key (LastName) and a minor key (FirstName).

```
USE AdventureWorks2012
GO


SELECT  TOP 100 *
FROM    Person.Person ORDER BY LastName, FirstName
-- (100 row(s) affected) - Partial results.
```

BusinessEntityID	PersonType	Title	FirstName	LastName	EmailPromotion
285	SP	Mr.	Syed	Abbas	0
293	SC	Ms.	Catherine	Abel	1
295	SC	Ms.	Kim	Abercrombie	0
2170	GC	NULL	Kim	Abercrombie	2
38	EM	NULL	Kim	Abercrombie	2
211	EM	NULL	Hazem	Abolrous	0
2357	GC	NULL	Sam	Abolrous	1
297	SC	Sr.	Humberto	Acevedo	2
291	SC	Mr.	Gustavo	Achong	2
299	SC	Sra.	Pilar	Ackerman	0

The total population of the Person.Person table is 19,972 rows.

```
SELECT  * FROM    Person.Person ORDER BY LastName, FirstName
-- (19972 row(s) affected)
```

We can also count the rows applying the COUNT function.

```
SELECT  RowsCount = count(*)  FROM    Person.Person
-- 19972
```

When counting, it is safe to count the PRIMARY KEY (ProductID) values.

```
SELECT  RowsCount = count(ProductID)   FROM    Production.Product;
-- 504
```

```
SELECT  RowsCount = count(Color)   FROM    Production.Product;      -- 256
```

CHAPTER 6: Basic SELECT Statement Syntax & Examples

Using the WHERE Clause in SELECT Queries

The WHERE clause filters the rows to be returned according the one or more predicates. The next T-SQL scripts demonstrate simple WHERE clause predicates, including multiple WHERE conditions.

```
-- Last name starts with S
SELECT *
FROM    Person.Person
WHERE   LEFT(LastName,1) = 'S'
ORDER BY LastName;
-- (2130 row(s) affected)
```

```
-- First name is Shelly
SELECT  *
FROM    Person.Person
WHERE   FirstName = 'Shelly'
ORDER BY LastName;
-- (1 row(s) affected)
```

```
-- First name is John
SELECT  *
FROM    Person.Person
WHERE   FirstName = 'John'
ORDER BY LastName;
-- (58 row(s) affected)
```

```
-- First name John, last name starts with S - Multiple WHERE conditions
SELECT  *
FROM    Person.Person
WHERE   FirstName = 'John'
    AND LEFT(LastName,1) = 'S'
ORDER BY LastName ;
-- (2 row(s) affected)
```

```
-- Last name starts with S OR first name starts with J
SELECT  *
FROM    Person.Person
WHERE   LEFT(FirstName,1) = 'J'  OR LEFT(LastName,1) = 'S'
ORDER BY LastName;
-- (4371 row(s) affected)
```

```
-- Last name starts with S AND first name starts with J
SELECT  *
FROM    Person.Person  WHERE   LEFT(FirstName,1) = 'J'    AND LEFT(LastName,1) = 'S'
ORDER BY LastName;   -- (221 row(s) affected)
```

Using Literals in SELECT Queries

Literals or constants are used commonly in T-SQL queries, also as defaults for columns, local variables, and parameters. The format of a literal depends on the data type of the value it represents. The database engine may perform implicit conversion to match data types. Explicit conversion of literals can be achieved with the CONVERT or CAST functions. T-SQL scripts demonstrate literal use in WHERE clause predicates.

```
USE AdventureWorks2012;
-- Integer literal  in WHERE clause predicate
SELECT * FROM Production.Product
WHERE ProductID = 800;
-- (1 row(s) affected)


-- String literal in WHERE clause predicate
SELECT * FROM Production.Product WHERE Color = 'Blue';
-- (26 row(s) affected)


USE AdventureWorksDW2012;
-- UNICODE (2 bytes per character) string literal
SELECT * FROM DimProduct
WHERE SpanishProductName = N'Jersey clásico de manga corta, G';
-- (1 row(s) affected)


-- UNICODE string literal
SELECT * FROM DimProduct
WHERE FrenchProductName = N'Roue arrière de vélo de randonnée';
-- (1 row(s) affected)


USE AdventureWorks2012;
-- Money literal in WHERE clause predicate
SELECT * FROM Production.Product
WHERE ListPrice > = $2000.0;
-- (35 row(s) affected)


-- Floating point literal with implicit conversion to MONEY
SELECT * FROM Production.Product  WHERE ListPrice > = 2.000E+3;
-- (35 row(s) affected)


-- Hex (binary) literal
SELECT * FROM Production.Product  WHERE rowguid >= 0x23D89CEE9F444F3EB28963DE6BA2B737
-- (302 row(s) affected)


-- The rest of the 504 products
SELECT * FROM Production.Product  WHERE rowguid < 0x23D89CEE9F444F3EB28963DE6BA2B737
-- (202 row(s) affected)
```

CHAPTER 6: Basic SELECT Statement Syntax & Examples

Date & Time Literals in SELECT Queries

Date and time literals appear to come from an infinite pool. Every country has tens of string date & time variations. Despite the many external string representation, **date, datetime, datetime, time, smalldatetime** and other temporal data types have unique, well-defined representation within the database engine.

ymd date literal format is the cleanest. There is eternal confusion about the North American mdy string date format and the European dmy string date format. The date and time format with "T" separator (last one) is the ISO date time format literal. ANSI Date literal - YYYYMMDD - the best choice since it work in any country.

CONVERT or CAST Date Time Literal	Result
SELECT [Date] = CAST('20160228' AS date)	2016-02-28
SELECT [Datetime] = CAST('20160228' AS datetime)	2016-02-28 00:00:00.000
SELECT [SmallDatetime] = CAST('20160228' AS smalldatetime)	2016-02-28 00:00:00
SELECT [Datetime] = CONVERT(datetime,'2016-02-28')	2016-02-28 00:00:00.000
SELECT [Datetime2] = CONVERT(datetime2,'2016-02-28')	2016-02-28 00:00:00.0000000
SELECT [Datetime] = CONVERT(datetime, '20160228')	2016-02-28 00:00:00.000
SELECT [Datetime2] = CONVERT(datetime2,'20160228')	2016-02-28 00:00:00.0000000
SELECT [Datetime] = CAST('Mar 15, 2016' AS datetime)	2016-03-15 00:00:00.000
SELECT [Datetime2] = CAST('Mar 15, 2016' AS datetime2)	2016-03-15 00:00:00.0000000
SELECT [Date] = CAST('Mar 15, 2016' AS date)	2016-03-15
SELECT CAST('16:40:31' AS datetime)	1900-01-01 16:40:31.000
SELECT CAST('16:40:31' AS time)	16:40:31.0000000
SELECT [Datetime] = CAST('Mar 15, 2016 12:07:34.444' AS datetime)	2016-03-15 12:07:34.443
SELECT [Datetime2] = CAST('Mar 15, 2016 12:07:34.4445555' AS datetime2)	2016-03-15 12:07:34.4445555
SELECT [Datetime] = CAST('2016-03-15T12:07:34.513' AS datetime)	2016-03-15 12:07:34.513

CHAPTER 6: Basic SELECT Statement Syntax & Examples

ymd, dmy & mdy String Date Format Literals

Date and time string literals are the least understood part of the T-SQL language by database developers. It is a constant source of confusion and frustration, in addition huge economic cost of lost programmer's productivity. ymd, dmy & mdy are the main string date formats. Some countries use ydm format. Setting dateformat overrides the implicit setting by language.

The basic principles:

> **There is only one DATETIME data type internal format**, independent where SQL Server is operated: New York, London, Amsterdam, Berlin, Moscow, Hong Kong, Singapore, Tokyo, Melbourne or Rio de Janeiro.
> There are hundreds of national string date & time formats which have nothing to do with SQL Server.
> String date must be properly converted to DATETIME format.

```
SET DATEFORMAT ymd
SELECT convert(datetime,'16/05/08')             -- 2016-05-08 00:00:00.000


-- Setting DATEFORMAT to UK-Style (European)
SET DATEFORMAT dmy
SELECT convert(datetime,'20/05/16')             -- 2016-05-20 00:00:00.000


-- Setting DATEFORMAT to US-Style
SET DATEFORMAT mdy
SELECT convert(datetime,'05/20/16')             -- 2016-05-20 00:00:00.000
SELECT convert(datetime,'05/20/2016')           -- 2016-05-20 00:00:00.000
Interestingly we can achieve the same implicit conversion action by setting language.

-- Setting DATEFORMAT ymd  via language
SET LANGUAGE Japanese;  SELECT convert(datetime,'16/05/08') ;       -- 2016-05-08 00:00:00.000


-- Setting DATEFORMAT to UK-Style (European) via language
SET LANGUAGE British;  SELECT convert(datetime,'20/05/16');          -- 2016-05-20 00:00:00.000
SELECT convert(datetime,'05/20/16');
/* Msg 242, Level 16, State 3, Line 3
The conversion of a varchar data type to a datetime data type resulted in an out-of-range value. */


-- Setting DATEFORMAT to US-Style via language
SET LANGUAGE English;  SELECT convert(datetime,'05/20/16');          -- 2016-05-20 00:00:00.000
SELECT convert(datetime,'05/20/2016');                  -- 2016-05-20 00:00:00.000
SELECT convert(datetime,'20/05/2016');
/* Msg 242, Level 16, State 3, Line 4
The conversion of a varchar data type to a datetime data type resulted in an out-of-range value. */
```

CHAPTER 6: Basic SELECT Statement Syntax & Examples

Setting DATEFIRST with Literal

DATEFIRST indicates the first day of the week which may vary by country, culture or business. The next T-SQL script demonstrates how it can be set by integer literal 1-7. It overrides the implicit setting by language. @@DATEFIRST is a system (SQL Server database engine) variable.

```
SET DATEFIRST 7  -- Sunday as first day of the week
SELECT DATEPART(dw, '20160315');            -- 3
SELECT DATENAME(dw, '20160315');            -- Tuesday
SELECT @@DATEFIRST                          -- 7
```

```
SET DATEFIRST 1  -- Monday as first day of the week
SELECT DATEPART(dw, '20160315');            -- 2
SELECT DATENAME(dw, '20160315');            -- Tuesday
SELECT @@DATEFIRST                          -- 1
```

Language Setting - SET LANGUAGE

DATEFIRST is tied to the language setting, just the like the date format (ymd, dmy, or mdy).

```
SET LANGUAGE us_english
SELECT DATEPART(dw, '20160315');            -- 3
SELECT DATENAME(dw, '20160315');            -- Tuesday
SELECT @@DATEFIRST                          -- 7
```

```
SET LANGUAGE german
SELECT DATEPART(dw, '20160315');            -- 2
SELECT DATENAME(dw, '20160315');            -- Dienstag
SELECT @@DATEFIRST                          -- 1
```

```
SET LANGUAGE british
SELECT DATEPART(dw, '20160315');            -- 2
SELECT DATENAME(dw, '20160315');            -- Tuesday
SELECT @@DATEFIRST                          -- 1
```

```
SET LANGUAGE hungarian
SELECT DATEPART(dw, '20160315');            -- 2
SELECT DATENAME(dw, '20160315');            -- kedd
SELECT @@DATEFIRST                          -- 1
```

```
SET LANGUAGE spanish
SELECT DATEPART(dw, '20160315');            -- 2
SELECT DATENAME(dw, '20160315');            -- Martes
SELECT @@DATEFIRST                          -- 1
```

The sys.syslanguages System View

The syslanguages table contains not only language related information, but date related settings as well.

```
SELECT
        langid,
        dateformat,
        datefirst,
        name                            AS native_language,
        alias                           AS english,
        left(shortmonths, 15)           AS shortmonths,
        left(days,15)                   AS days
FROM AdventureWorks2012.sys.syslanguages
ORDER BY langid;
GO
-- (34 row(s) affected)  -  Partial results.
```

langid	dateformat	datefirst	native_language	english	shortmonths	days
0	mdy	7	us_english	English	Jan,Feb,Mar,Apr	Monday,Tuesday,
1	dmy	1	Deutsch	German	Jan,Feb,Mär,Apr	Montag,Dienstag
2	dmy	1	Français	French	janv,févr,mars,	lundi,mardi,mer
3	ymd	7	日本語	Japanese	01,02,03,04,05,	月曜日,火曜日,水曜日,木曜日
4	dmy	1	Dansk	Danish	jan,feb,mar,apr	mandag,tirsdag,
5	dmy	1	Español	Spanish	Ene,Feb,Mar,Abr	Lunes,Martes,Mi
6	dmy	1	Italiano	Italian	gen,feb,mar,apr	lunedì,martedì,
7	dmy	1	Nederlands	Dutch	jan,feb,mrt,apr	maandag,dinsdag
8	dmy	1	Norsk	Norwegian	jan,feb,mar,apr	mandag,tirsdag,
9	dmy	7	Português	Portuguese	jan,fev,mar,abr	segunda-feira,t
10	dmy	1	Suomi	Finnish	tammi,helmi,maa	maanantai,tiist
11	ymd	1	Svenska	Swedish	jan,feb,mar,apr	måndag,tisdag,o
12	dmy	1	čeština	Czech	I,II,III,IV,V,V	pondělí,úterý,s
13	ymd	1	magyar	Hungarian	jan,febr,márc,á	hétfő,kedd,szer
14	dmy	1	polski	Polish	I,II,III,IV,V,V	poniedziałek,wt
15	dmy	1	română	Romanian	Ian,Feb,Mar,Apr	luni,marţi,mier
16	ymd	1	hrvatski	Croatian	sij,vel,ožu,tra	ponedjeljak,uto
17	dmy	1	slovenčina	Slovak	I,II,III,IV,V,V	pondelok,utorok
18	dmy	1	slovenski	Slovenian	jan,feb,mar,apr	ponedeljek,tore
19	dmy	1	ελληνικά	Greek	Ιαν,Φεβ,Μαρ,Απρ	Δευτέρα,Τρίτη,Τ
20	dmy	1	български	Bulgarian	януари,февруари	понеделник,втор
21	dmy	1	русский	Russian	янв,фев,мар,апр	понедельник,вто
22	dmy	1	Türkçe	Turkish	Oca,Şub,Mar,Nis	Pazartesi,Salı,
23	dmy	1	British	British English	Jan,Feb,Mar,Apr	Monday,Tuesday,
24	dmy	1	eesti	Estonian	jaan,veebr,märt	esmaspäev,teisi
25	ymd	1	latviešu	Latvian	jan,feb,mar,apr	pirmdiena,otrdi
26	ymd	1	lietuvių	Lithuanian	sau,vas,kov,bal	pirmadienis,ant
27	dmy	7	Português (Brasil)	Brazilian	Jan,Fev,Mar,Abr	Segunda-Feira,T
28	ymd	7	繁體中文	Traditional Chinese	01,02,03,04,05,	星期一,星期二,星期三,星期四
29	ymd	7	한국어	Korean	01,02,03,04,05,	월요일,화요일,수요일,목요일
30	ymd	7	简体中文	Simplified Chinese	01,02,03,04,05,	星期一,星期二,星期三,星期四
31	dmy	1	Arabic	Arabic	Jan,Feb,Mar,Apr	Monday,Tuesday,
32	dmy	7	ไทย	Thai	ม.ค.,ก.พ.,มี.ค.	จันทร์,อังคาร,พ
33	dmy	1	norsk (bokmål)	Bokmål	jan,feb,mar,apr	mandag,tirsdag,

DBCC USEROPTIONS

The DBCC USEROPTIONS command displays some of the connection (session) settings. As we have seen these settings play an important part on how date literals are interpreted by the system such as dateformat.

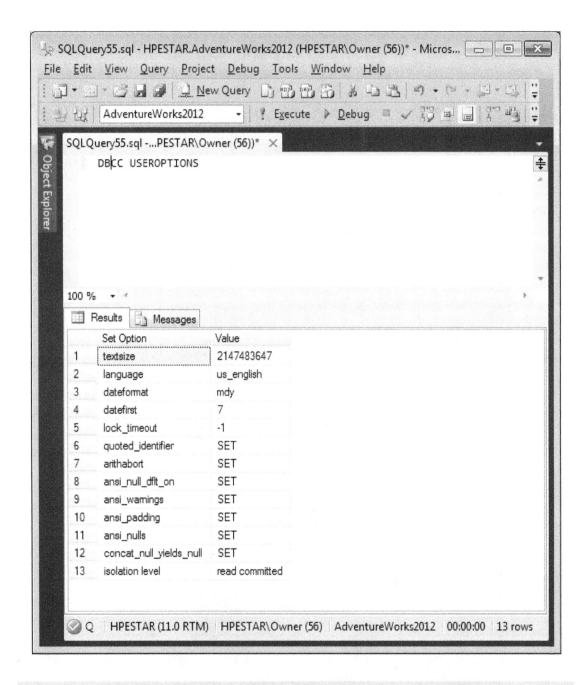

Easy SELECT Queries for Fun & Learning

T-SQL scripts to demonstrate simple, easy-to-read SELECT query variations. Important note: alias column names cannot be reused in successive computed columns by expressions or anywhere else in the query except the ORDER BY clause.

```
-- Datetime range with string literal date
SELECT  *  FROM    Person.Person
WHERE   ModifiedDate <= '2002-08-09 00:00:00.000'  ORDER BY LastName;
-- (38 row(s) affected)
```

NOTE

The string literal above looks like datetime, but it is not. It is only a string literal. The database engine will try to convert it to datetime data type at runtime (implicit conversion), and if successful the query will be executed.

The syntax of the following query is OK, however, it will fail at execution time.

```
SELECT  *  FROM    Person.Person  WHERE   ModifiedDate <= 'New York City'  ORDER BY LastName;
/* Msg 241, Level 16, State 1, Line 1 Conversion failed when converting date and/or time from character string. */
```

```
-- Complimentary (remaining) datetime range specified again with string literal
SELECT * FROM    Person.Person  WHERE   ModifiedDate > '2002-08-09 00:00:00.000'  ORDER BY
LastName;
-- (19934 row(s) affected)
```

```
-- Total rows in Person.Person
SELECT ( 38 + 19934 ) AS TotalRows;   -- 19972
```

```
SELECT count(* ) FROM  Person.Person -- 19972
```

```
SELECT TableRows = count(* ),  Calc = 38 + 19934  FROM   Person.Person; -- 19972     19972
```

```
-- Get prefix left of comma or entire string if there is no comma present
SELECT TOP 4                                                              ProductNumber,
      LEFT(Name, COALESCE(NULLIF(CHARINDEX(',',Name)-1,-1),LEN(Name)))    AS NamePrefix,
      Name                                                               AS ProductName
FROM AdventureWorks2012.Production.Product   WHERE CHARINDEX(',',Name) > 0
ORDER BY ProductName;
```

ProductNumber	NamePrefix	ProductName
VE-C304-L	Classic Vest	Classic Vest, L
VE-C304-M	Classic Vest	Classic Vest, M
VE-C304-S	Classic Vest	Classic Vest, S
GL-F110-L	Full-Finger Gloves	Full-Finger Gloves, L

CHAPTER 6: Basic SELECT Statement Syntax & Examples

NULL refers to no information available. Note: "=" and "!=" operators are not used with NULL; "IS" or "IS NOT" operators are applicable.

```
SELECT *
FROM    Person.Person
WHERE   AdditionalContactInfo IS NOT NULL
ORDER BY LastName;
-- (10 row(s) affected)
```

```
SELECT *
FROM    Person.Person
WHERE   AdditionalContactInfo IS NULL
ORDER BY LastName;
-- (19962 row(s) affected)
```

```
SELECT  DISTINCT FirstName
FROM    Person.Person
ORDER BY FirstName;     -- (1018 row(s) affected)
```

```
-- Summary revenue by product, interesting sort
USE AdventureWorks2012;
GO
SELECT  TOP 10 p.Name                                                   AS ProductName,
  FORMAT(SUM(((OrderQty * UnitPrice) * (1.0 - UnitPriceDiscount))),'c','en-US') AS SubTotal
FROM Production.Product AS p
INNER JOIN Sales.SalesOrderDetail AS sod
ON p.ProductID = sod.ProductID
GROUP BY p.Name
ORDER BY REVERSE(p.Name);
```

ProductName	SubTotal
Water Bottle - 30 oz.	$28,654.16
Hydration Pack - 70 oz.	$105,826.42
LL Mountain Frame - Black, 40	$1,198.99
ML Mountain Frame - Black, 40	$14,229.41
Mountain-300 Black, 40	$501,648.88
Mountain-500 Black, 40	$101,734.12
LL Mountain Frame - Silver, 40	$69,934.28
ML Mountain Frame-W - Silver, 40	$195,826.39
Mountain-500 Silver, 40	$145,089.43
Mountain-400-W Silver, 40	$323,703.82

CHAPTER 6: Basic SELECT Statement Syntax & Examples

DISTINCT & GROUP BY operations are generally "expensive".

```
SELECT  DISTINCT LastName FROM   Person.Person ORDER BY LastName;  -- (1206 row(s) affected)

-- LastName popularity descending
SELECT LastName,    Frequency = count(* )
FROM    Person.Person
GROUP BY LastName
ORDER BY Frequency DESC;
GO
```

LastName	Frequency
Diaz	211
Hernandez	188
Sanchez	175
Martinez	173
Torres	172
Martin	171
Perez	170
Gonzalez	169
Lopez	168
Rodriguez	166

```
-- Sort on column not in SELECT list - Note: demo only, confusing to end user
SELECT   LastName
FROM    Person.Person
ORDER BY FirstName;
-- (19972 row(s) affected)

-- Sort on column not in SELECT list
SELECT   Name = CONCAT(LastName, ', ', FirstName )
FROM    Person.Person
ORDER BY LastName;
-- (19972 row(s) affected)

-- Sort on column alias
SELECT   Name = CONCAT(LastName, ', ', FirstName )
FROM    Person.Person
ORDER BY Name;
-- (19972 row(s) affected)

SELECT   CONCAT(LastName, ', ', FirstName ) AS FullName
FROM    Person.Person
WHERE    LastName >= 'K'  ORDER BY LastName;
-- (12057 row(s) affected)
```

CHAPTER 6: Basic SELECT Statement Syntax & Examples

The NULLIF Function Actually Creates A NULL

```
SELECT  CONCAT(LastName, ', ', FirstName )  AS FullName
FROM    Person.Person  WHERE    LastName < 'K'  ORDER BY LastName;
-- (7915 row(s) affected)


-- Cardinality check
SELECT Difference= ((count(*)) - (12057 + 7915)) FROM  Person.Person; -- 0


-- Using the NULLIF function in counting
-- Count of all list prices - no NULLs in column
SELECT COUNT(ListPrice) FROM   AdventureWorks2012.Production.Product
-- 504


-- Counts only when ListPrice != 0 - does not count NULLs (ListPrice = 0.0)
SELECT COUNT(NULLIF(ListPrice,0.0)) FROM   AdventureWorks2012.Production.Product
-- 304


SELECT COUNT(ListPrice)  FROM  AdventureWorks2012.Production.Product  WHERE ListPrice = 0;
-- 200
```

Cardinality of DISTINCT & GROUP BY Clauses

The cardinality of DISTINCT and the cardinality of GROUP BY are the same with the same column(s).

```
-- FirstName by popularity descending
SELECT FirstName,
        Freq = count(* )
FROM    Person.Person
GROUP BY FirstName
ORDER BY Freq DESC;
-- (1018 row(s) affected)
```

FirstName	Freq
Richard	103
Katherine	99
Marcus	97
James	97
Jennifer	96
Dalton	93
Lucas	93
Alexandra	93
Morgan	92
Seth	92

```
SELECT  DISTINCT FirstName  FROM    Person.Person  ORDER BY FirstName;  -- (1018 row(s) affected)
```

CHAPTER 6: Basic SELECT Statement Syntax & Examples

Column Alias Can only Be Used in ORDER BY

Column aliases cannot be used in other computed columns (expressions), neither in the WHERE clause or GROUP BY clause.

```
SELECT   TableRows = count(* ),
         Calculated = 38 + 19934,
         Difference = (count(*) - 38 - 19934)
FROM   Person.Person;
```

TableRows	Calculated	Difference
19972	19972	0

Workarounds for Column Alias Use Restriction

There is a simple workaround for recycling column aliases in other clauses than just the ORDER BY: make the query into a derived table (x) and include it in an outer query. Similarly, CTEs can be used instead of derived tables.

```
-- Derived table workaround
SELECT TableRows, Calculated, Difference = TableRows - Calculated
FROM (
        SELECT   TableRows = count(* ),     Calculated = 38 + 19934,
        FROM   Person.Person
        ) x ;  -- Derived table
GO
```

TableRows	Calculated	Difference
19972	19972	0

```
-- CTE workaround
;WITH CTE AS (
        SELECT   TableRows = count(* ),     Calculated = 38 + 19934
        FROM   Person.Person)
-- Outer query
SELECT TableRows, Calculated, Difference = TableRows - Calculated
FROM CTE;
```

TableRows	Calculated	Difference
19972	19972	0

When the Clock Strikes Midnight: datetime Behaviour

This is one of the most troublesome issues in T-SQL programming (midnight bug, Cinderella syndrom): the predicate YYYYMMDD (date string literal) = DatetimeColumn does not include the entire day, only records with time at midnight: 00:00:00.000 .

```
USE AdventureWorks2012;

-- Note: only midnight 2003-08-09 included
-- Even a second after midnight is not included like 2003-08-09 00:00:01.000
SELECT  *
FROM    Person.Person
WHERE       ModifiedDate BETWEEN '2002-08-09 00:00:00.000'
            AND '2003-08-09 00:00:00.000'
ORDER BY LastName;
GO
-- (396 row(s) affected)
```

```
-- Entire day of 2003-08-09 included
-- The count same as before because no records after midnight 2003-08-09
SELECT  *
FROM    Person.Person
WHERE      ModifiedDate >= '2002-08-09 00:00:00.000'
           AND ModifiedDate <  '2003-08-10 00:00:00.000'
ORDER BY LastName;
GO
-- (396 row(s) affected)
```

LEFT(), RIGHT() & SUBSTRING() String Functions

```
SELECT  FirstCharOfFirstName = LEFT(FirstName,1),        -- column alias
        FirstCharOfLastName = LEFT(LastName,1),          -- column alias
        LastCharOfLastName = RIGHT(LastName,1),          -- column alias
        FullName = CONCAT(FirstName, SPACE(1), LastName) , -- column alias
        *                                                -- wild card, all columns
FROM    Person.Person
WHERE   SUBSTRING(FirstName,1,1) = 'J'
    AND SUBSTRING (LastName,1,1) = 'S'
    AND (RIGHT(LastName,1) = 'H' OR RIGHT(LastName,1) = 'Z')
ORDER BY LastName;
-- (59 row(s) affected) - Partial result.
```

FirstCharOfFirstName	FirstCharOfLastName	LastCharOfLastName	FullName	BusinessEntityID
J	S	z	Jacqueline Sanchez	8975
J	S	z	Jada Sanchez	9499
J	S	z	Jade Sanchez	9528
J	S	z	Janelle Sanchez	18590
J	S	z	Jared Sanchez	15266
J	S	z	Jarrod Sanchez	2948
J	S	z	Jay Sanchez	10298
J	S	z	Jennifer Sanchez	20440
J	S	z	Jeremiah Sanchez	15292
J	S	z	Jermaine Sanchez	8040

```
-- Sort on first column
SELECT BusinessEntityID, JobTitle, SUBSTRING(JobTitle, 5, 7)  AS MiddleOfJobTitle
FROM   HumanResources.Employee
WHERE  BirthDate <= '1960/12/31'    -- date literal (constant)
ORDER BY 1;
-- (27 row(s) affected) - Partial results.
```

BusinessEntityID	JobTitle	MiddleOfJobTitle
5	Design Engineer	gn Engi
6	Design Engineer	gn Engi
12	Tool Designer	Design
15	Design Engineer	gn Engi
23	Marketing Specialist	eting S
27	Production Supervisor - WC60	uction

```
-- String functions usage in formatting
DECLARE @SSN char(9) = '123456789';
SELECT SSN=CONCAT(LEFT(@SSN,3),'-', SUBSTRING(@SSN,4,2),'-', RIGHT(@SSN,4));
-- 123-45-6789
```

CHAPTER 6: Basic SELECT Statement Syntax & Examples

ASCII value range is 0-127. Extended ASCII: 128-255. Size is 8-bit, one byte.

```
SELECT TOP 5     ProductNumber,
                 SUBSTRING(ProductNumber,9,1)             AS MiddleSubstring,
                 ASCII(SUBSTRING(ProductNumber,9,1))      AS ASCIIValue
FROM AdventureWorks2008.Production.Product
WHERE LEN(ProductNumber) > 8
ORDER BY Name;                        - OK syntax, but does not make sense
```

ProductNumber	MiddleSubstring	ASCIIValue
VE-C304-L	L	76
VE-C304-M	M	77
VE-C304-S	S	83
GL-F110-L	L	76
GL-F110-M	M	77

NOTE
Table columns and columns by expressions (computed) can be mixed in a query at will.

```
-- Computed (expressions) & table columns
SELECT FirstCharOfFirstName = LEFT(FirstName,1),        -- string expression
       FirstCharOfLastName  = LEFT(LastName,1),         -- string expression
       FullName = CONCAT(LastName, ', ', FirstName ),   -- string expression
       SquareOfID = SQUARE(BusinessEntityID),           -- math expression
       *                                                -- wild card, all table columns
FROM    Person.Person
WHERE   LEFT(FirstName,1) = 'J'
    AND LEFT(LastName,2) = 'Sm'
ORDER BY FullName;
-- (14 row(s) affected)   - Partial results.
```

FirstCharOfFirstName	FirstCharOfLastName	FullName	SquareOfID	BusinessEntityID
J	S	Smith, Jacob	348680929	18673
J	S	Smith, James	308986084	17578
J	S	Smith, Jasmine	129572689	11383
J	S	Smith, Jeff	3139984	1772
J	S	Smith, Jennifer	122699929	11077
J	S	Smith, Jeremiah	20511841	4529
J	S	Smith, Jessica	145829776	12076
J	S	Smith, John	332041284	18222
J	S	Smith, Jonathan	312228900	17670
J	S	Smith, Jose	300710281	17341
J	S	Smith, Joseph	357474649	18907
J	S	Smith, Joshua	351825049	18757
J	S	Smith, Julia	121616784	11028
J	S	Smith, Justin	324900625	18025

Transact-SQL Reserved Keywords

List of reserved keywords in SQL Server 2012 Transact-SQL. Keywords can only be used as delimited identifiers such as [Inner] or "Order".

ADD	EXTERNAL	PROCEDURE
ALL	FETCH	PUBLIC
ALTER	FILE	RAISERROR
AND	FILLFACTOR	READ
ANY	FOR	READTEXT
AS	FOREIGN	RECONFIGURE
ASC	FREETEXT	REFERENCES
AUTHORIZATION	FREETEXTTABLE	REPLICATION
BACKUP	FROM	RESTORE
BEGIN	FULL	RESTRICT
BETWEEN	FUNCTION	RETURN
BREAK	GOTO	REVERT
BROWSE	GRANT	REVOKE
BULK	GROUP	RIGHT
BY	HAVING	ROLLBACK
CASCADE	HOLDLOCK	ROWCOUNT
CASE	IDENTITY	ROWGUIDCOL
CHECK	IDENTITY_INSERT	RULE
CHECKPOINT	IDENTITYCOL	SAVE
CLOSE	IF	SCHEMA
CLUSTERED	IN	SECURITYAUDIT
COALESCE	INDEX	SELECT
COLLATE	INNER	SEMANTICKEYPHRASETABLE
COLUMN	INSERT	SEMANTICSIMILARITYDETAILSTABLE
COMMIT	INTERSECT	SEMANTICSIMILARITYTABLE
COMPUTE	INTO	SESSION_USER
CONSTRAINT	IS	SET
CONTAINS	JOIN	SETUSER
CONTAINSTABLE	KEY	SHUTDOWN
CONTINUE	KILL	SOME
CONVERT	LEFT	STATISTICS
CREATE	LIKE	SYSTEM_USER
CROSS	LINENO	TABLE
CURRENT	LOAD	TABLESAMPLE
CURRENT_DATE	MERGE	TEXTSIZE
CURRENT_TIME	NATIONAL	THEN
CURRENT_TIMESTAMP	NOCHECK	TO
CURRENT_USER	NONCLUSTERED	TOP
CURSOR	NOT	TRAN
DATABASE	NULL	TRANSACTION
DBCC	NULLIF	TRIGGER
DEALLOCATE	OF	TRUNCATE
DECLARE	OFF	TRY_CONVERT
DEFAULT	OFFSETS	TSEQUAL
DELETE	ON	UNION
DENY	OPEN	UNIQUE
DESC	OPENDATASOURCE	UNPIVOT
DISK	OPENQUERY	UPDATE
DISTINCT	OPENROWSET	UPDATETEXT
DISTRIBUTED	OPENXML	USE
DOUBLE	OPTION	USER
DROP	OR	VALUES
DUMP	ORDER	VARYING
ELSE	OUTER	VIEW
END	OVER	WAITFOR
ERRLVL	PERCENT	WHEN
ESCAPE	PIVOT	WHERE
EXCEPT	PLAN	WHILE
EXEC	PRECISION	WITH
EXECUTE	PRIMARY	WITHIN GROUP
EXISTS	PRINT	WRITETEXT
EXIT	PROC	

CHAPTER 6: Basic SELECT Statement Syntax & Examples

Case Sensitive Sort with Latin1_General_CS_AI

For case sensitive sort on a column with case insensitive collation, we have use a case sensitive (CS) collation such as Latin1_General_CS_AI.

```
-- CASE INSENSITIVE sort using default collation
SELECT lname FROM
        (SELECT TOP 5 UPPER (LastName) AS lname FROM Person.Person ORDER BY FirstName) x
UNION ALL   SELECT lname FROM
        (SELECT TOP 5 LOWER (LastName) AS lname FROM Person.Person ORDER BY FirstName) y
ORDER BY lname;
-- ADAMS, adams, alexander, ALEXANDER, leonetti, LEONETTI, WRIGHT, WRIGHT, wright, wright
```

```
-- CASE SENSITIVE sort using %CS% collation
SELECT lname FROM ( SELECT lname FROM
  (SELECT TOP 5 UPPER (LastName) AS lname FROM Person.Person ORDER BY FirstName) x
  UNION ALL  SELECT lname FROM
  (SELECT TOP 5 LOWER (LastName) AS lname FROM Person.Person ORDER BY FirstName) y  ) z
ORDER BY lname COLLATE Latin1_General_CS_AI;
-- adams,ADAMS,alexander,ALEXANDER,leonetti,LEONETTI,wright,wright,WRIGHT,WRIGHT
```

CHAPTER 6: Basic SELECT Statement Syntax & Examples

The ORDER BY Clause for Sorting Query Results

The ORDER BY clause is located at the very end of the query. In fact the sorting itself takes place after the query executed and generated **an unordered result set**. Although frequently, especially for small sets, the results appear to be sorted, **only an ORDER BY clause can guarantee proper sorting**. INSERT, UPDATE, DELETE & MERGE statement do not support sorting, **the database engine performs all set operations unordered**. T-SQL scripts demonstrate the many variations of the ORDER BY clause.

```
USE AdventureWorks2012;
GO


-- A column can be used for sorting even though not explicitly used in the SELECT list
SELECT *
FROM   Production.Product
ORDER  BY Name ASC;
GO


-- Sort on the second column, whatever it may be
SELECT *
FROM   Production.Product
ORDER  BY 2 DESC;
GO


-- ASCending is the default sort order, it is not necessary to use
SELECT  Name AS ProductName,
        *

FROM   Production.Product
ORDER  BY ProductName ASC;
GO


SELECT  TOP (10) Name AS ProductName,              *
FROM   Production.Product  ORDER  BY 1 ASC;
```

ProductName	ProductID	Name	ProductNumber	MakeFlag	FinishedGoodsFlag	Color	SafetyStockLevel
Adjustable Race	1	Adjustable Race	AR-5381	0	0	NULL	1000
All-Purpose Bike Stand	879	All-Purpose Bike Stand	ST-1401	0	1	NULL	4
AWC Logo Cap	712	AWC Logo Cap	CA-1098	0	1	Multi	4
BB Ball Bearing	3	BB Ball Bearing	BE-2349	1	0	NULL	800
Bearing Ball	2	Bearing Ball	BA-8327	0	0	NULL	1000
Bike Wash - Dissolver	877	Bike Wash - Dissolver	CL-9009	0	1	NULL	4
Blade	316	Blade	BL-2036	1	0	NULL	800
Cable Lock	843	Cable Lock	LO-C100	0	1	NULL	4
Chain	952	Chain	CH-0234	0	1	Silver	500
Chain Stays	324	Chain Stays	CS-2812	1	0	NULL	1000

CHAPTER 6: Basic SELECT Statement Syntax & Examples

Using Column Alias in the ORDER BY Clause

Column alias can be used in an ORDER BY clause. In fact, it should be used to make the query more readable.

```
-- ProductName is a column alias, it can only be used in the ORDER BY clause, not anywhere before
SELECT ProductName = Name, *
FROM Production.Product
WHERE ProductName like '%glove%'
ORDER BY ProductName ASC ;
GO
/* ERROR
Msg 207, Level 16, State 1, Line 3
Invalid column name 'ProductName'.
*/
```

```
-- The TOP clause uses the ORDER BY sorting to select the 5 rows
SELECT TOP (5) ProductName = Name, *
FROM Production.Product
WHERE Name like '%glove%'
ORDER BY ProductName ASC ;
```

ProductName	ProductID	Name	ProductNumber	MakeFlag	FinishedGoodsFlag	Color	SafetyStockLevel
Full-Finger Gloves, L	863	Full-Finger Gloves, L	GL-F110-L	0	1	Black	4
Full-Finger Gloves, M	862	Full-Finger Gloves, M	GL-F110-M	0	1	Black	4
Full-Finger Gloves, S	861	Full-Finger Gloves, S	GL-F110-S	0	1	Black	4
Half-Finger Gloves, L	860	Half-Finger Gloves, L	GL-H102-L	0	1	Black	4
Half-Finger Gloves, M	859	Half-Finger Gloves, M	GL-H102-M	0	1	Black	4

```
-- Descending sort on name which is string data type
SELECT TOP (10) ProductName = Name, *
FROM Production.Product
WHERE Name like '%road%'
ORDER BY ProductName DESC ;
```

ProductName	ProductID	Name	ProductNumber	MakeFlag	FinishedGoodsFlag	Color	SafetyStockLevel
Road-750 Black, 58	977	Road-750 Black, 58	BK-R19B-58	1	1	Black	100
Road-750 Black, 52	999	Road-750 Black, 52	BK-R19B-52	1	1	Black	100
Road-750 Black, 48	998	Road-750 Black, 48	BK-R19B-48	1	1	Black	100
Road-750 Black, 44	997	Road-750 Black, 44	BK-R19B-44	1	1	Black	100
Road-650 Red, 62	761	Road-650 Red, 62	BK-R50R-62	1	1	Red	100
Road-650 Red, 60	760	Road-650 Red, 60	BK-R50R-60	1	1	Red	100
Road-650 Red, 58	759	Road-650 Red, 58	BK-R50R-58	1	1	Red	100
Road-650 Red, 52	764	Road-650 Red, 52	BK-R50R-52	1	1	Red	100
Road-650 Red, 48	763	Road-650 Red, 48	BK-R50R-48	1	1	Red	100
Road-650 Red, 44	762	Road-650 Red, 44	BK-R50R-44	1	1	Red	100

Using Table Alias in the ORDER BY Clause

Unlike the column alias, table alias can be used anywhere in the query within the scope of the alias.

```
-- Using table alias in ORDER BY
SELECT P.*
FROM   Production.Product P
ORDER  BY P.Name ASC;
GO
```

ProductID	Name	ProductNumber	MakeFlag	FinishedGoodsFlag	Color	SafetyStockLevel
958	Touring-3000 Blue, 54	BK-T18U-54	1	1	Blue	100
959	Touring-3000 Blue, 58	BK-T18U-58	1	1	Blue	100
960	Touring-3000 Blue, 62	BK-T18U-62	1	1	Blue	100
961	Touring-3000 Yellow, 44	BK-T18Y-44	1	1	Yellow	100
962	Touring-3000 Yellow, 50	BK-T18Y-50	1	1	Yellow	100
963	Touring-3000 Yellow, 54	BK-T18Y-54	1	1	Yellow	100
964	Touring-3000 Yellow, 58	BK-T18Y-58	1	1	Yellow	100
965	Touring-3000 Yellow, 62	BK-T18Y-62	1	1	Yellow	100
842	Touring-Panniers, Large	PA-T100	0	1	Grey	4
870	Water Bottle - 30 oz.	WB-H098	0	1	NULL	4
869	Women's Mountain Shorts, L	SH-W890-L	0	1	Black	4
868	Women's Mountain Shorts, M	SH-W890-M	0	1	Black	4
867	Women's Mountain Shorts, S	SH-W890-S	0	1	Black	4
854	Women's Tights, L	TG-W091-L	0	1	Black	4
853	Women's Tights, M	TG-W091-M	0	1	Black	4
852	Women's Tights, S	TG-W091-S	0	1	Black	4

```
-- Specific column list instead of all (*)
SELECT   Name,
         ProductNumber,
         ListPrice AS PRICE
FROM   Production.Product  P
ORDER  BY P.Name ASC;
GO


SELECT        Name,
              ProductNumber,
              ListPrice AS PRICE
FROM   Production.Product  P
ORDER  BY P.ListPrice DESC;

-- Equivalent to above with column alias usage
SELECT        Name,
              ProductNumber,
              ListPrice AS PRICE
FROM   Production.Product  P ORDER  BY PRICE DESC;
```

CHAPTER 6: Basic SELECT Statement Syntax & Examples

Easy ORDER BY Queries for Exercises

T-SQL scripts demonstrate easily readable queries with sorted result sets.

```
USE pubs ;
```

```
SELECT TYPE,  AvgPrice=FORMAT(AVG(price) , 'c', 'en-US')
FROM   titles WHERE  royalty = 10 GROUP  BY TYPE ORDER  BY TYPE ;
```

TYPE	AvgPrice
business	$17.31
popular_comp	$20.00
psychology	$14.14
trad_cook	$17.97

```
SELECT          type = type,
                AvgPrice = FORMAT(AVG(price),'c', 'en-US')
FROM   titles  WHERE  royalty = 10  GROUP  BY type  ORDER  BY AvgPrice;
```

type	AvgPrice
psychology	$14.14
business	$17.31
trad_cook	$17.97
popular_comp	$20.00

```
SELECT   type                         AS [type],
         FORMAT(AVG(price),'c', 'en-US')    AS AvgPrice
FROM   titles  GROUP  BY [type]  ORDER  BY [type] desc;
```

type	AvgPrice
UNDECIDED	NULL
trad_cook	$15.96
psychology	$13.50
popular_comp	$21.48
mod_cook	$11.49
business	$13.73

An Aggregate Function Can Be Used in an ORDER BY Clause

The NULL related warning message can be turned off: SET ANSI_WARNINGS OFF; alternately ISNULL function can be used in the query.

```
SELECT TYPE, AVG(price) Avg FROM titles  GROUP  BY TYPE ORDER  BY AVG(price);
/* Warning: Null value is eliminated by an aggregate or other SET operation.
(6 row(s) affected) */
```

CHAPTER 6: Basic SELECT Statement Syntax & Examples

Eliminate NULL in result with COALESCE or ISNULL functions

```
SELECT [type] = type,
       AvgPrice = COALESCE(FORMAT(AVG(price),'c', 'en-US') ,'')
FROM  titles  GROUP BY [type]  ORDER BY [type] desc;
```

type	AvgPrice
UNDECIDED	
trad_cook	$15.96
psychology	$13.50
popular_comp	$21.48
mod_cook	$11.49
business	$13.73

```
SELECT          pub_name                           Publisher,
                FORMAT(AVG(price),'c', 'en-US')    AvgPrice
FROM  titles
   INNER JOIN publishers
     ON  titles.pub_id = publishers.pub_id
GROUP  BY pub_name
ORDER  BY pub_name;
```

Publisher	AvgPrice
Algodata Infosystems	$18.98
Binnet & Hardley	$15.41
New Moon Books	$9.78

```
SELECT TOP(3) * FROM   titles ORDER  BY title;
```

title_id	title	type	pub_id	price	advance	royalty	ytd_sales	notes	pubdate
PC1035	But Is It User Friendly?	popular_comp	1389	22.95	7000.00	16	8780	A survey of software for the naive user, focusing on the 'friendliness' of each.	1991-06-30 00:00:00.000
PS1372	Computer Phobic AND Non-Phobic Individuals: Behavior Variations	psychology	0877	21.59	7000.00	10	375	A must for the specialist, this book examines the difference between those who hate and fear computers and those who don't.	1991-10-21 00:00:00.000
BU1111	Cooking with Computers: Surreptitious Balance Sheets	business	1389	11.95	5000.00	10	3876	Helpful hints on how to use your electronic resources to the best advantage.	1991-06-09 00:00:00.000

```
SELECT TOP(3) *  FROM   publishers  ORDER  BY pub_name;
```

pub_id	pub_name	city	state	country
1389	Algodata Infosystems	Berkeley	CA	USA
0877	Binnet & Hardley	Washington	DC	USA
1622	Five Lakes Publishing	Chicago	IL	USA

CHAPTER 6: Basic SELECT Statement Syntax & Examples

Sorting Products by Attributes

USE Northwind;

SELECT   UnitsInStock,
          ProductID,
          ProductName,
          QuantityPerUnit,
          FORMAT(UnitPrice, 'c', 'en-US') AS UnitPrice -- Column alias is same as column
FROM   Northwind.dbo.Products WHERE UnitsInStock BETWEEN 15 AND 25 ORDER BY UnitsInStock;

UnitsInStock	ProductID	ProductName	QuantityPerUnit	UnitPrice
15	7	Uncle Bob's Organic Dried Pears	12 - 1 lb pkgs.	$30.00
15	26	Gumbär Gummibärchen	100 - 250 g bags	$31.23
15	48	Chocolade	10 pkgs.	$12.75
15	70	Outback Lager	24 - 355 ml bottles	$15.00
17	38	Côte de Blaye	12 - 75 cl bottles	$263.50
17	43	Ipoh Coffee	16 - 500 g tins	$46.00
17	62	Tarte au sucre	48 pies	$49.30
17	2	Chang	24 - 12 oz bottles	$19.00
19	60	Camembert Pierrot	15 - 300 g rounds	$34.00
20	24	Guaraná Fantástica	12 - 355 ml cans	$4.50
20	35	Steeleye Stout	24 - 12 oz bottles	$18.00
20	51	Manjimup Dried Apples	50 - 300 g pkgs.	$53.00
21	54	Tourtière	16 pies	$7.45
21	56	Gnocchi di nonna Alice	24 - 250 g pkgs.	$38.00
22	11	Queso Cabrales	1 kg pkg.	$21.00
22	64	Wimmers gute Semmelknödel	20 bags x 4 pieces	$33.25
24	13	Konbu	2 kg box	$6.00
24	63	Vegie-spread	15 - 625 g jars	$43.90
25	19	Teatime Chocolate Biscuits	10 boxes x 12 pieces	$9.20

-- A second key is necessary for unique ordering
SELECT TOP(8) UnitsInStock,
          ProductID,
          ProductName,
          QuantityPerUnit,
          FORMAT(UnitPrice, 'c', 'en-US') AS UnitPrice
FROM   Northwind.dbo.Products
WHERE UnitsInStock BETWEEN 15 AND 25 ORDER BY UnitsInStock, ProductName;

UnitsInStock	ProductID	ProductName	QuantityPerUnit	UnitPrice
15	48	Chocolade	10 pkgs.	$12.75
15	26	Gumbär Gummibärchen	100 - 250 g bags	$31.23
15	70	Outback Lager	24 - 355 ml bottles	$15.00
15	7	Uncle Bob's Organic Dried Pears	12 - 1 lb pkgs.	$30.00
17	2	Chang	24 - 12 oz bottles	$19.00
17	38	Côte de Blaye	12 - 75 cl bottles	$263.50
17	43	Ipoh Coffee	16 - 500 g tins	$46.00
17	62	Tarte au sucre	48 pies	$49.30

Changing WHERE condition changes the cardinality of result set

```
SELECT          UnitsInStock,
                ProductID,
                ProductName,
                QuantityPerUnit,
                FORMAT( UnitPrice, 'c', 'en-US')          AS UnitPrice
FROM   Northwind.dbo.Products
WHERE  UnitsInStock = 15 or UnitsInStock = 25  -- same as UnitsInStock IN (15, 25)
ORDER  BY UnitsInStock, ProductName;
```

UnitsInStock	ProductID	ProductName	QuantityPerUnit	UnitPrice
15	48	Chocolade	10 pkgs.	$12.75
15	26	Gumbär Gummibärchen	100 - 250 g bags	$31.23
15	70	Outback Lager	24 - 355 ml bottles	$15.00
15	7	Uncle Bob's Organic Dried Pears	12 - 1 lb pkgs.	$30.00
25	19	Teatime Chocolate Biscuits	10 boxes x 12 pieces	$9.20

```
SELECT  TOP(7)  UnitsInStock,
                ProductID,
                ProductName,
                QuantityPerUnit,
                FORMAT( UnitPrice, 'c', 'en-US')          AS UnitPrice
FROM   Northwind.dbo.Products  ORDER  BY UnitsInStock DESC, ProductName ASC;
```

UnitsInStock	ProductID	ProductName	QuantityPerUnit	UnitPrice
125	75	Rhönbräu Klosterbier	24 - 0.5 l bottles	$7.75
123	40	Boston Crab Meat	24 - 4 oz tins	$18.40
120	6	Grandma's Boysenberry Spread	12 - 8 oz jars	$25.00
115	55	Pâté chinois	24 boxes x 2 pies	$24.00
113	61	Sirop d'érable	24 - 500 ml bottles	$28.50
112	33	Geitost	500 g	$2.50
112	36	Inlagd Sill	24 - 250 g jars	$19.00

```
SELECT  TOP(5)  UnitsInStock, ProductID, ProductName,          QuantityPerUnit,
                FORMAT( UnitPrice, 'c', 'en-US') AS UnitPrice
FROM   Northwind.dbo.Products
WHERE  UnitsInStock > 15  AND UnitsInStock < 25  ORDER  BY UnitsInStock DESC, ProductName ASC;
```

UnitsInStock	ProductID	ProductName	QuantityPerUnit	UnitPrice
24	13	Konbu	2 kg box	$6.00
24	63	Vegie-spread	15 - 625 g jars	$43.90
22	11	Queso Cabrales	1 kg pkg.	$21.00
22	64	Wimmers gute Semmelknödel	20 bags x 4 pieces	$33.25
21	56	Gnocchi di nonna Alice	24 - 250 g pkgs.	$38.00

CHAPTER 6: Basic SELECT Statement Syntax & Examples

The "Tricky" BETWEEN & NOT BETWEEN Operators
They are very English-like, but results should be verified to make sure they work as intended.

```
SELECT   TOP(5)   UnitsInStock, ProductID, ProductName,      QuantityPerUnit,
                  FORMAT( UnitPrice, 'c', 'en-US') AS UnitPrice
FROM   Northwind.dbo.Products
WHERE  UnitsInStock BETWEEN 15 AND 25
ORDER  BY UnitsInStock DESC, ProductName ASC;
GO
```

UnitsInStock	ProductID	ProductName	QuantityPerUnit	UnitPrice
25	19	Teatime Chocolate Biscuits	10 boxes x 12 pieces	$9.20
24	13	Konbu	2 kg box	$6.00
24	63	Vegie-spread	15 - 625 g jars	$43.90
22	11	Queso Cabrales	1 kg pkg.	$21.00
22	64	Wimmers gute Semmelknödel	20 bags x 4 pieces	$33.25

```
SELECT   TOP(5)   UnitsInStock, ProductID, ProductName,      QuantityPerUnit,
                  FORMAT( UnitPrice, 'c', 'en-US') AS UnitPrice
FROM   Northwind.dbo.Products
WHERE  UnitsInStock NOT BETWEEN 15 AND 25
ORDER  BY UnitsInStock DESC, ProductName ASC;
```

UnitsInStock	ProductID	ProductName	QuantityPerUnit	UnitPrice
125	75	Rhönbräu Klosterbier	24 - 0.5 l bottles	$7.75
123	40	Boston Crab Meat	24 - 4 oz tins	$18.40
120	6	Grandma's Boysenberry Spread	12 - 8 oz jars	$25.00
115	55	Pâté chinois	24 boxes x 2 pies	$24.00
113	61	Sirop d'érable	24 - 500 ml bottles	$28.50

```
SELECT          Orders.OrderID,
                Shippers.*
FROM   Shippers
    INNER JOIN Orders
    ON ( Shippers.ShipperID = Orders.ShipVia )
ORDER  BY Orders.OrderID;
GO
-- (830 row(s) affected) - Partial results.
```

OrderID	ShipperID	CompanyName	Phone
10248	3	Federal Shipping	(503) 555-9931
10249	1	Speedy Express	(503) 555-9831
10250	2	United Package	(503) 555-3199
10251	1	Speedy Express	(503) 555-9831
10252	2	United Package	(503) 555-3199
10253	2	United Package	(503) 555-3199

A second key is frequently required in sorting exception is PRIMARY KEY column.

```
SELECT  OrderID,
        ProductID,
        FORMAT( UnitPrice, 'c', 'en-US')            AS UnitPrice,
        Quantity,
        Discount
FROM    [Order Details]  ORDER  BY OrderID ASC, ProductID ASC;
GO
-- (2155 row(s) affected) - Partial results.
```

OrderID	ProductID	UnitPrice	Quantity	Discount
10248	11	$14.00	12	0
10248	42	$9.80	10	0
10248	72	$34.80	5	0
10249	14	$18.60	9	0
10249	51	$42.40	40	0
10250	41	$7.70	10	0
10250	51	$42.40	35	0.15
10250	65	$16.80	15	0.15

```
-- Sort keys are different from expression column EmployeeName
SELECT  CONCAT(LastName,', ', FirstName)  AS EmployeeName ,
        Title, City, Country
FROM  Northwind.dbo.Employees ORDER  BY LastName,  FirstName ASC;
```

EmployeeName	Title	City	Country
Buchanan, Steven	Sales Manager	London	UK
Callahan, Laura	Inside Sales Coordinator	Seattle	USA
Davolio, Nancy	Sales Representative	Seattle	USA
Dodsworth, Anne	Sales Representative	London	UK
Fuller, Andrew	Vice President, Sales	Tacoma	USA
King, Robert	Sales Representative	London	UK
Leverling, Janet	Sales Representative	Kirkland	USA
Peacock, Margaret	Sales Representative	Redmond	USA
Suyama, Michael	Sales Representative	London	UK

```
-- Equivalent sort
SELECT TOP(3)     CONCAT(LastName,', ', FirstName) AS EmployeeName ,     Title, City, Country
FROM  Northwind.dbo.Employees  ORDER  BY EmployeeName ASC;
```

EmployeeName	Title	City	Country
Buchanan, Steven	Sales Manager	London	UK
Callahan, Laura	Inside Sales Coordinator	Seattle	USA
Davolio, Nancy	Sales Representative	Seattle	USA

CHAPTER 6: Basic SELECT Statement Syntax & Examples

Using Multiple Keys in the ORDER BY Clause

If a single sort key does not result in unique ordering, multiple keys can be used. In the next example the Price (major) key is based on a column which is not unique. If we add Name as a second (minor) key, unique ordering will be guaranteed since Name is a unique column, it has a unique index and not null. It's worth noting if Name would allow nulls, we would need a third key for unique ordering.

```
-- Single key sort
SELECT   P.Name,
         P.ProductNumber,
         P.ListPrice              AS PRICE
FROM   Production.Product  P
WHERE  P.ProductLine = 'R'   AND P.DaysToManufacture < 4    ORDER  BY  P. ListPrice DESC;
```

Name	ProductNumber	PRICE
HL Road Frame - Black, 58	FR-R92B-58	1431.50
HL Road Frame - Red, 58	FR-R92R-58	1431.50
HL Road Frame - Red, 62	FR-R92R-62	1431.50
HL Road Frame - Red, 44	FR-R92R-44	1431.50
HL Road Frame - Red, 48	FR-R92R-48	1431.50
HL Road Frame - Red, 52	FR-R92R-52	1431.50
HL Road Frame - Red, 56	FR-R92R-56	1431.50
HL Road Frame - Black, 62	FR-R92B-62	1431.50
HL Road Frame - Black, 44	FR-R92B-44	1431.50
HL Road Frame - Black, 48	FR-R92B-48	1431.50
HL Road Frame - Black, 52	FR-R92B-52	1431.50
ML Road Frame-W - Yellow, 40	FR-R72Y-40	594.83

```
-- Double key sort - PRICE is the major key, Name is the minor key
SELECT   P.Name,
         P.ProductNumber,
         P.ListPrice              AS PRICE
FROM   Production.Product  P
WHERE  P.ProductLine = 'R'  AND P.DaysToManufacture < 4   ORDER  BY  PRICE DESC, Name;
```

Name	ProductNumber	PRICE
HL Road Frame - Black, 44	FR-R92B-44	1431.50
HL Road Frame - Black, 48	FR-R92B-48	1431.50
HL Road Frame - Black, 52	FR-R92B-52	1431.50
HL Road Frame - Black, 58	FR-R92B-58	1431.50
HL Road Frame - Black, 62	FR-R92B-62	1431.50
HL Road Frame - Red, 44	FR-R92R-44	1431.50
HL Road Frame - Red, 48	FR-R92R-48	1431.50
HL Road Frame - Red, 52	FR-R92R-52	1431.50
HL Road Frame - Red, 56	FR-R92R-56	1431.50
HL Road Frame - Red, 58	FR-R92R-58	1431.50
HL Road Frame - Red, 62	FR-R92R-62	1431.50
ML Road Frame - Red, 44	FR-R72R-44	594.83

ORDER BY in Complex Queries

An ORDER BY can be in a complex query and/or ORDER BY can be complex itself. T-SQL scripts demonstrate complex ORDER BY usage.


```
-- We cannot tell just by query inspection if the second key is sufficient for unique ordering or not
-- If we inspect the result set it becomes obvious that we need a third key at least (SalesOrderID unsorted)
SELECT   ProductName            = P.Name,
         NonDiscountSales        = ( OrderQty * UnitPrice ),
         Discounts               = ( ( OrderQty * UnitPrice ) * UnitPriceDiscount ) ,
         SalesOrderID
FROM   Production.Product P
    INNER JOIN Sales.SalesOrderDetail SOD
        ON P.ProductID = SOD.ProductID
ORDER  BY        ProductName DESC,
                 NonDiscountSales DESC;
GO
```

ProductName	NonDiscountSales	Discounts	SalesOrderID
Women's Tights, S	1049.86	104.986	47355
Women's Tights, S	824.89	41.2445	46987
Women's Tights, S	783.6455	39.1823	47400
Women's Tights, S	742.401	37.1201	50206
Women's Tights, S	701.1565	35.0578	46993
Women's Tights, S	701.1565	35.0578	46671
Women's Tights, S	701.1565	35.0578	50688
Women's Tights, S	701.1565	35.0578	49481
Women's Tights, S	659.912	32.9956	48295
Women's Tights, S	659.912	32.9956	46967
Women's Tights, S	618.6675	30.9334	46652
Women's Tights, S	608.9188	12.1784	46672
Women's Tights, S	608.9188	12.1784	47365
Women's Tights, S	565.4246	11.3085	47004
Women's Tights, S	565.4246	11.3085	50663

NOTE
Even though SELECT DISTINCT results may appear to be sorted, **only ORDER BY clause can guarantee sort**. This holds true for any kind of SELECT statement, simple or complex.

```
SELECT DISTINCT JobTitle  FROM  HumanResources.Employee ;

SELECT DISTINCT JobTitle  FROM  HumanResources.Employee ORDER  BY JobTitle;
```

CHAPTER 6: Basic SELECT Statement Syntax & Examples

ORDER BY with ROW_NUMBER()

T-SQL queries demonstrate sorting with not matching and matching ROW_NUMBER() sequence number.

```
SELECT
  ROW_NUMBER()  OVER( PARTITION BY CountryRegionName   ORDER BY SalesYTD ASC) AS SeqNo,
  CountryRegionName AS Country,  FirstName, LastName,  JobTitle,
  FORMAT(SalesYTD, 'c', 'en-US') AS SalesYTD,
  FORMAT(SalesLastYear, 'c', 'en-US') AS SalesLastYear
FROM  Sales.vSalesPerson        ORDER  BY JobTitle,   SalesYTD DESC;
```

SeqNo	Country	FirstName	LastName	JobTitle	SalesYTD	SalesLastYear
2	United States	Amy	Alberts	European Sales Manager	$519,905.93	$0.00
3	United States	Stephen	Jiang	North American Sales Manager	$559,697.56	$0.00
1	United States	Syed	Abbas	Pacific Sales Manager	$172,524.45	$0.00
11	United States	Linda	Mitchell	Sales Representative	$4,251,368.55	$1,439,156.03
1	United Kingdom	Jae	Pak	Sales Representative	$4,116,871.23	$1,635,823.40
10	United States	Michael	Blythe	Sales Representative	$3,763,178.18	$1,750,406.48
9	United States	Jillian	Carson	Sales Representative	$3,189,418.37	$1,997,186.20
1	France	Ranjit	Varkey Chudukatil	Sales Representative	$3,121,616.32	$2,396,539.76
2	Canada	José	Saraiva	Sales Representative	$2,604,540.72	$2,038,234.65
8	United States	Shu	Ito	Sales Representative	$2,458,535.62	$2,073,506.00
7	United States	Tsvi	Reiter	Sales Representative	$2,315,185.61	$1,849,640.94
1	Germany	Rachel	Valdez	Sales Representative	$1,827,066.71	$1,307,949.79
6	United States	Tete	Mensa-Annan	Sales Representative	$1,576,562.20	$0.00
5	United States	David	Campbell	Sales Representative	$1,573,012.94	$1,371,635.32
1	Canada	Garrett	Vargas	Sales Representative	$1,453,719.47	$1,620,276.90
1	Australia	Lynn	Tsoflias	Sales Representative	$1,421,810.92	$2,278,548.98
4	United States	Pamela	Ansman-Wolfe	Sales Representative	$1,352,577.13	$1,927,059.18

```
-- ROW_NUMBER() ORDER BY in synch with sort ORDER BY
SELECT  ROW_NUMBER()  OVER( ORDER BY JobTitle, SalesYTD DESC) AS SeqNo,
    CountryRegionName AS Country,  FirstName, LastName,  JobTitle,
    FORMAT(SalesYTD, 'c', 'en-US') AS SalesYTD, FORMAT(SalesLastYear, 'c', 'en-US') AS SalesLastYear
FROM  Sales.vSalesPerson ORDER  BY      SeqNo;
```

SeqNo	Country	FirstName	LastName	JobTitle	SalesYTD	SalesLastYear
1	United States	Amy	Alberts	European Sales Manager	$519,905.93	$0.00
2	United States	Stephen	Jiang	North American Sales Manager	$559,697.56	$0.00
3	United States	Syed	Abbas	Pacific Sales Manager	$172,524.45	$0.00
4	United States	Linda	Mitchell	Sales Representative	$4,251,368.55	$1,439,156.03
5	United Kingdom	Jae	Pak	Sales Representative	$4,116,871.23	$1,635,823.40
6	United States	Michael	Blythe	Sales Representative	$3,763,178.18	$1,750,406.48
7	United States	Jillian	Carson	Sales Representative	$3,189,418.37	$1,997,186.20
8	France	Ranjit	Varkey Chudukatil	Sales Representative	$3,121,616.32	$2,396,539.76
9	Canada	José	Saraiva	Sales Representative	$2,604,540.72	$2,038,234.65
10	United States	Shu	Ito	Sales Representative	$2,458,535.62	$2,073,506.00
11	United States	Tsvi	Reiter	Sales Representative	$2,315,185.61	$1,849,640.94
12	Germany	Rachel	Valdez	Sales Representative	$1,827,066.71	$1,307,949.79
13	United States	Tete	Mensa-Annan	Sales Representative	$1,576,562.20	$0.00
14	United States	David	Campbell	Sales Representative	$1,573,012.94	$1,371,635.32
15	Canada	Garrett	Vargas	Sales Representative	$1,453,719.47	$1,620,276.90
16	Australia	Lynn	Tsoflias	Sales Representative	$1,421,810.92	$2,278,548.98
17	United States	Pamela	Ansman-Wolfe	Sales Representative	$1,352,577.13	$1,927,059.18

ORDER BY Clause with CASE Conditional Expression

Sort by LastName, MiddleName if exists else FirstName, and FirstName in case MiddleName is used.

```
USE AdventureWorks;

SELECT          FirstName,
                COALESCE(MiddleName, '')        AS MName,  -- ISNULL can also be used
                LastName,
                AddressLine1,
                COALESCE(AddressLine2, '')       AS Addr2,
                City,
                SP.Name                          AS [State],
                CR.Name                          AS Country,
                I.CustomerID
FROM   Person.Contact AS C
    INNER JOIN Sales.Individual AS I
        ON C.ContactID = I.ContactID
    INNER JOIN Sales.CustomerAddress AS CA
        ON CA.CustomerID = I.CustomerID
    INNER JOIN Person.[Address] AS A
        ON A.AddressID = CA.AddressID
    INNER JOIN Person.StateProvince SP
        ON SP.StateProvinceID = A.StateProvinceID
    INNER JOIN Person.CountryRegion CR
        ON CR.CountryRegionCode = SP.CountryRegionCode
ORDER  BY LastName,
    CASE
      WHEN MiddleName != '' THEN MiddleName
      ELSE FirstName
    END,
    FirstName;
-- (18508 row(s) affected) -Partial results.
```

FirstName	MName	LastName	AddressLine1	Addr2	City	State	Country	CustomerID
Chloe	A	Adams	3001 N. 48th Street		Marysville	Washington	United States	19410
Eduardo	A	Adams	4283 Meaham Drive		San Diego	California	United States	25292
Kaitlyn	A	Adams	3815 Berry Dr.		Westminster	British Columbia	Canada	11869
Mackenzie	A	Adams	9639 Ida Drive		Langford	British Columbia	Canada	14640
Sara	A	Adams	7503 Hill Drive		Milwaukie	Oregon	United States	16986
Adam		Adams	9381 Bayside Way		Newport Beach	California	United States	13323
Amber		Adams	9720 Morning Glory Dr.		Brisbane	Queensland	Australia	26746
Angel		Adams	9556 Lyman Rd.		Burlingame	California	United States	18504
Aaron	B	Adams	4116 Stanbridge Ct.		Downey	California	United States	28866
Noah	B	Adams	6738 Wallace Dr.		El Cajon	California	United States	16977
Bailey		Adams	1817 Adobe Drive		Kirkland	Washington	United States	13280
Ben		Adams	1534 Land Ave		Bremerton	Washington	United States	28678
Alex	C	Adams	237 Bellwood Dr.		Lake Oswego	Oregon	United States	21139
Courtney	C	Adams	6089 Santa Fe Dr.		Torrance	California	United States	18075
Ian	C	Adams	7963 Elk Dr	#4	Versailles	Yveline	France	29422

Special Sorting, Like United States On Top Of The Country Pop-Up List
It requires CASE or IIF conditional expression.

```
-- Major sort key is Color if not null, else product name
-- Minor sort on ProductNumber
SELECT ProductID,
    ProductNumber,
    Name AS ProductName,
    FORMAT(ListPrice, 'c', 'en-US')  AS ListPrice,
    Color
FROM   Production.Product
WHERE  Name LIKE ( '%Road%' )
ORDER  BY        CASE
                    WHEN Color IS NULL THEN Name
                    ELSE Color
            END,
            ProductNumber DESC;
-- (103 row(s) affected) - Partial results.
```

ProductID	ProductNumber	ProductName	ListPrice	Color
768	BK-R50B-44	Road-650 Black, 44	$782.99	Black
977	BK-R19B-58	Road-750 Black, 58	$539.99	Black
999	BK-R19B-52	Road-750 Black, 52	$539.99	Black
998	BK-R19B-48	Road-750 Black, 48	$539.99	Black
997	BK-R19B-44	Road-750 Black, 44	$539.99	Black
813	HB-R956	HL Road Handlebars	$120.27	NULL
512	RM-R800	HL Road Rim	$0.00	NULL
519	SA-R522	HL Road Seat Assembly	$196.92	NULL
913	SE-R995	HL Road Seat/Saddle	$52.64	NULL
933	TI-R982	HL Road Tire	$32.60	NULL
811	HB-R504	LL Road Handlebars	$44.54	NULL
510	RM-R436	LL Road Rim	$0.00	NULL
517	SA-R127	LL Road Seat Assembly	$133.34	NULL
911	SE-R581	LL Road Seat/Saddle	$27.12	NULL
931	TI-R092	LL Road Tire	$21.49	NULL
812	HB-R720	ML Road Handlebars	$61.92	NULL
511	RM-R600	ML Road Rim	$0.00	NULL
518	SA-R430	ML Road Seat Assembly	$147.14	NULL
912	SE-R908	ML Road Seat/Saddle	$39.14	NULL
932	TI-R628	ML Road Tire	$24.99	NULL
717	FR-R92R-62	HL Road Frame - Red, 62	$1,431.50	Red
706	FR-R92R-58	HL Road Frame - Red, 58	$1,431.50	Red
721	FR-R92R-56	HL Road Frame - Red, 56	$1,431.50	Red

T-SQL queries demonstrate complex sorting with the CASE expression usage.
CASE expression returns a SINGLE SCALAR VALUE of the same data type.

```
SELECT  SellStartDate,
        SellEndDate,
        *
FROM   Production.Product
WHERE  Name LIKE ( '%mountain%' )
ORDER  BY CASE
                WHEN SellEndDate IS NULL THEN SellStartDate
                ELSE SellEndDate
          END DESC, Name;
GO
-- (94 row(s) affected) -Partial results.
```

SellStartDate	SellEndDate	ProductID	Name	ProductNumber
2007-07-01 00:00:00.000	NULL	986	Mountain-500 Silver, 44	BK-M18S-44
2007-07-01 00:00:00.000	NULL	987	Mountain-500 Silver, 48	BK-M18S-48
2007-07-01 00:00:00.000	NULL	988	Mountain-500 Silver, 52	BK-M18S-52
2007-07-01 00:00:00.000	NULL	869	Women's Mountain Shorts, L	SH-W890-L
2007-07-01 00:00:00.000	NULL	868	Women's Mountain Shorts, M	SH-W890-M
2007-07-01 00:00:00.000	NULL	867	Women's Mountain Shorts, S	SH-W890-S
2006-07-01 00:00:00.000	2007-06-30 00:00:00.000	817	HL Mountain Front Wheel	FW-M928
2006-07-01 00:00:00.000	2007-06-30 00:00:00.000	825	HL Mountain Rear Wheel	RW-M928
2006-07-01 00:00:00.000	2007-06-30 00:00:00.000	815	LL Mountain Front Wheel	FW-M423
2006-07-01 00:00:00.000	2007-06-30 00:00:00.000	823	LL Mountain Rear Wheel	RW-M423
2006-07-01 00:00:00.000	2007-06-30 00:00:00.000	814	ML Mountain Frame - Black, 38	FR-M63B-38
2006-07-01 00:00:00.000	2007-06-30 00:00:00.000	830	ML Mountain Frame - Black, 40	FR-M63B-40

```
-- 2 keys descending sort
SELECT       PRODUCTNAME  = P.Name,
             SALETOTAL    = ( OrderQty * UnitPrice ),
             NETSALETOTAL = ( ( OrderQty - RejectedQty ) * UnitPrice )
FROM   Production.Product P
    INNER JOIN Purchasing.PurchaseOrderDetail SOD
        ON P.ProductID = SOD.ProductID
ORDER  BY PRODUCTNAME  DESC,  SALETOTAL DESC;

-- Column alias sorting of GROUP BY aggregation results
SELECT [YEAR]=YEAR(OrderDate), Orders = COUNT(*)
FROM AdventureWorks2012.Sales.SalesOrderHeader
GROUP BY YEAR(OrderDate)  ORDER BY [YEAR];
```

YEAR	Orders
2005	1379
2006	3692
2007	12443
2008	13951

CHAPTER 6: Basic SELECT Statement Syntax & Examples

ORDER BY Clause with IIF Conditional Function

Sort by LastName, MiddleName if exists else FirstName, and FirstName in case MiddleName is used.

```
USE AdventureWorks;

SELECT          FirstName,
                COALESCE(MiddleName, '')          AS MName,  -- ISNULL can also be used
                LastName,
                AddressLine1,
                COALESCE(AddressLine2, '')         AS Addr2,
                City,
                SP.Name                           AS [State],
                CR.Name                           AS Country,
                I.CustomerID
FROM   Person.Contact AS C
   INNER JOIN Sales.Individual AS I
       ON C.ContactID = I.ContactID
   INNER JOIN Sales.CustomerAddress AS CA
       ON CA.CustomerID = I.CustomerID
   INNER JOIN Person.[Address] AS A
       ON A.AddressID = CA.AddressID
   INNER JOIN Person.StateProvince SP
       ON SP.StateProvinceID = A.StateProvinceID
   INNER JOIN Person.CountryRegion CR
       ON CR.CountryRegionCode = SP.CountryRegionCode
ORDER  BY       LastName,
                IIF( MiddleName != '',
                        MiddleName,               -- TRUE condition return value
                        FirstName),               -- FALSE condition return value
                FirstName;
GO
-- (18508 row(s) affected) -Partial results.
```

FirstName	MName	LastName	AddressLine1	Addr2	City	State	Country	CustomerID
Chloe	A	Adams	3001 N. 48th Street		Marysville	Washington	United States	19410
Eduardo	A	Adams	4283 Meaham Drive		San Diego	California	United States	25292
Kaitlyn	A	Adams	3815 Berry Dr.		Westminster	British Columbia	Canada	11869
Mackenzie	A	Adams	9639 Ida Drive		Langford	British Columbia	Canada	14640
Sara	A	Adams	7503 Hill Drive		Milwaukie	Oregon	United States	16986
Adam		Adams	9381 Bayside Way		Newport Beach	California	United States	13323
Amber		Adams	9720 Morning Glory Dr.		Brisbane	Queensland	Australia	26746
Angel		Adams	9556 Lyman Rd.		Burlingame	California	United States	18504
Aaron	B	Adams	4116 Stanbridge Ct.		Downey	California	United States	28866
Noah	B	Adams	6738 Wallace Dr.		El Cajon	California	United States	16977
Bailey		Adams	1817 Adobe Drive		Kirkland	Washington	United States	13280
Ben		Adams	1534 Land Ave		Bremerton	Washington	United States	28678
Alex	C	Adams	237 Bellwood Dr.		Lake Oswego	Oregon	United States	21139
Courtney	C	Adams	6089 Santa Fe Dr.		Torrance	California	United States	18075
Ian	C	Adams	7963 Elk Dr	#4	Versailles	Yveline	France	29422

ORDER BY Clause with the RANK() Function

T-SQL query demonstrates the combination of CASE expression and RANK() function in an ORDER BY clause. Note that while such a complex sort is technically impressive, ultimately it has to make sense to the user, the Business Intelligence consumer.

```
-- SQL complex sorting
USE AdventureWorks;

SELECT          ContactID,
                FirstName,
                LastName,
                COALESCE(Title, '')  AS Title
FROM   Person.Contact
WHERE  LEFT(FirstName, 1) = 'M'
ORDER  BY CASE
                WHEN LEFT(LastName, 1) = 'A' THEN RANK()
                        OVER( ORDER BY CONCAT(FirstName, SPACE(1), LastName))
                WHEN LEFT(LastName, 1) = 'M' THEN RANK()
                        OVER( ORDER BY CONCAT(LastName,', ', FirstName), Title)
                WHEN LEFT(LastName, 1) = 'U' THEN RANK()
                        OVER(  ORDER BY CONCAT(LastName,', ', FirstName)  DESC)
                ELSE RANK()
                        OVER( ORDER BY LastName ASC, FirstName DESC)
        END;
```

ContactID	FirstName	LastName	Title
9500	Mackenzie	Adams	
10144	Mackenzie	Allen	
10128	Madeline	Allen	
11708	Madison	Alexander	
11527	Madison	Anderson	
19872	Morgan	Bailey	
8059	Michelle	Bailey	
8080	Melissa	Bailey	
18291	Megan	Bailey	
8070	Mariah	Bailey	
2432	Maria	Bailey	
14378	Marcus	Bailey	
8063	Makayla	Bailey	
8032	Mackenzie	Bailey	
9521	Morgan	Baker	
3320	Miguel	Baker	
15437	Mason	Baker	
9546	Mary	Baker	
1082	Mary	Baker	
9539	Maria	Baker	

CHAPTER 6: Basic SELECT Statement Syntax & Examples

ORDER BY Clause with Custom Mapped Sort Sequence

Typically we rely on alphabets or numbers for sorting. What if, for example, we don't want United States way down on a website drop-down menu, rather than on the top with Canada and United Kingdom just above "lucky" Australia? We have to do custom mapping for such a sort in the ORDER BY clause.

```
USE AdventureWorks;
SELECT          AddressLine1,
                City,
                SP.StateProvinceCode                AS State,
                PostalCode,
                CR.Name                             AS  Country
FROM   Person.[Address] A
    INNER JOIN Person.StateProvince SP              ON A.StateProvinceID = SP.StateProvinceID
    INNER JOIN Person.CountryRegion CR              ON SP.CountryRegionCode = CR.CountryRegionCode
ORDER  BY (     CASE    WHEN CR.Name = 'United States' THEN 0
                        WHEN CR.Name = 'Canada' THEN 1
                        WHEN CR.Name = 'United Kingdom' THEN 2   ELSE 3  END ),
                Country,
                City
                AddressLine1;
-- (19614 row(s) affected) - Partial results.
```

AddressLine1	City	State	PostalCode	Country
9355 Armstrong Road	York	ENG	YO15	United Kingdom
939 Vista Del Diablo	York	ENG	YO15	United Kingdom
9458 Flame Drive	York	ENG	YO15	United Kingdom
9557 Steven Circle	York	ENG	YO3 4TN	United Kingdom

Sorting on the Last Word of a String

```
USE tempdb;
SELECT BusinessEntityID, FULLNAME = CONCAT(FirstName , SPACE(1), LastName )
INTO   People FROM   AdventureWorks2012.Person.Person ORDER  BY BusinessEntityID ;

SELECT *  FROM   People
ORDER  BY REVERSE(LEFT(REVERSE(FullName), charindex(' ', REVERSE(FullName) + ' '  ) - 1)),
     FullName ;
GO -- (19972 row(s) affected) - Partial results.
```

BusinessEntityID	FULLNAME
285	Syed Abbas
293	Catherine Abel
295	Kim Abercrombie

ORDER BY Clause with Custom Alphanumeric Sort Sequence

A frequent requirement is custom sorting on alphanumeric field (column). The next T-SQL query demonstrates special alphanumeric sorting.

```
USE AdventureWorks;

SELECT AddressLine1,
            isnull(AddressLine2, '')    AS Addressline2,
            City,
            SP.StateProvinceCode    AS State,
            PostalCode,
            CR.Name                 AS Country
FROM   Person.[Address] A
    INNER JOIN Person.StateProvince SP
     ON A.StateProvinceID = SP.StateProvinceID
    INNER JOIN Person.CountryRegion CR
     ON SP.CountryRegionCode = CR.CountryRegionCode
ORDER  BY (     CASE
                    WHEN Ascii([AddressLine1]) BETWEEN 65 AND 90 THEN 0 -- Upper case alpha
                    WHEN Ascii([AddressLine1]) BETWEEN 48 AND 57 THEN 1 -- Digits
                    ELSE 2
                END ),
            AddressLine1,
            City;
GO
-- (19614 row(s) affected) - Partial results.
```

AddressLine1	Addressline2	City	State	PostalCode	Country
Zur Lindung 46		Leipzig	NW	04139	Germany
Zur Lindung 6		Saarlouis	SL	66740	Germany
Zur Lindung 6		Solingen	NW	42651	Germany
Zur Lindung 609		Sulzbach Taunus	SL	66272	Germany
Zur Lindung 7		Berlin	HE	14129	Germany
Zur Lindung 7		Neunkirchen	SL	66578	Germany
Zur Lindung 764		Paderborn	HH	33041	Germany
Zur Lindung 78		Berlin	HH	10791	Germany
Zur Lindung 787		München	NW	80074	Germany
00, rue Saint-Lazare		Dunkerque	59	59140	France
02, place de Fontenoy		Verrieres Le Buisson	91	91370	France
035, boulevard du Montparnasse		Verrieres Le Buisson	91	91370	France
081, boulevard du Montparnasse		Saint-Denis	93	93400	France
081, boulevard du Montparnasse		Seattle	WA	98104	United States
084, boulevard du Montparnasse		Les Ulis	91	91940	France
1 Corporate Center Drive		Miami	FL	33127	United States
1 Mt. Dell Drive		Portland	OR	97205	United States
1 Smiling Tree Court	Space 55	Los Angeles	CA	90012	United States
1, allée des Princes		Courbevoie	92	92400	France

CHAPTER 6: Basic SELECT Statement Syntax & Examples

Working with Synonyms

A synonym is a shorthand name for a longer name including multi-part names. **While prefix like "sn" or "syn" is not required, it is a good practice since otherwise a synonym can be confused with a (real) table for example, leading to loss of DBA or developer productivity.**

```
USE tempdb;
GO


-- Create synonyms for a 3-part names
CREATE SYNONYM snCustomerAW  FOR AdventureWorks.Sales.Customer;
CREATE SYNONYM snCustomerAW12  FOR AdventureWorks2012.Sales.Customer;


-- Create a synonym for 4-part name linked server
CREATE SYNONYM snCustomerLDNAW12  FOR
        [LONDONPROD8].AdventureWorks2012.Sales.Customer;
GO -- Command(s) completed successfully.


-- Query the Customer tables by using the synonyms
SELECT * FROM snCustomerAW ORDER BY AccountNumber;    -- (19185 row(s) affected)
SELECT * FROM snCustomerAW12 ORDER BY AccountNumber;  -- (19820 row(s) affected)
GO


-- Delete a synonym
DROP SYNONYM snCustomerAW;  -- Command(s) completed successfully.
GO


-- Enumerating all synonyms in database
SELECT  name                              AS "Name"
        ,base_object_name                 AS "Definition"
        ,PARSENAME(base_object_name, 4)   AS "Server"
        ,PARSENAME(base_object_name, 3)   AS "Database"
        ,PARSENAME(base_object_name, 2)   AS "Schema"
        ,PARSENAME(base_object_name, 1)   AS "Object"
   FROM sys.synonyms ORDER BY Definition;
```

Name	Definition	Server	Database	Schema	Object
CustomerAW12	[AdventureWorks2012].[Sales].[Customer]	NULL	AdventureW orks2012	Sales	Customer
CustomerLNDA W12	[LONDONPROD8].[AdventureWorks2012].[Sales].[C ustomer]	LONDONPRO D8	AdventureW orks2012	Sales	Customer

Date & Time Conversion To / From String

While there are only a few internal representation of date and time, string representations are many, even not deterministic since they may change from one country to another such as weekday and month names.   T-SQL scripts demonstrate the myriad of date and time conversion possibilities.

The CONVERT() Function with Style Number Parameter

```
-- String source  format: mon dd yyyy hh:mmAM (or PM)
-- 100 is the style number parameter for CONVERT
SELECT [Date&Time] = convert(datetime, 'Oct 23 2020 11:01AM', 100)
```

> Date&Time
> 2020-10-23 11:01:00.000

```
-- Default without style number
SELECT convert(datetime, 'Oct 23 2020 11:01AM')                -- 2020-10-23 11:01:00.000
```

```
-- Without century (yy) string date conversion with style number 0
-- Input format: mon dd yy hh:mmAM (or PM)
SELECT [Date&Time] = convert(datetime, 'Oct 23 20 11:01AM', 0)
```

> Date&Time
> 2020-10-23 11:01:00.000

```
-- Default without style number
SELECT convert(datetime, 'Oct 23 20 11:01AM')                  -- 2020-10-23 11:01:00.000
```

 Convert string date & time to datetime (8-bytes internal representation) data type.

```
SELECT convert(datetime, '10/23/2016', 101)        -- mm/dd/yyyy

SELECT convert(datetime, '2016.10.23', 102)          -- yyyy.mm.dd ANSI date with century

SELECT convert(datetime, '23/10/2016', 103)          -- dd/mm/yyyy

SELECT convert(datetime, '23.10.2016', 104)-- dd.mm.yyyy

SELECT convert(datetime, '23-10-2016', 105)          -- dd-mm-yyyy

-- mon (month) types are nondeterministic conversions, dependent on language setting.
SELECT convert(datetime, '23 OCT 2016', 106)          -- dd mon yyyy
```

String Datetime Formats With "Mon" Are Nondeterministic, Language Dependent

SELECT [Date&Time] = convert(datetime, 'Oct 23, 2016', 107) -- mon dd, yyyy

> Date&Time
> 2016-10-23 00:00:00.000

SELECT [Date&Time]=convert(datetime, '20:10:44', 108)   -- hh:mm:ss

> Date&Time
> 1900-01-01 20:10:44.000

SELECT [Date&Time]=convert(datetime, 'Oct 23 2016 11:02:44:013AM', 109) -- mon dd yyyy hh:mm:ss:mmmAM (or PM)

> Date&Time
> 2016-10-23 11:02:44.013

SELECT convert(datetime, '10-23-2016', 110)   -- mm-dd-yyyy
SELECT convert(datetime, '2016/10/23', 111)   -- yyyy/mm/dd

-- YYYYMMDD ISO date format works at any language setting - international standard
SELECT [Date&Time]=convert(datetime, '20161023')

> Date&Time
> 2016-10-23 00:00:00.000

SELECT [Date&Time]=convert(datetime, '20161023', 112)   -- ISO yyyymmdd

> Date&Time
> 2016-10-23 00:00:00.000

SELECT [Date&Time]=convert(datetime, '23 Oct 2016 11:02:07:577', 113) -- dd mon yyyy hh:mm:ss:mmm

> Date&Time
> 2016-10-23 11:02:07.577

SELECT [Date&Time]=convert(datetime, '20:10:25:300', 114)   -- hh:mm:ss:mmm(24h)

> Date&Time
> 1900-01-01 20:10:25.300

SELECT [Date&Time]=convert(datetime, '2016-10-23 20:44:11', 120)   -- yyyy-mm-dd hh:mm:ss(24h)
> Date&Time
> 2016-10-23 20:44:11.000

Style 126 Is ISO 8601 Format: International Standard; Works With Any Language Setting

SELECT [Date&Time]=convert(datetime, '2018-10-23T18:52:47.513', 126) -- yyyy-mm-ddThh:mm:ss(.mmm)

>   Date&Time
>   2018-10-23 18:52:47.513

SELECT [Date&Time]=convert(datetime, '2016-10-23 20:44:11.500', 121)   -- yyyy-mm-dd hh:mm:ss.mmm

>   Date&Time
>   2016-10-23 20:44:11.500

-- Islamic / Hijri date conversion

SELECT CONVERT(nvarchar(32), convert(datetime,'2016-10-23'), 130);
-- 22 محرم 1438 12:00:00:000AM

SELECT [Date&Time]=convert(datetime, N'23 شوال 1441 6:52:47:513PM', 130)

>   Date&Time
>   2020-06-14 18:52:47.513

SELECT [Date&Time]=convert(datetime, '23/10/1441 6:52:47:513PM',   131)

>   Date&Time
>   2020-06-14 18:52:47.513

-- Convert DDMMYYYY format to datetime with intermediate conversion using STUFF().

SELECT STUFF(STUFF('31012016',3,0,'-'),6,0,'-');
-- 31-01-2016

SELECT [Date&Time]=convert(datetime, STUFF(STUFF('31012016',3,0,'-'),6,0,'-'), 105)

>   Date&Time
>   2016-01-31 00:00:00.000

-- Equivalent
SELECT STUFF(STUFF('31012016',3,0,'/'),6,0,'/'); -- 31/01/2016
SELECT [Date&Time]=convert(datetime, STUFF(STUFF('31012016',3,0,'/'),6,0,'/'), 103)

CHAPTER 6: Basic SELECT Statement Syntax & Examples

String to Datetime Conversion Without Century

String to datetime conversion without century - some exceptions. Nondeterministic means language setting (also regional setting) dependent such as Mar/Mär/mars/márc .

SELECT [Date&Time]=convert(datetime, 'Oct 23 16 11:02:44AM')   -- Default

Date&Time
2016-10-23 11:02:44.000

SELECT convert(datetime, '10/23/16', 1)	mm/dd/yy	U.S.
SELECT convert(datetime, '16.10.23', 2)	yy.mm.dd	ANSI
SELECT convert(datetime, '23/10/16', 3)	dd/mm/yy	UK/FR
SELECT convert(datetime, '23.10.16', 4)	dd.mm.yy	German
SELECT convert(datetime, '23-10-16', 5)	dd-mm-yy	Italian
SELECT convert(datetime, '23 OCT 16', 6)	dd mon yy	non-det.
SELECT convert(datetime, 'Oct 23, 16', 7)	mon dd, yy	non-det.
SELECT convert(datetime, '20:10:44', 8)	hh:mm:ss	
SELECT convert(datetime, 'Oct 23 16 11:02:44:013AM', 9)	Default with msec	
SELECT convert(datetime, '10-23-16', 10)	mm-dd-yy	U.S.
SELECT convert(datetime, '16/10/23', 11)	yy/mm/dd	Japan
SELECT convert(datetime, '161023', 12)	yymmdd	ISO
SELECT convert(datetime, '23 Oct 16 11:02:07:577', 13)	dd mon yy hh:mm:ss:mmm EU dflt	
SELECT convert(datetime, '20:10:25:300', 14)	hh:mm:ss:mmm(24h)	
SELECT convert(datetime, '2016-10-23 20:44:11',20)	yyyy-mm-dd hh:mm:ss(24h) ODBC can.	
SELECT convert(datetime, '2016-10-23 20:44:11.500', 21)	yyyy-mm-dd hh:mm:ss.mmm ODBC	

Combine Date & Time String into Datetime

```
DECLARE @DateTimeValue varchar(32), @DateValue char(8), @TimeValue char(6)
 SELECT @DateValue = '20200718',          @TimeValue = '211920'
SELECT          @DateTimeValue =
                CONCAT(
                convert(varchar, convert(datetime, @DateValue), 111),
                ' ', substring(@TimeValue, 1, 2) , ':', substring(@TimeValue, 3, 2) , ':',
substring(@TimeValue, 5, 2)  )

SELECT  DateInput = @DateValue, TimeInput = @TimeValue,  DateTimeOutput = @DateTimeValue;
GO
```

DateInput	TimeInput	DateTimeOutput
20200718	211920	2020/07/18 21:19:20

```
SELECT DATETIMEFROMPARTS (2020, 07, 1, 21, 01, 20, 700)          -- New in SQL Server 2012
```

Date and Time Internal Storage Format

DATETIME 8 bytes internal storage structure:

- ➢ 1st 4 bytes: number of days after the base date 1900-01-01
- ➢ 2nd 4 bytes: number of clock-ticks (3.33 milliseconds) since midnight

```
SELECT CONVERT(binary(8), CURRENT_TIMESTAMP);
```

Hex
0x0000A09C00F23CE1

DATE 3 bytes internal storage structure:

- ➢ 3 bytes integer: number of days after the first date 0001-01-01
- ➢ Note: hex byte order reversed

SMALLDATETIME 4 bytes internal storage structure

- ➢ 1st 2 bytes: number of days after the base date 1900-01-01
- ➢ 2nd 2 bytes: number of minutes since midnight

```
SELECT Hex=CONVERT(binary(4), convert(smalldatetime, getdate()));
```

Hex
0xA09C0375

CHAPTER 6: Basic SELECT Statement Syntax & Examples

Date & Time Operations Using System Operators & Functions

```
-- Conversion from hex (binary) to datetime value
DECLARE @dtHex binary(8)= 0x00009966002d3344;  DECLARE @dt datetime = @dtHex;
SELECT @dt;   -- 2007-07-09 02:44:34.147
```

```
-- SQL convert seconds to HH:MM:SS -
DECLARE  @Seconds INT;  SET @Seconds = 20000 ;
SELECT HH = @Seconds / 3600, MM = (@Seconds%3600) / 60, SS = (@Seconds%60) ;
```

HH	MM	SS
5	33	20

Extract Date Only from DATETIME Data Type

```
DECLARE @Now datetime = CURRENT_TIMESTAMP -- getdate()

SELECT  DateAndTime        = @Now     -- Date portion and Time portion
        ,DateString               = REPLACE(LEFT(CONVERT (varchar, @Now, 112),10),' ','-')
        ,[Date]                   = CONVERT(DATE, @Now)  -- SQL Server 2008 and on - date part
        ,Midnight1                = dateadd(day, datediff(day,0, @Now), 0)
        ,Midnight2                = CONVERT(DATETIME,CONVERT(int, @Now))
        ,Midnight3                = CONVERT(DATETIME,CONVERT(BIGINT,@Now) &
(POWER(Convert(bigint,2),32)-1));
```

DateAndTime	DateString	Date	Midnight1	Midnight2	Midnight3
2020-07-28 15:01:51.960	20200728	2020-07-28	2020-07-28 00:00:00.000	2020-07-29 00:00:00.000	2020-07-29 00:00:00.000

```
-- Compare today with database dates
SELECT          TOP (10) OrderDate = CONVERT(date, OrderDate),
                Today = CONVERT(date, getdate()),
                DeltaDays = DATEDIFF(DD, OrderDate, getdate())
FROM AdventureWorks2012.Sales.SalesOrderHeader  ORDER BY NEWID(); -- random sort
```

OrderDate	Today	DeltaDays
2008-01-15	2012-08-10	1669
2006-07-14	2012-08-10	2219
2008-07-05	2012-08-10	1497
2008-03-01	2012-08-10	1623
2007-10-01	2012-08-10	1775
2007-01-15	2012-08-10	2034
2008-05-27	2012-08-10	1536
2008-04-18	2012-08-10	1575
2008-04-25	2012-08-10	1568
2006-12-17	2012-08-10	2063

String Date Formats Without Time

```
-- String date format yyyy/mm/dd from datetime
SELECT CONVERT(VARCHAR(10), GETDATE(), 111) AS [YYYY/MM/DD] ;
```

> YYYY/MM/DD
> 2012/07/28

```
SELECT CONVERT(VARCHAR(10), GETDATE(), 112) AS [YYYYMMDD];
```

> YYYYMMDD
> 20120728

```
SELECT REPLACE(CONVERT(VARCHAR(10), GETDATE(), 111),'/',' ') AS [YYYY MM DD];
```

> YYYY MM DD
> 2020 07 28

```
-- Converting to special (non-standard) date formats: DD-MMM-YY
SELECT UPPER(REPLACE(CONVERT(VARCHAR,GETDATE(),6),' ','-')) AS CustomDate;
```

> CustomDate
> 28-JUL-20

```
-- SQL convert date string to datetime - time set to 00:00:00.000 or 12:00AM

PRINT CONVERT(datetime,'07-10-2020',110) ;        -- Jul 10 2020 12:00AM
PRINT CONVERT(datetime,'2020/07/10',111) ;        -- Jul 10 2020 12:00AM
PRINT CONVERT(datetime,'20200710',  112);         -- Jul 10 2020 12:00AM
GO
```

```
-- SQL Server cast string to date / datetime
DECLARE @DateValue char(8) = '20200718'

SELECT [Date] = CAST (@DateValue AS datetime);
GO
```

> Date
> 2020-07-18 00:00:00.000

CHAPTER 6: Basic SELECT Statement Syntax & Examples

String date to string date conversion with nested CONVERT

```
SELECT CONVERT(varchar, CONVERT(datetime, '20140508'), 100) AS StringDate;
```

> StringDate
> May 8 2014 12:00AM

```
-- T-SQL convert date to integer
DECLARE @Date datetime;  SET @Date = getdate();
SELECT DateAsInteger = CAST (CONVERT(varchar,@Date,112) as INT);
GO
```

> DateAsInteger
> 20120728

```
-- SQL Server convert integer to datctime
DECLARE @iDate int = 20151225;
SELECT IntegerToDatetime = CAST(convert(varchar,@iDate) as datetime)
GO
```

> IntegerToDatetime
> 2015-12-25 00:00:00.000

```
-- Alternates: date-only datetime values

SELECT [DATE-ONLY]=CONVERT(DATETIME, FLOOR(CONVERT(FLOAT, GETDATE())));

SELECT [DATE-ONLY]=CONVERT(DATETIME, FLOOR(CONVERT(MONEY, GETDATE())));

SELECT [DATE-ONLY]=CONVERT(DATETIME, CONVERT(DATE, GETDATE()));
```

```
-- CAST string to datetime
-- String date preparation, length is 10 characters
SELECT CONVERT(varchar, GETDATE(), 101), LEN (CONVERT(varchar, GETDATE(), 101))
--       07/28/2018       10
```

```
SELECT [DATE-ONLY]=CAST(CONVERT(varchar, GETDATE(), 101) AS DATETIME);
```

> DATE-ONLY
> 2018-07-28 00:00:00.000

DATEADD() and DATEDIFF() Functions

```
-- T-SQL strip time from date
SELECT getdate() AS [DateTime], dateadd(dd, datediff(dd, 0, getdate()), 0) [DateOnly];
```

DateTime	DateOnly
2012-07-28 17:24:07.300	2012-07-28 00:00:00.000

```
-- First day of current month
SELECT dateadd(month, datediff(month, 0, getdate()), 0)  AS FirstDayOfCurrentMonth;
SELECT dateadd(dd,1, EOMONTH(getdate(),-1));  -- New to SQL Server 2012
```

FirstDayOfCurrentMonth
2020-07-01 00:00:00.000

```
-- 15th day of current month
SELECT dateadd(day,14,dateadd(month, datediff(month,0,getdate()),0))
                                                    AS MiddleOfCurrentMonth;
SELECT dateadd(dd,15, EOMONTH(getdate(),-1));  -- New to SQL Server 2012
```

MiddleOfCurrentMonth
2012-07-15 00:00:00.000

```
-- First Monday of current month
SELECT  dateadd(day, (9-datepart(weekday,
        dateadd(month, datediff(month, 0, getdate()), 0)))%7,
        dateadd(month, datediff(month, 0, getdate()), 0)) AS [First Monday Of Current Month];
GO
```

First Monday Of Current Month
2012-07-02 00:00:00.000

```
-- Next Monday calculation from the reference date which was a Monday
DECLARE @Now datetime = GETDATE();
DECLARE @NextMonday datetime = dateadd(dd, ((datediff(dd, '19000101', @Now)
            / 7) * 7) + 7, '19000101');
SELECT [Now]=@Now, [Next Monday]=@NextMonday;
GO
```

Now	Next Monday
2012-07-28 17:35:29.657	2012-07-30 00:00:00.000

Last Date & First Date Calculations

```
-- Last Friday of current month

SELECT   dateadd(day, -7+(6-datepart(weekday,

        dateadd(month, datediff(month, 0, getdate())+1, 0)))%7,

        dateadd(month, datediff(month, 0, getdate())+1, 0)) ;

-- First day of next month

SELECT dateadd(month, datediff(month, 0, getdate())+1, 0) ;

-- 15th of next month

SELECT dateadd(day,14, dateadd(month, datediff(month, 0, getdate())+1, 0));

-- First Monday of next month

SELECT   dateadd(day, (9-datepart(weekday,
        dateadd(month, datediff(month, 0, getdate())+1, 0)))%7,
        dateadd(month, datediff(month, 0, getdate())+1, 0));


-- Next 12 months start & end - EOMONTH is new to SQL Server 2012
SELECT TOP 12
        DATEADD(DD,1, EOMONTH(getdate(),number-1))     AS Start,
        EOMONTH(getdate(),number)                      AS [End]
FROM master.dbo.spt_values   -- get integer sequence
WHERE type='P'  ORDER BY number;
GO
```

Start	End
2016-08-01	2016-08-31
2016-09-01	2016-09-30
2016-10-01	2016-10-31
2016-11-01	2016-11-30
2016-12-01	2016-12-31
2017-01-01	2017-01-31
2017-02-01	2017-02-28
2017-03-01	2017-03-31
2017-04-01	2017-04-30
2017-05-01	2017-05-31
2017-06-01	2017-06-30
2017-07-01	2017-07-31

BETWEEN Operator for Date Range

Date time range SELECT using the using >= and < operators. Count Sales Orders for date range 2007 OCT-NOV.

```
DECLARE  @StartDate DATETIME,  @EndDate DATETIME
SET @StartDate = convert(DATETIME,'10/01/2007',101)
SET @EndDate   = convert(DATETIME,'11/30/2007',101)
SELECT @StartDate, @EndDate
-- 2007-10-01 00:00:00.000  2007-11-30 00:00:00.000
SELECT dateadd(DAY,1,@EndDate),    dateadd(ms,-3,dateadd(DAY,1,@EndDate))
-- 2007-12-01 00:00:00.000  2007-11-30 23:59:59.997

SELECT [Sales Orders for 2007 OCT-NOV] = COUNT(* )
FROM   AdventureWorks2012.Sales.SalesOrderHeader
WHERE  OrderDate >= @StartDate
       AND OrderDate < dateadd(DAY,1,@EndDate)
```

```
        Sales Orders for 2007 OCT-NOV
        3668
```

Equivalent date range query using BETWEEN comparison. It requires a bit of trick programming. 23.59.59.997 is the last available time in a day.

```
SELECT [Sales Orders for 2007 OCT-NOV] = COUNT(* )
FROM   AdventureWorks2012.Sales.SalesOrderHeader
WHERE   OrderDate BETWEEN @StartDate
        AND dateadd(ms,-3, dateadd(DAY, 1, @EndDate))
GO
```

```
        Sales Orders for 2007 OCT-NOV
        3668
```

The BETWEEN operator can be used with string dates as well. Note: anything after midnight on 2004-02-10 is not included.

```
USE AdventureWorks;
SELECT POs=COUNT(*) FROM Purchasing.PurchaseOrderHeader
WHERE OrderDate BETWEEN '20040201' AND '20040210'
GO
```

```
        POs
        108
```

CHAPTER 6: Basic SELECT Statement Syntax & Examples

BETWEEN Dates Without Time: Entire 2004-02-10 Day Included This Fashion

```
SELECT POs=COUNT(*) FROM Purchasing.PurchaseOrderHeader
WHERE datediff(dd,0,OrderDate)
        BETWEEN datediff(dd,0,'20040201 12:11:39') AND datediff(dd,0,'20040210 14:33:19')
```

POs
108

The datetime range BETWEEN is equivalent to >=...AND....<= operators.

```
SELECT POs=COUNT(*) FROM Purchasing.PurchaseOrderHeader
WHERE OrderDate  BETWEEN '2004-02-01 00:00:00.000' AND '2004-02-10  00:00:00.000'
```

POs
108

Orders with datetime OrderDate-s of

'2004-02-10 00:00:01.000'	1 second after midnight (start of day at 12:00AM)
'2004-02-10 00:01:00.000'	1 minute after midnight
'2004-02-10 01:00:00.000'	1 hour after midnight
'2004-02-10 23:00:00.000'	23 hours after midnight

would not included in the preceding two queries. Only datetime OrderDate of '2004-02-10
00:00:00.000' would be included. That would be OK if the time part is not used. But even in that
case and order can be entered accidentally with a time part, that would throw off the count.

To include the entire day of 2004-02-10, move the day up by one and use the < operator:

```
SELECT POs=COUNT(*) FROM Purchasing.PurchaseOrderHeader
WHERE OrderDate >= '20040201' AND OrderDate < '20040211';
```

POs
108

The reason we cannot detect a difference is due to lack of data passed midnight on 2004-02-11.

```
SELECT  [PurchaseOrderID], [RevisionNumber], [Status],
        [EmployeeID], [VendorID], [ShipMethodID], [OrderDate]
FROM [AdventureWorks].[Purchasing].[PurchaseOrderHeader] WHERE PurchaseOrderID = 1665;
```

PurchaseOrderID	RevisionNumber	Status	EmployeeID	VendorID	ShipMethodID	OrderDate
1665	0	4	261	43	5	2004-02-10 00:00:00.000

CHAPTER 6: Basic SELECT Statement Syntax & Examples

Advance the datetime one second from midnight, the BETWEEN datetime query is not going to count it

```
UPDATE [AdventureWorks].[Purchasing].[PurchaseOrderHeader]
      SET OrderDate = '2004-02-10 00:00:01.000'
WHERE PurchaseOrderID = 1665;  -- (1 row(s) affected)
```

This is the current value for OrderDate datetime.

PurchaseOrderID	RevisionNumber	Status	EmployeeID	VendorID	ShipMethodID	OrderDate
1665	0	4	261	43	5	2004-02-10 00:00:01.000

The following queries are not going to count this passed midnight record any more.

```
SELECT POs=COUNT(*) FROM Purchasing.PurchaseOrderHeader
WHERE OrderDate BETWEEN '2004-02-01 00:00:00.000' AND '2004-02-10  00:00:00.000'
```

POs
107

```
USE AdventureWorks; SELECT POs=COUNT(*) FROM Purchasing.PurchaseOrderHeader
WHERE OrderDate BETWEEN '20040201' AND '20040210'
```

POs
107

While the query we designed specifically for a case like this will count it correctly.

```
SELECT POs=COUNT(*) FROM Purchasing.PurchaseOrderHeader
WHERE OrderDate >= '20040201' AND OrderDate < '20040211'
```

POs
108

We restore the data to its original value.

```
UPDATE [AdventureWorks].[Purchasing].[PurchaseOrderHeader]
      SET OrderDate = '2004-02-10 00:00:00.000'
WHERE PurchaseOrderID = 1665;     -- (1 row(s) affected)
```

CHAPTER 6: Basic SELECT Statement Syntax & Examples

Date Validation Function ISDATE()

```
DECLARE @StringDate varchar(32);
SET @StringDate = '2011-03-15 18:50';
IF EXISTS( SELECT * WHERE ISDATE(@StringDate) = 1)
   PRINT 'VALID DATE: ' + @StringDate
ELSE
   PRINT 'INVALID DATE: ' + @StringDate;
```

> VALID DATE: 2011-03-15 18:50

```
DECLARE @StringDate varchar(32) ;
SET @StringDate = '20112-03-15 18:50';
IF EXISTS( SELECT * WHERE ISDATE(@StringDate) = 1)
   PRINT 'VALID DATE: ' + @StringDate
ELSE  PRINT 'INVALID DATE: ' + @StringDate;
GO
```

> INVALID DATE: 20112-03-15 18:50

First and Last Day of Date Periods

Calculating date periods markers is a very important task in T-SQL programming, especially related to reporting queries.

```
DECLARE @Date DATE = '20161023';  SELECT ReferenceDate  = @Date;

SELECT FirstDayOfYear  = CONVERT(DATE, dateadd(yy, datediff(yy,0, @Date),0));

SELECT LastDayOfYear   = CONVERT(DATE, dateadd(yy, datediff(yy,0, @Date)+1,-1));

SELECT FDofSemester = CONVERT(DATE, dateadd(qq,((datediff(qq,0,@Date)/2)*2),0));

SELECT LastDayOfSemester  = CONVERT(DATE, dateadd(qq,((datediff(qq,0,@Date)/2)*2)+2,-1));

SELECT FirstDayOfQuarter = CONVERT(DATE, dateadd(qq, datediff(qq,0, @Date),0));

SELECT LastDayOfQuarter = CONVERT(DATE, dateadd(qq, datediff(qq,0,@Date)+1,-1));
```

LastDayOfQuarter
2016-12-31

The brand-new EOMonth() function simplifies month start/end formulas

```
SELECT LastDayOfMonth = EOMonth (@Date);  -- New in SQL Server 2012

SELECT FirstDayOfMonth = CONVERT(DATE, dateadd(mm, datediff(mm,0, @Date),0));

SELECT LastDayOfMonth  = CONVERT(DATE, dateadd(mm, datediff(mm,0, @Date)+1,-1));

SELECT FirstDayOfWeek  = CONVERT(DATE, dateadd(wk, datediff(wk,0, @Date),0));

SELECT LastDayOfWeek   = CONVERT(DATE, dateadd(wk, datediff(wk,0, @Date)+1,-1));
GO
```

Month Sequence Generator

Sometimes date based data may have gaps missing months. For reporting purposes we may want to include all months from start date to end date. To do that we have to generate a continuous sequence of months, and use it to fill in the gaps. Calendar table can also be used for such a task.

```
DECLARE @Date date = '2000-01-01'
SELECT MonthStart=dateadd(MM, number, @Date)
FROM  master.dbo.spt_values
WHERE type='P' AND  dateadd(MM, number, @Date) <= CURRENT_TIMESTAMP
ORDER BY MonthStart;    -- (151 row(s) affected) - Partial results.
```

MonthStart
2000-01-01
2000-02-01
2000-03-01
2000-04-01
2000-05-01
2000-06-01
2000-07-01
2000-08-01
2000-09-01
2000-10-01
2000-11-01
2000-12-01
2001-01-01
2001-02-01
2001-03-01
2001-04-01

Selected U.S. & International Date Styles

The U.S. date style is m/d/y.

DECLARE @DateTimeValue varchar(32) = '10/23/2016';

SELECT StringDate=@DateTimeValue, [SSMS-Style] = CONVERT(datetime, @DatetimeValue);

SELECT @DateTimeValue = '10/23/2016 23:01:05';

SELECT StringDate = @DateTimeValue, [SSMS-Style] = CONVERT(datetime, @DatetimeValue);
GO

StringDate	SSMS-Style
10/23/2016	2016-10-23 00:00:00.000

StringDate	SSMS-Style
10/23/2016 23:01:05	2016-10-23 23:01:05.000

The UK or British/French style is dmy.

DECLARE @DateTimeValue varchar(32) = '23/10/16 23:01:05';

SELECT StringDate = @DateTimeValue, [SSMS-Style] = CONVERT(datetime, @DatetimeValue, 3);

 SELECT @DateTimeValue = '23/10/2016 04:01 PM';

SELECT StringDate = @DateTimeValue, [SSMS-Style] = CONVERT(datetime, @DatetimeValue, 103);
GO

The German style is dmy as well with a new twist to it: period instead of slash.

DECLARE @DateTimeValue varchar(32) = '23.10.16 23:01:05';
SELECT StringDate = @DateTimeValue, [SSMS -Style] = CONVERT(datetime, @DatetimeValue, 4);
 SELECT @DateTimeValue = '23.10.2016 04:01 PM';
SELECT StringDate = @DateTimeValue, [SSMS -Style] = CONVERT(datetime, @DatetimeValue, 104);
GO

```
-- Nondeterministic month name (mon)
SET LANGUAGE Spanish; SELECT CONVERT(varchar, getdate(), 100);        -- Ago 10 2018  4:43PM
SET LANGUAGE Turkish; SELECT CONVERT(varchar, getdate(), 100);        -- Agu 10 2018  4:44PM
SET LANGUAGE Polish; SELECT CONVERT(varchar, getdate(), 100);         -- VIII 10 2018  4:46PM
SET LANGUAGE Hungarian; SELECT CONVERT(varchar, getdate(), 100);      -- aug 10 2018  4:46PM
SET LANGUAGE Russian; SELECT CONVERT(nvarchar, getdate(), 100);       -- авг 10 2018  4:47PM
```

The DATEPART() Function to Decompose a Date

The DATEPART() function returns a part of a date.

```
DECLARE @dt datetime = getdate();
SELECT DATEPART(YEAR, @dt)        AS YYYY,
       DATEPART(MONTH, @dt)       AS MM,
       DATEPART(DAY, @dt)         AS DD;
```

YYYY	MM	DD
2016	7	29

```
SELECT * FROM Northwind.dbo.Orders
WHERE DATEPART(YEAR, OrderDate)        = '1996' AND
      DATEPART(MONTH,OrderDate)        = '07'   AND
      DATEPART(DAY, OrderDate)         = '10'
```

```
/*OrderID      CustomerID     EmployeeID    OrderDate          RequiredDate        ShippedDate
     ShipVia  Freight  ShipName       Shipaddress      ShipCity  ShipRegion      ShipPostalCode
     ShipCountry
10253   HANAR   3        1996-07-10 00:00:00.000 1996-07-24 00:00:00.000 1996-07-16 00:00:00.000
        2       58.17    Hanari Carnes    Rua do Paço, 67  Rio de Janeiro    RJ        05454-876
        Brazil */
```

Alternate syntax for DATEPART.

```
SELECT * FROM Northwind.dbo.Orders
WHERE          YEAR(OrderDate)     = 1996      AND
               MONTH(OrderDate)    = 07        AND
               DAY(OrderDate)      = 10
GO
```

```
-- Additional datepart parameters including Julian date
DECLARE @dt datetime = getdate();
SELECT DATEPART(DAY, @dt)          AS DD,
       DATEPART(WEEKDAY, @dt)      AS WD,
       DATEPART(DAYOFYEAR, @dt)    AS JulianDate,
       DATEPART(WEEK, @dt)         AS Week,
       DATEPART(ISO_WEEK, @dt)     AS ISOWeek,
       DATEPART(HOUR, @dt)         AS HH;
```

DD	WD	JulianDate	Week	ISOWeek	HH
10	5	223	33	32	17

CHAPTER 6: Basic SELECT Statement Syntax & Examples

The DATENAME() Function to Get Date Part Names

The DATENAME() function can be used to find out the words for months and weekdays.

```
SELECT DayName=DATENAME(weekday, OrderDate), SalesPerWeekDay = COUNT(*)
FROM AdventureWorks2008.Sales.SalesOrderHeader
GROUP BY DATENAME(weekday, OrderDate), DATEPART(weekday,OrderDate)
ORDER BY DATEPART(weekday,OrderDate);
```

DayName	SalesPerWeekDay
Sunday	4482
Monday	4591
Tuesday	4346
Wednesday	4244
Thursday	4483
Friday	4444
Saturday	4875

DATENAME application for month names

```
SELECT MonthName=DATENAME(month, OrderDate), SalesPerMonth = COUNT(*)
FROM AdventureWorks2008.Sales.SalesOrderHeader
GROUP BY DATENAME(month, OrderDate), MONTH(OrderDate) ORDER BY MONTH(OrderDate);
```

MonthName	SalesPerMonth
January	2483
February	2686
March	2750
April	2740
May	3154
June	3079
July	2094
August	2411
September	2298
October	2282
November	2474
December	3014

```
SELECT DATENAME(MM,dateadd(MM,7,-1))  -- July  - Month name from month number
```

Extract Date from Text with PATINDEX Pattern Matching

```
USE tempdb;
go

CREATE TABLE InsiderTransaction (
    InsiderTransactionID int identity primary key,
    TradeDate datetime,
    TradeMsg varchar(256),
    ModifiedDate datetime default (getdate())  );

-- Populate table with dummy data
INSERT InsiderTransaction (TradeMsg)
VALUES ('INSIDER TRAN QABC Hammer, Bruce D. CSO 09-02-08 Buy 2,000 6.10');
INSERT InsiderTransaction (TradeMsg)
VALUES ('INSIDER TRAN QABC Schmidt, Steven CFO 08-25-08 Buy 2,500 6.70') ;
INSERT InsiderTransaction (TradeMsg)
VALUES ('INSIDER TRAN QABC  Hammer, Bruce D. CSO  08-20-08 Buy 3,000 8.59');
INSERT InsiderTransaction (TradeMsg)
VALUES ('INSIDER TRAN QABC Walters,  Jeff CTO 08-15-08  Sell 5,648 8.49');
INSERT InsiderTransaction (TradeMsg)
VALUES  ('INSIDER TRAN  QABC  Walters, Jeff CTO   08-15-08 Option Exercise 5,648 2.15');
INSERT InsiderTransaction (TradeMsg)
VALUES('INSIDER TRAN QABC Hammer, Bruce D. CSO 07-31-08  Buy 5,000 8.05');
INSERT InsiderTransaction (TradeMsg)
VALUES('INSIDER TRAN QABC Lennot, Mark  Director  08-31-07 Buy 1,500 9.97');
INSERT InsiderTransaction (TradeMsg)
VALUES('INSIDER TRAN QABC  O''Neal, Linda COO  08-01-08 Sell 5,000 6.50');
```

Pattern match for MM-DD-YY using the PATINDEX string function to extract dates from stock trade message text.

```
SELECT  InsiderTransactionID ,      substring(TradeMsg,
        patindex('%[01][0-9]-[0123][0-9]-[0-9][0-9]%', TradeMsg),8) AS TradeDate
FROM InsiderTransaction  WHERE  patindex('%[01][0-9]-[0123][0-9]-[0-9][0-9]%', TradeMsg) > 0;
```

InsiderTransactionID	TradeDate
1	09-02-08
2	08-25-08
3	08-20-08
4	08-15-08
5	08-15-08
6	07-31-08
7	08-31-07
8	08-01-08

CHAPTER 6: Basic SELECT Statement Syntax & Examples

Valid Ranges for Date & Time Data Types

- ➢ DATE (3 bytes) date range:

- ➢ January 1, 1 through December 31, 9999 A.D.

- ➢ SMALLDATETIME (4 bytes) date range:

- ➢ January 1, 1900 through June 6, 2079

- ➢ DATETIME (8 bytes) date range:

- ➢ January 1, 1753 through December 31, 9999

- ➢ DATETIME2 (6-8 bytes) date range:

- ➢ January 1, 1 A.D. through December 31, 9999 A.D.

Smalldatetime has limited range. The statement below will give a date range error.

```
SELECT CONVERT(smalldatetime, '2110-01-01')
/* Msg 242, Level 16, State 3, Line 1
The conversion of a varchar data type to a smalldatetime data type
resulted in an out-of-range value. */
```

```
-- Date Columbus discovers America
SELECT CONVERT(datetime, '14921012');
/* Msg 242, Level 16, State 3, Line 2
The conversion of a varchar data type to a datetime data type resulted in an out-of-range value. */
```

```
SELECT CONVERT(datetime2, '14921012');   -- 1492-10-10 00:00:00.0000000
```

```
SELECT CONVERT(date, '14921012');                 -- 1492-10-12
```

CHAPTER 6: Basic SELECT Statement Syntax & Examples

Last Week Calculations

```
-- SQL last Friday - Implied string to datetime conversions in dateadd & datediff
DECLARE @BaseFriday CHAR(8), @LastFriday datetime, @LastMonday datetime;
SET @BaseFriday = '19000105';
SELECT  @LastFriday = dateadd(dd,
        (datediff (dd, @BaseFriday, CURRENT_TIMESTAMP) / 7) * 7, @BaseFriday) ;
SELECT [Last Friday] = @LastFriday ;
```

Last Friday
2012-07-27 00:00:00.000

```
-- Last Monday (last week's Monday)
SELECT  @LastMonday=dateadd(dd, (datediff (dd, @BaseFriday,
        CURRENT_TIMESTAMP) / 7) * 7 - 4, @BaseFriday)
SELECT [Last Monday]= @LastMonday;
```

Last Monday
2012-07-23 00:00:00.000

```
-- Last week - SUN - SAT
SELECT          [Last Week] = CONCAT(CONVERT(varchar,dateadd(day, -1, @LastMonday), 101), ' - ',
                CONVERT(varchar, dateadd(day, 1,  @LastFriday), 101))
```

Last Week
07/22/2012 - 07/28/2012

```
-- Next 10 weeks including this one; SUN - SAT
SELECT  TOP 10  [ Week] = CONCAT(CONVERT(varchar,dateadd(day, -1+number*7, @LastMonday), 101),
        ' - ',      CONVERT(varchar, dateadd(day, 1+number*7, @LastFriday), 101))
FROM master.dbo.spt_values  WHERE type = 'P';
```

Week
08/05/2012 - 08/11/2012
08/12/2012 - 08/18/2012
08/19/2012 - 08/25/2012
08/26/2012 - 09/01/2012
09/02/2012 - 09/08/2012
09/09/2012 - 09/15/2012
09/16/2012 - 09/22/2012
09/23/2012 - 09/29/2012
09/30/2012 - 10/06/2012
10/07/2012 - 10/13/2012

Specific Day Calculations

```
-- First day of current month
SELECT dateadd(month, datediff(month, 0, getdate()), 0);
```

```
-- 15th day of current month
SELECT dateadd(day,14,dateadd(month,datediff(month,0,getdate()),0));
```

```
-- First Monday of current month
SELECT   dateadd(day, (9-datepart(weekday,
         dateadd(month, datediff(month, 0, getdate()), 0)))%7,
         dateadd(month, datediff(month, 0, getdate()), 0)) ;
```

```
-- Next Monday calculation from the reference date which was a Monday
DECLARE @Now datetime = GETDATE();
DECLARE @NextMonday datetime = dateadd(dd, ((datediff(dd, '19000101', @Now)  / 7) * 7) + 7,
'19000101');
SELECT [Now]=@Now, [Next Monday]=@NextMonday;
```

```
-- Last Friday of current month
SELECT   dateadd(day, -7+(6-datepart(weekday,
         dateadd(month, datediff(month, 0, getdate())+1, 0)))%7,
         dateadd(month, datediff(month, 0, getdate())+1, 0)) ;
```

```
-- First day of next month
SELECT dateadd(month, datediff(month, 0, getdate())+1, 0);
```

```
-- 15th of next month
SELECT dateadd(day,14, dateadd(month, datediff(month, 0, getdate())+1, 0));
```

```
-- First Monday of next month
SELECT   dateadd(day, (9-datepart(weekday,
         dateadd(month, datediff(month, 0, getdate())+1, 0)))%7,
          dateadd(month, datediff(month, 0, getdate())+1, 0))  AS NextMonthMonday;
```

NextMonthMonday
2012-08-06 00:00:00.000

CHAPTER 6: Basic SELECT Statement Syntax & Examples

CHAPTER 7: Subqueries in SELECT Statements

Subqueries

Subquery ("inner query") is query within a query which is called the "outer query".

When a subquery involves columns form the outer query, it is called correlated subquery.

When a subquery has a table alias, it is called a derived table.

With SQL Server 2005 a new kind of subquery was introduced: Common Table Expression (CTE). A query can have one or more CTEs. If they are related, they are called nested CTEs. CTEs support recursion.

Correlated subquery is used to retrieve the last freight cost for the customer.

```
-- Correlated subquery - it has reference to an outer query column: A.CustomerID
USE Northwind;

SELECT   A.CustomerID,
     FORMAT(MIN(A.OrderDate), 'd')                          AS FirstOrder,
     FORMAT(MAX(A.OrderDate), 'd')                          AS LastOrder,
     FORMAT( (SELECT   TOP 1 B.Freight
              FROM    Orders B
              WHERE   B.CustomerID = A.CustomerID
              ORDER BY OrderDate DESC),'c','en-US')         AS LastFreight
FROM    Orders A
GROUP BY A.CustomerID ORDER BY A.CustomerID;  -- (89 row(s) affected) - Partial results.
```

CustomerID	FirstOrder	LastOrder	LastFreight
ALFKI	8/25/1997	4/9/1998	$1.21
ANATR	9/18/1996	3/4/1998	$39.92
ANTON	11/27/1996	1/28/1998	$58.43
AROUT	11/15/1996	4/10/1998	$33.80
BERGS	8/12/1996	3/4/1998	$151.52
BLAUS	4/9/1997	4/29/1998	$31.14
BLONP	7/25/1996	1/12/1998	$7.09
BOLID	10/10/1996	3/24/1998	$16.16
BONAP	10/16/1996	5/6/1998	$38.28
BOTTM	12/20/1996	4/24/1998	$24.12
BSBEV	8/26/1996	4/14/1998	$123.83
CACTU	4/29/1997	4/28/1998	$0.33

CHAPTER 7: Subqueries in SELECT Statements

Non-Correlated Subqueries

In the next query, the inner query is not linked to the outer query at all (no outer column is used in the inner query). The implication is that the inner query can be executed by itself. The inner query needs to return a single value in this instance due to the ">=" operator. If it were to return multiple values, error would result.

```
-- Non-correlated subquery
SELECT          Name,
                FORMAT(ListPrice, 'c','en-US')              AS ListPrice,
                ProductNumber,
                FORMAT(StandardCost, 'c','en-US')           AS StandardCost
FROM AdventureWorks2012.Production.Product
WHERE ListPrice >=
                    (SELECT ListPrice
                     FROM AdventureWorks.Production.Product
                     WHERE Name = 'Road-250 Black, 48' )

ORDER BY ListPrice DESC, Name;
GO
```

Name	ListPrice	ProductNumber	StandardCost
Road-150 Red, 44	$3,578.27	BK-R93R-44	$2,171.29
Road-150 Red, 48	$3,578.27	BK-R93R-48	$2,171.29
Road-150 Red, 52	$3,578.27	BK-R93R-52	$2,171.29
Road-150 Red, 56	$3,578.27	BK-R93R-56	$2,171.29
Road-150 Red, 62	$3,578.27	BK-R93R-62	$2,171.29
Mountain-100 Silver, 38	$3,399.99	BK-M82S-38	$1,912.15
Mountain-100 Silver, 42	$3,399.99	BK-M82S-42	$1,912.15
Mountain-100 Silver, 44	$3,399.99	BK-M82S-44	$1,912.15
Mountain-100 Silver, 48	$3,399.99	BK-M82S-48	$1,912.15
Mountain-100 Black, 38	$3,374.99	BK-M82B-38	$1,898.09
Mountain-100 Black, 42	$3,374.99	BK-M82B-42	$1,898.09
Mountain-100 Black, 44	$3,374.99	BK-M82B-44	$1,898.09
Mountain-100 Black, 48	$3,374.99	BK-M82B-48	$1,898.09
Road-250 Black, 44	$2,443.35	BK-R89B-44	$1,554.95
Road-250 Black, 48	$2,443.35	BK-R89B-48	$1,554.95
Road-250 Black, 52	$2,443.35	BK-R89B-52	$1,554.95
Road-250 Black, 58	$2,443.35	BK-R89B-58	$1,554.95
Road-250 Red, 44	$2,443.35	BK-R89R-44	$1,518.79
Road-250 Red, 48	$2,443.35	BK-R89R-48	$1,518.79
Road-250 Red, 52	$2,443.35	BK-R89R-52	$1,518.79
Road-250 Red, 58	$2,443.35	BK-R89R-58	$1,554.95

Subquery returned more than 1 value Error

The following query fails. The reason: the ">=" requires a single value on the right side. The subquery returns 46 values.

```
-- Non-correlated subquery
SELECT          Name,
                FORMAT(ListPrice, 'c','en-US')              AS ListPrice,
                ProductNumber,
                FORMAT(StandardCost, 'c','en-US')           AS StandardCost
FROM AdventureWorks2012.Production.Product
WHERE ListPrice >=
   (SELECT ListPrice
    FROM AdventureWorks.Production.Product
    WHERE Name LIKE 'Road%' )
ORDER BY ListPrice DESC, Name;
GO
/* Msg 512, Level 16, State 1, Line 3
Subquery returned more than 1 value. This is not permitted when the subquery follows =, !=, <, <= , >, >=
or when the subquery is used as an expression. */
```

If we change the WHERE clause predicate operator from ">=" to "IN" then the query will execute correctly since the IN operator works with a set of values on the right side.

```
-- Non-correlated subquery
SELECT   Name,
         FORMAT(ListPrice, 'c','en-US')              AS ListPrice,
         ProductNumber,
         FORMAT(StandardCost, 'c','en-US')           AS StandardCost
FROM AdventureWorks2012.Production.Product
WHERE ListPrice IN
         (SELECT ListPrice
          FROM AdventureWorks.Production.Product  WHERE Name LIKE 'Road%' )
ORDER BY ListPrice DESC, Name;
-- (253 row(s) affected)  -- Partial results.
```

Name	ListPrice	ProductNumber	StandardCost
AWC Logo Cap	$8.99	CA-1098	$6.92
Racing Socks, L	$8.99	SO-R809-L	$3.36
Racing Socks, M	$8.99	SO-R809-M	$3.36
Road Bottle Cage	$8.99	BC-R205	$3.36
Road-650 Black, 44	$782.99	BK-R50B-44	$486.71
Road-650 Black, 48	$782.99	BK-R50B-48	$486.71
Road-650 Black, 52	$782.99	BK-R50B-52	$486.71

CHAPTER 7: Subqueries in SELECT Statements

Correlated Subqueries

In a correlated subquery there is a reference to an outer query column. In other words, the subquery by itself cannot be executed due to the correlation. In the next query, the inner query references soh.SalesOrderID column from the outer query in the WHERE clause predicate which is like an EQUI-JOIN.

```
SELECT          soh.SalesOrderID,
                FORMAT (soh.OrderDate, 'yyyy-MM-dd')                    AS OrderDate,

                ( SELECT FORMAT(MAX(sod.UnitPrice),'c','en-US')
                  FROM   AdventureWorks2012.Sales.SalesOrderDetail AS sod
                  WHERE  soh.SalesOrderID = sod.SalesOrderID )          AS MaxUnitPrice,

                FORMAT(TotalDue, 'c', 'en-US')                          AS TotalDue
FROM    AdventureWorks2012.Sales.SalesOrderHeader AS soh
ORDER BY MaxUnitPrice DESC, SalesOrderID;    -- (31465 row(s) affected) - Partial results.
```

SalesOrderID	OrderDate	MaxUnitPrice	TotalDue
51087	2007-07-01	$953.63	$2,721.27
51099	2007-07-01	$953.63	$5,276.64
51119	2007-07-01	$953.63	$2,040.14
51173	2007-07-01	$953.63	$1,457.54
51701	2007-08-01	$953.63	$2,634.93
51798	2007-08-01	$953.63	$907.09
51805	2007-08-01	$953.63	$907.09
51808	2007-08-01	$953.63	$1,827.45
51861	2007-08-01	$953.63	$11,762.43
53489	2007-09-01	$953.63	$1,814.18

The next query with correlated subquery list sales staff with 0.015 commission rate.

```
SELECT CONCAT(p.LastName,', ', p.FirstName) AS SalesPerson, e.BusinessEntityID AS EmployeeID
FROM AdventureWorks2012.Person.Person AS p
            INNER JOIN AdventureWorks2012.HumanResources.Employee AS e
            ON e.BusinessEntityID = p.BusinessEntityID
WHERE 0.015 IN  (SELECT CommissionPct   FROM AdventureWorks2012.Sales.SalesPerson sp
                 WHERE e.BusinessEntityID = sp.BusinessEntityID)  ORDER BY SalesPerson;
```

SalesPerson	EmployeeID
Carson, Jillian	277
Mitchell, Linda	276
Saraiva, José	282

CHAPTER 7: Subqueries in SELECT Statements

Single-Valued Correlated Subqueries

The query syntax determines if we can use a single-valued subquery or multiple-valued. A subquery can be the argument of a function.

USE AdventureWorks2012;

```
-- Single value subquery in SELECT list
SELECT   SOH.SalesOrderID                                AS SOID,
         CONVERT(DATE,SOH.OrderDate)                     AS OrderDate,
         FORMAT(SOH.Subtotal,'c0','en-US')               AS Subtotal,
         (SELECT MAX(SOD.UnitPrice)
          FROM Sales.SalesOrderDetail AS SOD
          WHERE SOH.SalesOrderID=SOD.SalesOrderID)       AS MaxUnitPrice
FROM Sales.SalesOrderHeader SOH    ORDER BY SOID;
--(31467 row(s) affected) - Partial results.
```

SOID	OrderDate	Subtotal	MaxUnitPrice
43659	2005-07-01	$20,566	2039.994
43660	2005-07-01	$1,294	874.794

```
-- Make the subquery the argument of the FORMAT function
SELECT   TOP (10)       SOH.SalesOrderID                 AS SOID,
                        CONVERT(DATE,SOH.OrderDate)       AS OrderDate,
                        FORMAT(SOH.Subtotal,'c0','en-US') AS Subtotal,
                        FORMAT(
    (SELECT MAX(SOD.UnitPrice)
    FROM Sales.SalesOrderDetail AS SOD
    WHERE SOH.SalesOrderID=SOD.SalesOrderID)
                        ,'c2','en-US')                    AS MaxUnitPrice
FROM Sales.SalesOrderHeader SOH   ORDER BY SOID;
```

SOID	OrderDate	Subtotal	MaxUnitPrice
43659	2005-07-01	$20,566	$2,039.99
43660	2005-07-01	$1,294	$874.79
43661	2005-07-01	$32,726	$2,039.99
43662	2005-07-01	$28,833	$2,146.96
43663	2005-07-01	$419	$419.46
43664	2005-07-01	$24,433	$2,039.99
43665	2005-07-01	$14,353	$2,039.99
43666	2005-07-01	$5,056	$2,146.96
43667	2005-07-01	$6,107	$2,039.99
43668	2005-07-01	$35,944	$2,146.96

CHAPTER 7: Subqueries in SELECT Statements

Correlated Subqueries with Same Table

In a correlated subquery, we can use a table from the outer query. In such a case table alias usage is required. In the next query with correlated subquery which lists same part suppliers, the ProductVendor table is referenced by both the outer query and inner query, therefore table alias is required.

```
SELECT          p.Name                          AS ProductName,
                v.Name                          AS Vendor,
                pv1.BusinessEntityID            AS VendorID
FROM AdventureWorks2012.Purchasing.ProductVendor pv1
   INNER JOIN AdventureWorks2012.Production.Product p ON p.ProductID = pv1.ProductID
   INNER JOIN AdventureWorks2012.Purchasing.Vendor v   ON v.BusinessEntityID = pv1.BusinessEntityID
WHERE pv1.ProductID IN    (       SELECT pv2.ProductID
                                  FROM AdventureWorks2012.Purchasing.ProductVendor pv2
                                  WHERE pv1.BusinessEntityID <> pv2.BusinessEntityID)
ORDER  BY ProductName, Vendor;           -- (347 row(s) affected) - Partial results.
```

ProductName	Vendor	VendorID
Internal Lock Washer 7	Aurora Bike Center	1616
Internal Lock Washer 7	Pro Sport Industries	1686
Internal Lock Washer 8	Aurora Bike Center	1616
Internal Lock Washer 8	Pro Sport Industries	1686
Internal Lock Washer 9	Aurora Bike Center	1616
Internal Lock Washer 9	Pro Sport Industries	1686
LL Crankarm	Proseware, Inc.	1678

CROSS APPLY with Correlated Subquery

The CROSS APPLY operator can connect tables with correlated subqueries as demonstrated following, INNER JOIN would not work in this case.

```
USE AdventureWorks;     DECLARE @Year  INT = 2003, @Month INT = 2;
SELECT   s.Name                                         AS Customer,
         FORMAT(SalesAmount.OrderTotal,'c','en-US')     AS [Total Sales]
FROM     Sales.Customer AS c  INNER JOIN Sales.Store AS s   ON s.CustomerID = c.CustomerID
     CROSS APPLY  (       SELECT  soh.CustomerId,   Sum(sod.LineTotal) AS OrderTotal
                          FROM    Sales.SalesOrderHeader AS soh
                 INNER JOIN Sales.SalesOrderDetail AS sod    ON sod.SalesOrderId = soh.SalesOrderId
                     WHERE soh.CustomerId = c.CustomerId
                 AND OrderDate > = DATEFROMPARTS(@Year, @Month, 1)
                 AND OrderDate <  DATEADD(mm, 1, DATEFROMPARTS(@Year, @Month, 1))
                     GROUP BY soh.CustomerId)              AS SalesAmount
ORDER BY Customer;       -- (132 row(s) affected) - Partial results.
```

Customer	Total Sales
Ace Bicycle Supply	$647.99
Affordable Sports Equipment	$50,953.32
Alpine Ski House	$939.59
Basic Sports Equipment	$159.56

CHAPTER 7: Subqueries in SELECT Statements

Derived Tables: SELECT from SELECT

A non-correlated subquery can be made into a derived table by enclosing it in parenthesis and assigning a table alias, such as "CAT" in the following example. It can then be used like a regular table for example in JOINs.

```
USE Northwind;

SELECT   c.CategoryName  AS Category,
         p.ProductName,   p.UnitPrice,   CAT.NoOfProducts
FROM     Categories c
    INNER JOIN Products p
      ON c.CategoryID = p.CategoryID
    INNER JOIN
                     (SELECT  c.CategoryID,
                             NoOfProducts = count(* )
                     FROM     Categories c
                       INNER JOIN Products p1
                            ON c.CategoryID = p1.CategoryID
                     GROUP BY c.CategoryID)                      AS CAT

      ON c.CategoryID = CAT.CategoryID
ORDER BY Category;
-- (77 row(s) affected)  - Partial results.
```

Category	ProductName	UnitPrice
Dairy Products	Raclette Courdavault	55.00
Dairy Products	Camembert Pierrot	34.00
Dairy Products	Gudbrandsdalsost	36.00
Dairy Products	Flotemysost	21.50
Dairy Products	Mozzarella di Giovanni	34.80
Grains/Cereals	Gustaf's Knäckebröd	21.00
Grains/Cereals	Tunnbröd	9.00
Grains/Cereals	Singaporean Hokkien Fried Mee	14.00
Grains/Cereals	Filo Mix	7.00
Grains/Cereals	Gnocchi di nonna Alice	38.00
Grains/Cereals	Ravioli Angelo	19.50

Results from the subquery (derived table).

CategoryID	NoOfProducts
1	12
2	12
3	13
4	10
5	7
6	6
7	5
8	12

CHAPTER 7: Subqueries in SELECT Statements

The UNION & UNION ALL Set Operators

UNION (distinct, duplicates eliminated) and UNION ALL (duplicates allowed) merge two or more sets of data into one set. Important points to remember about UNION:

> ➤ First SELECT column list establishes column names and data types; if INTO used it goes here
> ➤ Subsequent SELECTs must match the column structure; column names can be any; NULL if no data
> ➤ ORDER BY goes at the very end with the last SELECT

T-SQL UNION query merges data from different countries into a single result set.

```
USE NorthWind;
SELECT   ContactName,
         CompanyName,
         City,
         Country,
         Phone
FROM   Customers
WHERE  Country IN ( 'USA', 'Canada' )
-- (16 row(s) affected)
UNION
SELECT   ContactName,
         CompanyName            AS Company,
         City,     Country,
         Phone                  AS Telephone
FROM   Customers
WHERE  Country IN ( 'Germany', 'France' )
-- (22 row(s) affected)
UNION
SELECT   ContactName            AS Contact,
         CompanyName,    City,   Country,
         Phone                  AS Telephone
FROM   Customers
WHERE  Country IN ( 'Brazil', 'Spain' )
-- (14 row(s) affected)
ORDER  BY CompanyName,    ContactName ASC;
-- (52 row(s) affected)  - Partial results.
```

ContactName	CompanyName	City	Country	Phone
Maria Anders	Alfreds Futterkiste	Berlin	Germany	030-0074321
Hanna Moos	Blauer See Delikatessen	Mannheim	Germany	0621-08460
Frédérique Citeaux	Blondesddsl père et fils	Strasbourg	France	88.60.15.31
Martín Sommer	Bólido Comidas preparadas	Madrid	Spain	(91) 555 22 82

CHAPTER 7: Subqueries in SELECT Statements

CTE: Common Table Expression for Structured Coding

Common Table Expression is new in SQL Server 2005. It is similar to derived tables in one aspect with a difference: it is defined at the very beginning of a the query, above the main(outer) query. In addition, CTEs can be nested and defined as recursive.

```
USE AdventureWorks;

WITH CTE(ManagerID, StaffCount)
AS
(
    SELECT ManagerID, COUNT(*)
    FROM HumanResources.Employee AS e
    GROUP BY ManagerID
)

SELECT          CONCAT(LEFT(FirstName,1), '. ', LastName)          AS Manager,
                e.Title, StaffCount
FROM CTE s
        INNER JOIN HumanResources.Employee e
    ON s.ManagerID = e.EmployeeID
        INNER JOIN Person.Contact c
    ON c.ContactID = e.ContactID
ORDER BY Manager;
-- (47 row(s) affected) - Partial results.
```

Manager	Title	StaffCount
A. Alberts	European Sales Manager	3
A. Hill	Production Supervisor - WC10	7
A. Wright	Master Scheduler	4
B. Diaz	Production Supervisor - WC40	12
B. Welcker	Vice President of Sales	3
C. Kleinerman	Maintenance Supervisor	4
C. Petculescu	Production Supervisor - WC10	5
C. Randall	Production Supervisor - WC30	6
D. Bradley	Marketing Manager	8
D. Hamilton	Production Supervisor - WC40	6
D. Liu	Accounts Manager	7
D. Miller	Research and Development Manager	3
E. Gubbels	Production Supervisor - WC20	10
G. Altman	Facilities Manager	2
H. Abolrous	Quality Assurance Manager	2

Multiple CTEs Query

A query can have multiple CTEs, they can even be nested (CTE has reference to previous CTE). The two CTEs in the following query are first name and last name frequencies.

```
USE AdventureWorks2012;

WITH cteLastNameFreq

    AS (SELECT      LastName        AS [LastNames],
                    count(* )       AS [LNFrequency]
        FROM    Person.Person
        GROUP BY LastName),

    cteFirstNameFreq
    AS (SELECT      FirstName       AS [FirstNames],
                    count(* )       AS [FNFrequency]
        FROM    Person.Person
        GROUP BY FirstName)

SELECT    CONCAT(rtrim(FirstName), ' ', rtrim(LastName))    AS [Name],
                    isnull(Title,'')                        AS [Title] ,
                    f.FNFrequency,
                    l.LNFrequency
FROM    Person.Person c
    INNER JOIN cteFirstNameFreq AS f
    ON c.FirstName = f.FirstNames
    INNER JOIN cteLastNameFreq AS l
    ON c.LastName = l.LastNames
WHERE    LastName LIKE 'P%' ORDER BY [Name];
-- (1187 row(s) affected) - Partial results;
```

Name	Title	FNFrequency	LNFrequency
Aaron Patterson		56	117
Aaron Perez		56	170
Aaron Perry		56	122
Aaron Phillips		56	80
Aaron Powell		56	116
Abby Patel		19	86
Abby Perez		19	170
Abigail Patterson		76	117
Abigail Patterson		76	117
Abigail Perry		76	122
Abigail Peterson		76	92
Abigail Powell		76	116

Testing Common Table Expressions

A CTE can be tested independently of the main query if it does not have nesting (reference to a previous CTE). The following screen snapshot displays the execution of the first CTE SELECT query.

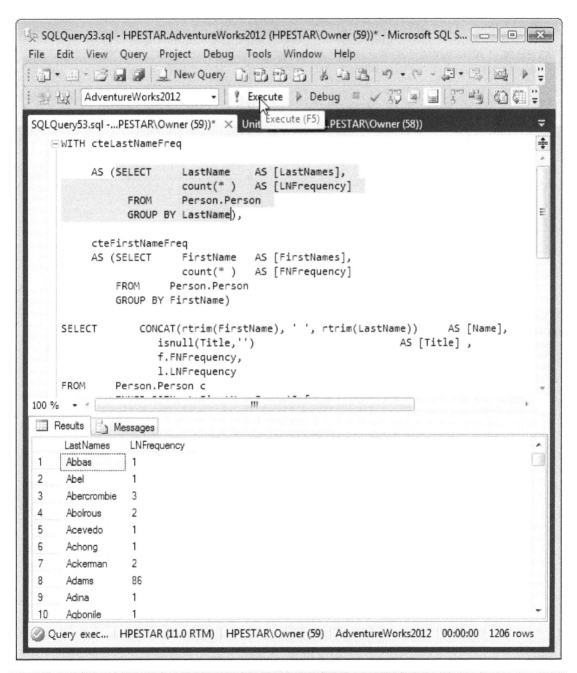

Nested CTEs Queries

CTEs can be nested by reference to a previous CTE like a table.

```
;WITH CTE1
   AS (SELECT 1 AS NUMBER
      UNION ALL
      SELECT 1),
   CTE2
   AS (SELECT 1 AS NUMBER
      FROM   CTE1 x,
          CTE1 y),
   CTE3
   AS (SELECT 1 AS NUMBER
      FROM   CTE2 x,
          CTE2 y),
   CTE4
   AS (SELECT 1 AS NUMBER
      FROM   CTE3 x,
          CTE3 y),
   CTE8BIT
   AS (SELECT ROW_NUMBER()
          OVER(ORDER BY NUMBER) AS INTSequence
      FROM   CTE4)
SELECT *
FROM   CTE8BIT
ORDER BY INTSequence;
-- (256 row(s) affected) - Partial results.
```

INTSequence
241
242
243
244
245
246
247
248
249
250
251
252
253
254
255
256

CTE nesting: cteLastSalary has a nested reference to cteLastSalaryChange

```
USE AdventureWorks2012;

WITH cteLastSalaryChange
   AS (SELECT    BusinessEntityID          AS EmployeeID,
                 Max(RateChangeDate)             AS ChangeDate
      FROM    HumanResources.EmployeePayHistory    GROUP BY BusinessEntityID),

   cteLastSalary
   AS (SELECT    eph.BusinessEntityID            AS EmployeeID,     Rate
      FROM   HumanResources.EmployeePayHistory eph
         INNER JOIN cteLastSalaryChange lsc
           ON lsc.EmployeeID = eph.BusinessEntityID
             AND lsc.ChangeDate = eph.RateChangeDate)

-- SELECT * FROM cteLastSalary  -- for testing & debugging

SELECT TOP 1 FORMAT( Rate, 'c', 'en-US') AS SecondHighestPayRate
FROM    (SELECT   TOP 2 Rate     FROM    cteLastSalary     ORDER BY Rate DESC) a   -- Derived table
ORDER BY Rate ASC;
```

SecondHighestPayRate
$84.13

Testing Nested CTEs

Nested CTEs can be tested independently of the main query the following way.

```
USE AdventureWorks2012;
WITH cteLastSalaryChange
   AS (SELECT    BusinessEntityID          AS EmployeeID,
                 Max(RateChangeDate)             AS ChangeDate
      FROM    HumanResources.EmployeePayHistory
      GROUP BY BusinessEntityID),
   cteLastSalary
   AS (SELECT    eph.BusinessEntityID            AS EmployeeID,
                 Rate
      FROM   HumanResources.EmployeePayHistory eph
         INNER JOIN cteLastSalaryChange lsc
           ON lsc.EmployeeID = eph.BusinessEntityID
             AND lsc.ChangeDate = eph.RateChangeDate)
SELECT * FROM cteLastSalary  -- for testing & debugging
```

CHAPTER 7: Subqueries in SELECT Statements

In Query Editor, uncomment the testing line, select (highlight) the top part of the query and execute it

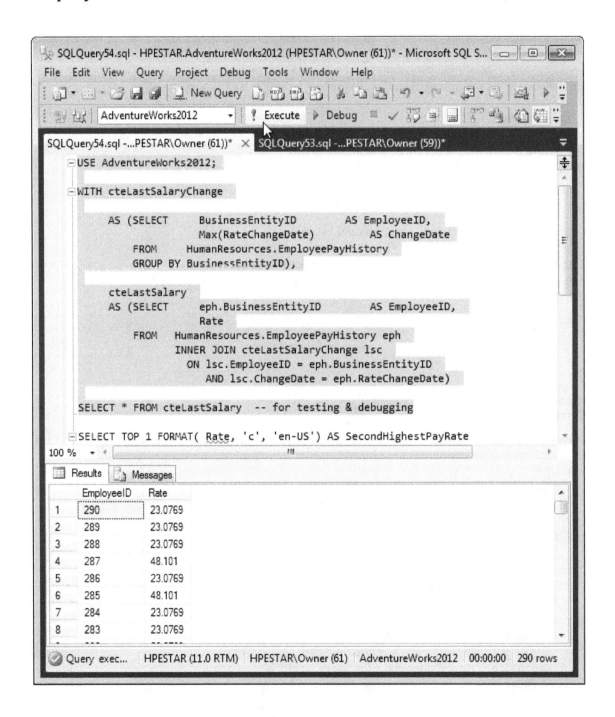

Recursive CTEs for Tree Hierarchy Processing

Recursive CTEs are one of the most exciting new features introduced with SQL Server 2005. They allow tree processing, such as organizational charts or bill of materials parts assembly, as well as generating sets of data without tables. The following recursive CTE generates 1 million integers all by itself. The query execution time is 10 seconds as it can be seen in the lower right.

Recursive Generation of Date & Month Sequences

Date sequence can be generated without a calendar table (Note: generally it is helpful to have a calendar table in the database) using recursive CTE.

```
DECLARE @StartDate date = '20160701', @Range smallint = 1000;

WITH cteSEQ ( SeqNo) as
(
    SELECT 0                              -- Anchor member
    UNION ALL                            -- Assemble set
    SELECT SeqNo + 1                     -- Recursive member
    FROM cteSEQ
    WHERE SeqNo < @Range
)
SELECT TOP 10 [DATE]=DATEADD(day, SeqNo, @StartDate)
FROM cteSEQ
OPTION ( MAXRECURSION 0);
GO
```

DATE
2016-07-01
2016-07-02
2016-07-03
2016-07-04
2016-07-05
2016-07-06
2016-07-07
2016-07-08
2016-07-09
2016-07-10

```
-- Month sequence generation
DECLARE @StartDate date = '20160701', @Range smallint = 100;
WITH cteSEQ ( SeqNo) as
(
    SELECT 0                              -- Anchor member
    UNION ALL                            -- Assemble set
    SELECT SeqNo + 1                     -- Recursive member
    FROM cteSEQ
    WHERE SeqNo < @Range
)
SELECT TOP 3 [DATE]=DATEADD(month, SeqNo, @StartDate)
FROM cteSEQ  OPTION ( MAXRECURSION 0);
```

CHAPTER 7: Subqueries in SELECT Statements

Generate Month Names in Different Languages

The following query can be used to generate month names in any of the SQL Server 2012 supported languages.

```
SET language Spanish;  -- Se cambió la configuración de idioma a Español.
;WITH CTE AS
(   SELECT    1 MonthNo, CONVERT(DATE, '19000101') MonthFirst
    UNION ALL
    SELECT    MonthNo+1, DATEADD(Month, 1, MonthFirst)
    FROM  CTE
    WHERE Month(MonthFirst) < 12    )
SELECT  MonthNo AS MonthNumber,  DATENAME(MONTH, MonthFirst) AS MonthName
FROM  CTE
ORDER BY MonthNo;
SET language English; -- Changed language setting to us_english.
```

```
SET language Hungarian;  -- Nyelvi beállítás átállítva a következőre: magyar.
;WITH CTE AS
(   SELECT    1 MonthNo, CONVERT(DATE, '19000101') MonthFirst
    UNION ALL
    SELECT    MonthNo+1, DATEADD(Month, 1, MonthFirst)
    FROM  CTE
    WHERE Month(MonthFirst) < 12    )
SELECT  MonthNo AS MonthNumber,  DATENAME(MONTH, MonthFirst) AS MonthName
FROM  CTE
ORDER BY MonthNo;
SET language English; -- Changed language setting to us_english.
```

MonthNumber	MonthName	MonthNumber	MonthName
1	Enero	1	január
2	Febrero	2	február
3	Marzo	3	március
4	Abril	4	április
5	Mayo	5	május
6	Junio	6	június
7	Julio	7	július
8	Agosto	8	augusztus
9	Septiembre	9	szeptember
10	Octubre	10	október
11	Noviembre	11	november
12	Diciembre	12	december

CHAPTER 7: Subqueries in SELECT Statements

Graphical Organizational Chart of AdventureWorks Cycles

T-SQL recursive CTE query generates the entire company chart of AdventureWorks Cycles. The anchor term is Ken Sanchez CEO with ManagerID as NULL. Everybody else in the company has a ManagerID which is not NULL.

```
USE AdventureWorks;

WITH cteEmployeeTree
  AS (SELECT     Root.EmployeeName,  Root.ManagerName,
                 Root.EmployeeId, Root.ManagerId,
                 CONVERT(VARCHAR(MAX),Root.PathSequence) AS PathLabel
     FROM   (SELECT EmployeeName = CONCAT(c.FirstName, SPACE(1), c.LastName),
            ManagerName = convert(VARCHAR(128),''),
            e.EmployeeId,
            e.ManagerId,
            char(64 + ROW_NUMBER()  OVER(ORDER BY e.EmployeeId)) AS PathSequence
        FROM   HumanResourccs.Employee e
        INNER JOIN Person.Contact c
        ON e.ContactID = c.ContactID
        WHERE  e.ManagerId IS NULL) Root          -- Anchor/root term (above)
  UNION ALL                                        -- Build a set
  SELECT      Branch.EmployeeName,                 -- Recursive term (below)
              Branch.ManagerName,
              Branch.EmployeeId, Branch.ManagerId,
              PathLabel = Branch.PathLabel + CONVERT(VARCHAR(MAX),  Branch.PathSequence)
  FROM   (SELECT EmployeeName = CONCAT(c.FirstName, SPACE(1), c.LastName),
        ManagerName = CONVERT(VARCHAR(128),CONCAT(cm.FirstName, SPACE(1), cm.LastName)),
        e.EmployeeId,
        e.ManagerId,
        cte.PathLabel,
        PathSequence = char(64 + ROW_NUMBER()  OVER(ORDER BY e.EmployeeId))
     FROM   cteEmployeeTree cte
        INNER JOIN HumanResources.Employee e
        ON e.ManagerId = cte.EmployeeId
        INNER JOIN Person.Contact c
        ON e.ContactID = c.ContactID
        INNER JOIN HumanResources.Employee em
        ON em.EmployeeID = e.ManagerID
        INNER JOIN Person.Contact cm
        ON em.ContactID = cm.ContactID) Branch)
-- Outer / main query
SELECT   CONCAT(REPLICATE(CHAR(9), LEN(PathLabel)-1),   -- tabs for indenting
            EmployeeName) AS EmployeeName
FROM     cteEmployeeTree ORDER BY PathLabel;
```

CHAPTER 7: Subqueries in SELECT Statements

The resulting organizational chart was generated by Word as tabs (CHAR(9)) were converted to table columns (partial results).

EmployeeName				
Ken Sánchez				
	David Bradley			
		Kevin Brown		
		Sariya Harnpadoungsataya		
		Mary Gibson		
		Jill Williams		
		Terry Eminhizer		
		Wanida Benshoof		
		John Wood		
		Mary Dempsey		
	Terri Duffy			
		Roberto Tamburello		
			Rob Walters	
			Gail Erickson	
			Jossef Goldberg	
			Dylan Miller	
				Diane Margheim
				Gigi Matthew
				Michael Raheem
			Ovidiu Cracium	
				Thierry D'Hers
				Janice Galvin
			Michael Sullivan	
			Sharon Salavaria	
	Jean Trenary			
		Janaina Bueno		
		Dan Bacon		
		François Ajenstat		
		Dan Wilson		
		Ramesh Meyyappan		
		Stephanie Conroy		
			Ashvini Sharma	
			Peter Connelly	
		Karen Berg		
	Laura Norman			
		Paula Barreto de Mattos		
			Willis Johnson	
			Mindy Martin	
			Vidur Luthra	
			Hao Chen	
			Grant Culbertson	
		Wendy Kahn		
			Sheela Word	
				Mikael Sandberg
				Arvind Rao
				Linda Meisner
				Fukiko Ogisu
				Gordon Hee
				Frank Pellow
				Eric Kurjan
				Erin Hagens
				Ben Miller
				Annette Hill
				Reinout Hillmann
		David Barber		
		David Liu		
			Deborah Poe	
			Candy Spoon	
			Bryan Walton	
			Dragan Tomic	
			Barbara Moreland	
			Janet Sheperdigian	
			Mike Seamans	
	James Hamilton			
		Peter Krebs		
			JoLynn Dobney	
				Simon Rapier
				James Kramer
				Nancy Anderson
				Bryan Baker
				Eugene Kogan
				Thomas Michaels
			Taylor Maxwell	
				Kendall Keil
				Bob Hohman
				Pete Male
				Diane Tibbott
				Denise Smith

Chain of Command Recursive Query

Find all ancestors (superiors) of a tree node(employee), all the up to the root of the tree (CEO in this instance).

```
USE AdventureWorks; DECLARE @EmployeeID INT = 100;
WITH CTE(Name, EmployeeID, ManagerID, Level)
   AS (SELECT      CONCAT(FirstName,' ', LastName),
                   EmployeeID,   ManagerID, 0 AS Level
      FROM   HumanResources.Employee AS E
         INNER JOIN Person.Contact AS C
            ON C.ContactID = E.ContactID
      WHERE  EmployeeID = @EmployeeID
      UNION ALL
      SELECT      CONCAT(C.FirstName,' ',C.LastName),
                  HRE.EmployeeID,  HRE.ManagerID,  Level + 1
      FROM   HumanResources.Employee AS HRE
         INNER JOIN Person.Contact AS C
            ON C.ContactID = HRE.ContactID
         INNER JOIN CTE AS E
            ON E.ManagerID = HRE.EmployeeID)
SELECT STUFF((SELECT CONCAT(', ', Name)
         FROM   CTE      ORDER  BY Level
         FOR XML path('')), 1, 2, '') AS [Chain of Command];
```

Chain of Command
Lane Sacksteder, Yuhong Li, Peter Krebs, James Hamilton, Ken Sánchez

CHAPTER 7: Subqueries in SELECT Statements

Graphical Bill of Materials for Mountain-100 Silver, 44 Bike

T-SQL query will generate bill of materials (assembly) listing for Mountain-100 Silver, 44 mountain bike. The AdventureWorks2012 database image for Mountain-100 Silver, 44 in Production.ProductPhoto table.

```
USE AdventureWorks2012;
DECLARE          @StartProductID int        = 773,            -- Mountain-100 Silver, 44
                 @CheckDate datetime      = '20080201';

  WITH cteBOM(ProductAssemblyID, ComponentID, ComponentName,  RecursionLevel)
  AS (
    SELECT b.ProductAssemblyID, b.ComponentID, p.Name,  0
         FROM Production.BillOfMaterials b
         INNER JOIN Production.Product p
         ON b.ComponentID = p.ProductID
    WHERE        b.ProductAssemblyID = @StartProductID
                 AND @CheckDate >= b.StartDate
                 AND @CheckDate <= ISNULL(b.EndDate, @CheckDate)      -- Anchor/root member (above)
    UNION ALL                                                        -- Build a set
    SELECT       b.ProductAssemblyID, b.ComponentID, p.Name,         -- Recursive member (below)
                 RecursionLevel + 1
    FROM cteBOM c
      INNER JOIN Production.BillOfMaterials b
      ON b.ProductAssemblyID = c.ComponentID
      INNER JOIN Production.Product p
      ON b.ComponentID = p.ProductID
    WHERE        @CheckDate >= b.StartDate          AND @CheckDate <= ISNULL(b.EndDate, @CheckDate)   )
-- Outer/main query
  SELECT CONCAT(REPLICATE(CHAR(9), RecursionLevel), -- Generate indents with tab character
               (SELECT Name FROM Production.Product WHERE ProductID=ProductAssemblyID)) AS PartName,
               ComponentName
      FROM cteBOM    GROUP BY  RecursionLevel,ProductAssemblyID,ComponentName
  ORDER BY       RecursionLevel, ProductAssemblyID,ComponentName    OPTION (MAXRECURSION 10);
-- (87 row(s) affected)
```

CHAPTER 7: Subqueries in SELECT Statements

The resulting graphical bill of materials for the mountain bike.

PartName	ComponentName	
Mountain-100 Silver, 44	Chain	
Mountain-100 Silver, 44	Front Brakes	
Mountain-100 Silver, 44	Front Derailleur	
Mountain-100 Silver, 44	HL Bottom Bracket	
Mountain-100 Silver, 44	HL Crankset	
Mountain-100 Silver, 44	HL Headset	
Mountain-100 Silver, 44	HL Mountain Frame - Silver, 44	
Mountain-100 Silver, 44	HL Mountain Front Wheel	
Mountain-100 Silver, 44	HL Mountain Handlebars	
Mountain-100 Silver, 44	HL Mountain Pedal	
Mountain-100 Silver, 44	HL Mountain Rear Wheel	
Mountain-100 Silver, 44	HL Mountain Seat Assembly	
Mountain-100 Silver, 44	Rear Brakes	
Mountain-100 Silver, 44	Rear Derailleur	
	HL Mountain Seat Assembly	HL Mountain Seat/Saddle
	HL Mountain Seat Assembly	Pinch Bolt
	HL Mountain Seat Assembly	Seat Lug
	HL Mountain Seat Assembly	Seat Post
	HL Mountain Frame - Silver, 44	Chain Stays
	HL Mountain Frame - Silver, 44	Decal 1
	HL Mountain Frame - Silver, 44	Decal 2
	HL Mountain Frame - Silver, 44	Down Tube
	HL Mountain Frame - Silver, 44	Head Tube
	HL Mountain Frame - Silver, 44	HL Fork
	HL Mountain Frame - Silver, 44	Paint - Silver
	HL Mountain Frame - Silver, 44	Seat Stays
	HL Mountain Frame - Silver, 44	Seat Tube
	HL Mountain Frame - Silver, 44	Top Tube
	HL Headset	Adjustable Race
	HL Headset	Crown Race
	HL Headset	Headset Ball Bearings
	HL Headset	Keyed Washer
	HL Headset	Lock Nut 19
	HL Headset	Lower Head Race
	HL Mountain Handlebars	Handlebar Tube
	HL Mountain Handlebars	HL Grip Tape
	HL Mountain Handlebars	Mountain End Caps
	HL Mountain Handlebars	Stem
	HL Mountain Front Wheel	HL Hub
	HL Mountain Front Wheel	HL Mountain Rim
	HL Mountain Front Wheel	HL Mountain Tire
	HL Mountain Front Wheel	HL Nipple
	HL Mountain Front Wheel	Mountain Tire Tube
	HL Mountain Front Wheel	Reflector
	HL Mountain Front Wheel	Spokes
	HL Mountain Rear Wheel	HL Hub
	HL Mountain Rear Wheel	HL Mountain Rim
	HL Mountain Rear Wheel	HL Mountain Tire
	HL Mountain Rear Wheel	HL Nipple
	HL Mountain Rear Wheel	Mountain Tire Tube
	HL Mountain Rear Wheel	Reflector
	HL Mountain Rear Wheel	Spokes
	Rear Derailleur	Guide Pulley
	Rear Derailleur	Rear Derailleur Cage
	Rear Derailleur	Tension Pulley
	Front Derailleur	Front Derailleur Cage
	Front Derailleur	Front Derailleur Linkage
	HL Crankset	Chainring
	HL Crankset	Chainring Bolts

CHAPTER 7: Subqueries in SELECT Statements

HL Crankset	Chainring Nut		
HL Crankset	Freewheel		
HL Crankset	HL Crankarm		
HL Bottom Bracket	BB Ball Bearing		
HL Bottom Bracket	HL Shell		
	BB Ball Bearing	Bearing Ball	
	BB Ball Bearing	Cone-Shaped Race	
	BB Ball Bearing	Cup-Shaped Race	
	BB Ball Bearing	Lock Ring	
	Chain Stays	Metal Sheet 5	
	Down Tube	Metal Sheet 3	
	Mountain End Caps	Metal Sheet 2	
	Handlebar Tube	Metal Sheet 6	
	Head Tube	Metal Sheet 4	
	HL Hub	HL Shell	
	HL Hub	HL Spindle/Axle	
	Stem	Metal Bar 1	
	Seat Stays	Metal Sheet 7	
	Seat Tube	Metal Bar 2	
	Top Tube	Metal Sheet 2	
	HL Fork	Blade	
	HL Fork	Fork Crown	
	HL Fork	Fork End	
	HL Fork	Steerer	
		Blade	Metal Sheet 5
		Fork End	Metal Sheet 2
		Fork Crown	Metal Sheet 5
		Steerer	Metal Sheet 6

CHAPTER 7: Subqueries in SELECT Statements

PIVOT Operator to Transform Rows Into Columns

The PIVOT operator, new to SQL Server 2005, can be used to create pivot table also called cross tabulation (crosstab). The data to be PIVOTed is generated by a CTE.

```
USE AdventureWorks2012;
;WITH CTE    AS (SELECT   YEAR              = YEAR(orderDate),
                          QUARTER           = DatePart(qq,OrderDate),
                          Sales             = Sum(TotalDue)
          FROM    Sales.SalesOrderHeader   GROUP BY YEAR(OrderDate), DatePart(qq,OrderDate))
SELECT * FROM CTE;
```

YEAR	QUARTER	Sales
2007	4	14886562.6775
2006	3	11555907.1472
2007	1	7492396.3224
2007	2	9379298.7027
2006	1	6562121.6796
2006	4	9397824.1785
2008	3	56178.9223
2007	3	15413231.8434
2005	3	5203127.8807
2008	1	12744940.3554
2005	4	7490122.7457
2008	2	16087078.2305
2006	2	6947995.43

PIVOT operator takes the data from the CTE source, aggregates it and transforms it to columns.

```
;WITH CTE    AS (SELECT   YEAR              = YEAR(orderDate),
                          QUARTER           = DatePart(qq,OrderDate),
                          Sales             = Sum(TotalDue)
          FROM    Sales.SalesOrderHeader   GROUP BY YEAR(OrderDate), DatePart(qq,OrderDate)    )
SELECT    YEAR
                 ,FORMAT ([1], 'c','en-US') AS Q1
                 ,FORMAT ([2], 'c','en-US') AS Q2
                 ,FORMAT ([3], 'c','en-US') AS Q3
                 ,FORMAT ([4], 'c','en-US') AS Q4
FROM    (SELECT * FROM CTE) AS PivotInput
      PIVOT    (SUM(Sales)  FOR QUARTER IN ( [1],[2],[3],[4] ) ) AS PivotOutput  ORDER BY YEAR;
```

YEAR	Q1	Q2	Q3	Q4
2005	NULL	NULL	$5,203,127.88	$7,490,122.75
2006	$6,562,121.68	$6,947,995.43	$11,555,907.15	$9,397,824.18
2007	$7,492,396.32	$9,379,298.70	$15,413,231.84	$14,886,562.68
2008	$12,744,940.36	$16,087,078.23	$56,178.92	NULL

UNPIVOT Crosstab View Results

The vSalesPersonSalesByFiscalYears view is a crosstab listing of sales person (rows) and sales by year (columns). The UNPIVOT operation transforms the year columns into rows.

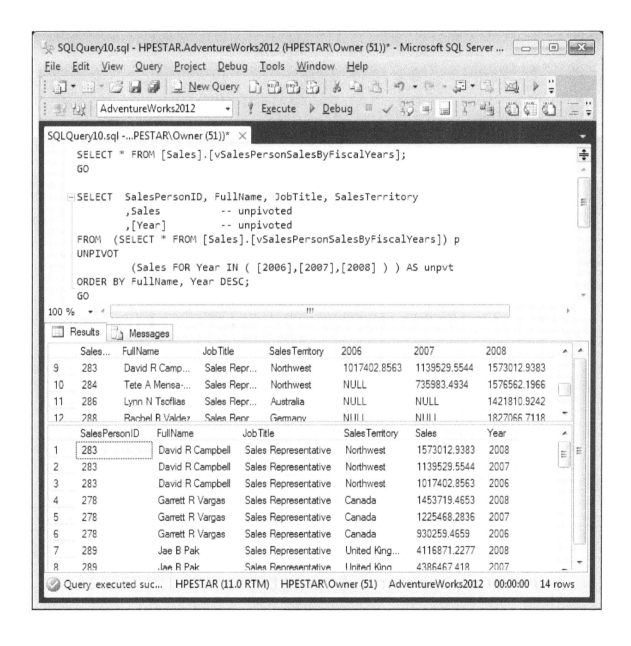

Using Subquery in Column List of SELECT

A subquery can be used in the column list of a SELECT statement.

```
USE Northwind;
GO
```

```
;WITH CTE AS
(
 SELECT ShipCity,
        CONVERT(DATE, OrderDate)                                AS OrderDate,
        (SELECT CONVERT(DATE, MAX(OrderDate))   FROM dbo.Orders)        AS CurrentOrderDate,
        DATEDIFF(dd,OrderDate,(SELECT MAX(OrderDate) FROM dbo.Orders)) AS DeltaDays,
        ROW_NUMBER() OVER (PARTITION BY ShipCity
                              ORDER BY OrderDate DESC)            AS RN
  FROM dbo.Orders
)

SELECT TOP 20 ShipCity, OrderDate, CurrentOrderDate, DeltaDays
FROM CTE
WHERE RN=1      ORDER BY DeltaDays DESC;
GO
```

ShipCity	OrderDate	CurrentOrderDate	DeltaDays
Walla Walla	1997-05-22	1998-05-06	349
Elgin	1997-09-08	1998-05-06	240
Montréal	1997-10-30	1998-05-06	188
Reims	1997-11-12	1998-05-06	175
Caracas	1997-12-18	1998-05-06	139
Lille	1997-12-22	1998-05-06	135
Vancouver	1998-01-01	1998-05-06	125
Kirkland	1998-01-08	1998-05-06	118
Strasbourg	1998-01-12	1998-05-06	114
Lyon	1998-01-23	1998-05-06	103
San Francisco	1998-02-12	1998-05-06	83
Luleå	1998-03-04	1998-05-06	63
Barcelona	1998-03-05	1998-05-06	62
Cowes	1998-03-06	1998-05-06	61
Resende	1998-03-09	1998-05-06	58
Leipzig	1998-03-12	1998-05-06	55
Bergamo	1998-03-16	1998-05-06	51
Münster	1998-03-23	1998-05-06	44
Nantes	1998-03-24	1998-05-06	43
Versailles	1998-03-24	1998-05-06	43

CHAPTER 8: Modify Data - INSERT, UPDATE, DELETE & MERGE

INSERT VALUES - Table Value Constructor

T-SQL scripts illustrate the use of INSERT VALUES with Table Value Constructor (a list of values). Because the text columns are defined as nvarchar the string literals are prefixed with "N" indicating UNICODE literal. Since only Latin letters used, the "N" can be omitted.

```
USE tempdb;
SELECT TOP 0 * INTO dbo.Department FROM AdventureWorks2012.HumanResources.Department;
-- This is necessary because IDENTITY property was inherited in the SELECT INTO
SET IDENTITY_INSERT dbo.Department ON;
GO
INSERT dbo.Department (DepartmentID, Name, GroupName, ModifiedDate) VALUES
(1, N'Engineering', N'Research and Development', getdate()),
(2, N'Tool Design', N'Research and Development', getdate()),
(3, N'Sales', N'Sales and Marketing', getdate()),
(4, N'Marketing', N'Sales and Marketing', getdate()),
(5, N'Purchasing', N'Inventory Management', getdate()),
(6, N'Research and Development', N'Research and Development', getdate()),
(7, N'Production', N'Manufacturing', getdate()),
(8, N'Production Control', N'Manufacturing', getdate()),
(9, N'Human Resources', N'Executive General and Administration', getdate()),
(10, N'Finance', N'Executive General and Administration', getdate()),
(11, N'Information Services', N'Executive General and Administration', getdate()),
(12, N'Document Control', N'Quality Assurance', getdate()),
(13, N'Quality Assurance', N'Quality Assurance', getdate()),
(14, N'Facilities and Maintenance', N'Executive General and Administration', getdate()),
(15, N'Shipping and Receiving', N'Inventory Management', getdate()),
(16, N'Executive', N'Executive General and Administration',getdate());
GO
SET IDENTITY_INSERT dbo.Department OFF;
GO
SELECT TOP 4 * FROM dbo.Department ORDER BY DepartmentID;
```

DepartmentID	Name	GroupName	ModifiedDate
1	Engineering	Research and Development	2016-08-02 06:35:44.623
2	Tool Design	Research and Development	2016-08-02 06:35:44.623
3	Sales	Sales and Marketing	2016-08-02 06:35:44.623
4	Marketing	Sales and Marketing	2016-08-02 06:35:44.623

INSERT VALUES - Ye Olde Way

T-SQL scripts illustrate the INSERT VALUES for single row insert, the only available method prior to SQL Server 2008.

```
USE AdventureWorks2012;
GO


CREATE TABLE Shift(
        ShiftID tinyint IDENTITY(1,1) NOT NULL,
        Name dbo.Name NOT NULL,
        StartTime time(7) NOT NULL,
        EndTime time(7) NOT NULL,
        ModifiedDate datetime NOT NULL,
        CONSTRAINT PK_Shift_ShiftID PRIMARY KEY CLUSTERED (ShiftID ASC) );
GO


SET IDENTITY_INSERT Shift ON;              -- To force insert into ShiftID

INSERT Shift (ShiftID, Name, StartTime, EndTime, ModifiedDate)
VALUES (1, N'Day', CAST(0x0700D85EAC3A0000 AS Time), CAST(0x07001882BA7D0000 AS Time),
CAST(0x0000921E00000000 AS DateTime))
INSERT Shift (ShiftID, Name, StartTime, EndTime, ModifiedDate)
VALUES (2, N'Evening', CAST(0x07001882BA7D0000 AS Time), CAST(0x070058A5C8C00000 AS Time),
getdate());
INSERT Shift (ShiftID, Name, StartTime, EndTime, ModifiedDate)
VALUES (3, N'Night', CAST(0x070058A5C8C00000 AS Time), CAST(0x0700D85EAC3A0000 AS Time),
CURRENT_TIMESTAMP);
GO


SET IDENTITY_INSERT Shift OFF;

ALTER TABLE Shift ADD  CONSTRAINT DF_Shift_ModifiedDate  DEFAULT (getdate()) FOR ModifiedDate
GO


SELECT * FROM Shift ORDER BY ShiftID;
GO
```

ShiftID	Name	StartTime	EndTime	ModifiedDate
1	Day	07:00:00.0000000	15:00:00.0000000	2002-06-01 00:00:00.000
2	Evening	15:00:00.0000000	23:00:00.0000000	2018-08-20 19:31:02.293
3	Night	23:00:00.0000000	07:00:00.0000000	2018-08-20 19:31:02.293

```
DROP TABLE Shift;
GO
```

CHAPTER 8: Modify Data - INSERT, UPDATE, DELETE & MERGE

INSERT SELECT

INSERT SELECT Literal List
T-SQL scripts demonstrate the insertion of literal records (rows) using INSERT SELECT.

```
USE tempdb;
GO
SELECT TOP 0 * INTO dbo.Department FROM AdventureWorks2012.HumanResources.Department;
GO
-- This is necessary because IDENTITY property was inherited in the SELECT INTO
SET IDENTITY_INSERT dbo.Department ON;
GO
INSERT dbo.Department (DepartmentID, Name, GroupName, ModifiedDate)
SELECT 1, N'Engineering', N'Research and Development', CURRENT_TIMESTAMP  UNION
SELECT 2, N'Tool Design', N'Research and Development', CURRENT_TIMESTAMP  UNION
SELECT 3, N'Sales', N'Sales and Marketing', CURRENT_TIMESTAMP  UNION
SELECT 4, N'Marketing', N'Sales and Marketing', CURRENT_TIMESTAMP  UNION
SELECT 5, N'Purchasing', N'Inventory Management', CURRENT_TIMESTAMP  UNION
SELECT 6, N'Research and Development', N'Research and Development', CURRENT_TIMESTAMP  UNION
SELECT 7, N'Production', N'Manufacturing', CURRENT_TIMESTAMP  UNION
SELECT 8, N'Production Control', N'Manufacturing', CURRENT_TIMESTAMP  UNION
SELECT 9, N'Human Resources', N'Executive General and Administration', CURRENT_TIMESTAMP  UNION
SELECT 10, N'Finance', N'Executive General and Administration', CURRENT_TIMESTAMP  UNION
SELECT 11, N'Information Services', N'Executive General and Administration', CURRENT_TIMESTAMP
UNION
SELECT 12, N'Document Control', N'Quality Assurance', CURRENT_TIMESTAMP  UNION
SELECT 13, N'Quality Assurance', N'Quality Assurance', CURRENT_TIMESTAMP  UNION
SELECT 14, N'Facilities and Maintenance', N'Executive General and Administration',
CURRENT_TIMESTAMP  UNION
SELECT 15, N'Shipping and Receiving', N'Inventory Management', CURRENT_TIMESTAMP  UNION
SELECT 16, N'Executive', N'Executive General and Administration', CURRENT_TIMESTAMP;
GO
SET IDENTITY_INSERT dbo.Department OFF;
GO
SELECT TOP 4 * FROM dbo.Department ORDER BY DepartmentID;
GO
```

DepartmentID	Name	GroupName	ModifiedDate
1	Engineering	Research and Development	2016-08-02 06:35:44.623
2	Tool Design	Research and Development	2016-08-02 06:35:44.623
3	Sales	Sales and Marketing	2016-08-02 06:35:44.623
4	Marketing	Sales and Marketing	2016-08-02 06:35:44.623

```
-- Cleanup
DROP TABLE tempdb.dbo.Department;
```

CHAPTER 8: Modify Data - INSERT, UPDATE, DELETE & MERGE

INSERT SELECT from Table

T-SQL script demonstrates table population with table SELECT.

```
USE tempdb;
SELECT TOP 0 * INTO dbo.Department FROM AdventureWorks2012.HumanResources.Department;
GO
-- This is necessary because IDENTITY property was inherited in the SELECT INTO
SET IDENTITY_INSERT dbo.Department ON;
GO
INSERT dbo.Department (DepartmentID, Name, GroupName, ModifiedDate)
SELECT TOP 15 DepartmentID, Name, GroupName, ModifiedDate
FROM AdventureWorks2012.HumanResources.Department  ORDER BY DepartmentID;
GO
-- (15 row(s) affected)
SELECT TOP 4 * FROM dbo.Department ORDER BY DepartmentID;
```

DepartmentID	Name	GroupName	ModifiedDate
1	Engineering	Research and Development	2016-08-02 06:35:44.623
2	Tool Design	Research and Development	2016-08-02 06:35:44.623
3	Sales	Sales and Marketing	2016-08-02 06:35:44.623
4	Marketing	Sales and Marketing	2016-08-02 06:35:44.623

SCOPE_IDENTITY() for Last-Inserted IDENTITY Value

The last inserted IDENTITY value can be returned with the SCOPE_IDENTITY() or @@IDENTITY system function (variable). SCOPE_IDENTITY() is better choice since it is within the current connection scope. @@IDENTITY is at server level. The best choice though is the OUTPUT clause.

```
INSERT dbo.Department (DepartmentID, Name, GroupName, ModifiedDate)
SELECT TOP 1 DepartmentID, Name, GroupName, ModifiedDate
FROM AdventureWorks2012.HumanResources.Department  ORDER BY DepartmentID DESC;
GO
-- (1 row(s) affected)
```

Alternate is SELECT @@IDENTITY; @@ variables are system variables.

```
DECLARE @LastID INT = SCOPE_IDENTITY();
SELECT @LastID;   -- 16
```

```
SET IDENTITY_INSERT dbo.Department OFF;
GO
```

```
-- Cleanup
DROP TABLE tempdb.dbo.Department;
```

CHAPTER 8: Modify Data - INSERT, UPDATE, DELETE & MERGE

INSERT with Subset of Columns

Only the required columns must be present in the INSERT column list. A column with default or NULL property can be omitted. In the next T-SQL script, ModifiedDate is filled by default with getdate().

```
USE tempdb;
SELECT TOP 0 * INTO dbo.Department FROM AdventureWorks2012.HumanResources.Department;
GO
ALTER TABLE dbo.Department ADD CONSTRAINT DF_Dept_ModDate
DEFAULT getdate() FOR ModifiedDate;
GO
SET IDENTITY_INSERT dbo.Department ON;
GO
INSERT dbo.Department (DepartmentID, Name, GroupName)
SELECT DepartmentID, Name, GroupName  FROM AdventureWorks2012.HumanResources.Department;
GO  -- (16 row(s) affected)
SELECT TOP 4 * FROM dbo.Department ORDER BY DepartmentID;
```

DepartmentID	Name	GroupName	ModifiedDate
1	Engineering	Research and Development	2016-08-02 06:35:44.623
2	Tool Design	Research and Development	2016-08-02 06:35:44.623
3	Sales	Sales and Marketing	2016-08-02 06:35:44.623
4	Marketing	Sales and Marketing	2016-08-02 06:35:44.623

Capturing Last-Inserted IDENTITY Set Values with OUTPUT

When more than one row is inserted with one statement, the OUTPUT clause can be used to capture the list of just inserted IDENTITY values.

```
DECLARE @LastInserted TABLE (ID INT);
INSERT dbo.Department (DepartmentID, Name, GroupName)
        OUTPUT inserted.DepartmentID INTO @LastInserted
SELECT DepartmentID+1000, Name, GroupName  FROM
AdventureWorks2012.HumanResources.Department;
SELECT TOP 5 * FROM @LastInserted ORDER BY ID;
GO
```

ID
1001
1002
1003
1004
1005

```
SET IDENTITY_INSERT dbo.Department OFF;
DROP TABLE tempdb.dbo.Department;
```

CHAPTER 8: Modify Data - INSERT, UPDATE, DELETE & MERGE

INSERT EXEC Stored Procedure

Data can be directly inserted from the execution of a user-defined stored procedure or system procedure. We create a table and a stored procedure, then perform INSERT EXEC.

```
USE AdventureWorks2012;
IF OBJECT_ID ('dbo.EmployeeSales', 'U') IS NOT NULL    DROP TABLE dbo.EmployeeSales;
IF OBJECT_ID ('dbo.uspGetEmployeeSales', 'P') IS NOT NULL    DROP PROCEDURE uspGetEmployeeSales;
CREATE TABLE dbo.EmployeeSales
 (
    BusinessEntityID        VARCHAR(11) NOT NULL PRIMARY KEY,
    LastName                VARCHAR(40) NOT NULL,
    SalesDollars            MONEY NOT NULL,
    DataSource              VARCHAR(20) NOT NULL
 );
GO


CREATE PROCEDURE dbo.uspGetEmployeeSales AS
 BEGIN
    SELECT          e.BusinessEntityID, c.LastName, sp.SalesYTD, 'PROCEDURE'
    FROM   HumanResources.Employee AS e
        INNER JOIN Sales.SalesPerson AS sp
            ON e.BusinessEntityID = sp.BusinessEntityID
        INNER JOIN Person.Person AS c
            ON e.BusinessEntityID = c.BusinessEntityID
    WHERE  e.BusinessEntityID > 280    ORDER  BY  e.BusinessEntityID,  c.LastName;
 END;
GO

--INSERT...EXECUTE user-defined stored procedure
INSERT EmployeeSales EXECUTE uspGetEmployeeSales;

SELECT * FROM   EmployeeSales;
```

BusinessEntityID	LastName	SalesDollars	DataSource
281	Ito	2458535.6169	PROCEDURE
282	Saraiva	2604540.7172	PROCEDURE
283	Campbell	1573012.9383	PROCEDURE
284	Mensa-Annan	1576562.1966	PROCEDURE
285	Abbas	172524.4512	PROCEDURE
286	Tsoflias	1421810.9242	PROCEDURE
287	Alberts	519905.932	PROCEDURE
288	Valdez	1827066.7118	PROCEDURE
289	Pak	4116871.2277	PROCEDURE
290	Varkey Chudukatil	3121616.3202	PROCEDURE

Insert Into A Table Via The Direct Execution Of An SQL Query With The EXEC Command

```
SELECT Population = count(*)  FROM   dbo.EmployeeSales;
```

Population
10

```
--INSERT...EXECUTE('string') example
INSERT EmployeeSales
EXECUTE ('       SELECT e.BusinessEntityID, c.LastName,     sp.SalesYTD, ''EXEC SQL STRING''
                 FROM HumanResources.Employee AS e        INNER JOIN Sales.SalesPerson AS sp
                 ON e.BusinessEntityID = sp.BusinessEntityID      INNER JOIN Person.Person AS c
                 ON e.BusinessEntityID = c.BusinessEntityID
                 WHERE e.BusinessEntityID BETWEEN 270 and 280
                 ORDER BY e.BusinessEntityID, c.LastName ');
GO
-- (7 row(s) affected)
```

Inserted number of rows can be captured for later use. **Capture must be done immediately after the monitored statement.** Any following statement will change @@ROWCOUNT value.

```
DECLARE @InsertCount int = @@ROWCOUNT;
SELECT @InsertCount;   -- 7
GO
```

```
SELECT * FROM   dbo.EmployeeSales ORDER BY BusinessEntityID ;
```

BusinessEntityID	LastName	SalesDollars	DataSource
274	Jiang	559697.5639	EXEC SQL STRING
275	Blythe	3763178.1787	EXEC SQL STRING
276	Mitchell	4251368.5497	EXEC SQL STRING
277	Carson	3189418.3662	EXEC SQL STRING
278	Vargas	1453719.4653	EXEC SQL STRING
279	Reiter	2315185.611	EXEC SQL STRING
280	Ansman-Wolfe	1352577.1325	EXEC SQL STRING
281	Ito	2458535.6169	PROCEDURE
282	Saraiva	2604540.7172	PROCEDURE
283	Campbell	1573012.9383	PROCEDURE
284	Mensa-Annan	1576562.1966	PROCEDURE
285	Abbas	172524.4512	PROCEDURE
286	Tsoflias	1421810.9242	PROCEDURE
287	Alberts	519905.932	PROCEDURE
288	Valdez	1827066.7118	PROCEDURE
289	Pak	4116871.2277	PROCEDURE
290	Varkey Chudukatil	3121616.3202	PROCEDURE

INSERT EXEC System Procedure

Data can be inserted into a table by the execution of a system procedure. We create a test table with SELECT INTO FROM OPENQUERY. We can also create the table manually if we know the data type of columns.

```
-- DATA ACCESS must be turned on at YOURSERVER SQL Server instance
SELECT TOP(0) * INTO #SPWHO
FROM OPENQUERY(YOURSERVER, 'exec sp_who');          -- will not work with sp_who2 due to duplicate
column name
```

```
/*  Table created
CREATE TABLE [dbo].[#SPWHO](
        [spid] [smallint] NOT NULL,
        [ecid] [smallint] NOT NULL,
        [status] [nchar](30) NOT NULL,
        [loginame] [nvarchar](128) NULL,
        [hostname] [nchar](128) NOT NULL,
        [blk] [char](5) NULL,
        [dbname] [nvarchar](128) NULL,
        [cmd] [nchar](16) NOT NULL,
        [request_id] [int] NOT NULL
); */
```

```
INSERT #SPWHO   EXEC sp_who
```

The blk column contains blocking spid if any. A large update for example may block other queries until it completes. The spid of the current session is @@SPID.

```
SELECT * FROM  #SPWHO
GO -- (42 row(s) affected) - Partial results.
```

spid	ecid	status	loginame	hostname	blk	dbname	cmd	request_id
21	0	background	sa		0	master	TASK MANAGER	0
22	0	background	sa		0	master	CHECKPOINT	0
23	0	sleeping	sa		0	master	TASK MANAGER	0
24	0	background	sa		0	master	BRKR TASK	0
25	0	sleeping	sa		0	master	TASK MANAGER	0
26	0	sleeping	sa		0	master	TASK MANAGER	0
27	0	sleeping	sa		0	master	TASK MANAGER	0
28	0	sleeping	sa		0	master	TASK MANAGER	0
29	0	sleeping	sa		0	master	TASK MANAGER	0
30	0	sleeping	sa		0	master	TASK MANAGER	0
40	0	background	sa		0	master	BRKR TASK	0
42	0	background	sa		0	master	BRKR TASK	0
43	0	background	sa		0	master	BRKR TASK	0
51	0	sleeping	YOURSERVER \Owner	YOURSERVER	0	AdventureWorks2012	AWAITING COMMAND	0
52	0	sleeping	NT SERVICE\SQLSERVERAGENT	YOURSERVER	0	msdb	AWAITING COMMAND	0

```
DROP TABLE #SPWHO
GO
```

INSERT Only New Rows Omit the Rest

INSERT only new records. If record exists, do nothing. Note: DELETE will not rollback IDENTITY current value. Therefore with repeated testing, the IDENTITY current value will roll ahead.

```
USE AdventureWorks2012;
SELECT COUNT(*) FROM HumanResources.Department;                -- 16


-- All rows exists, no new row insertion
INSERT HumanResources.Department (Name, GroupName)
SELECT Name, GroupName
FROM AdventureWorks2008.HumanResources.Department D
WHERE NOT EXISTS (      SELECT * FROM HumanResources.Department DD  -- Correlated subquery
                   WHERE D.Name = DD.Name
                      AND D.GroupName = DD.GroupName);
GO -- (0 row(s) affected)


-- Prefix Name with "ZZZ", 16 successful new inserted rows
INSERT HumanResources.Department (Name, GroupName)
SELECT CONCAT('ZZZ', Name), GroupName
FROM AdventureWorks2008.HumanResources.Department D
WHERE NOT EXISTS (      SELECT * FROM HumanResources.Department DD
        WHERE DD.Name = CONCAT('ZZZ', D.Name)   AND DD.GroupName = D.GroupName);
GO -- (16 row(s) affected)

DELETE TOP ( 7 ) HumanResources.Department WHERE Name LIKE ('ZZZ%');      -- (7 row(s) affected)
```

Only 7 rows will be inserted since the rest are duplicates.

```
INSERT HumanResources.Department (Name, GroupName)
SELECT CONCAT('ZZZ', Name), GroupName
FROM AdventureWorks2008.HumanResources.Department D
WHERE NOT EXISTS (      SELECT * FROM HumanResources.Department DD
             WHERE DD.Name = CONCAT('ZZZ', D.Name)    AND DD.GroupName = DD.GroupName);
GO
-- (7  row(s) affected)

SELECT * FROM HumanResources.Department;    -- (32 row(s) affected) -- Partial results;
```

DepartmentID	Name	GroupName	ModifiedDate
16	Executive	Executive General and Administration	2002-06-01 00:00:00.000
65	ZZZEngineering	Research and Development	2018-08-13 08:32:43.133

```
DELETE HumanResources.Department
WHERE Name LIKE ('ZZZ%');        -- (16 row(s) affected)
SELECT COUNT(*) FROM HumanResources.Department;                -- 16
```

CHAPTER 8: Modify Data - INSERT, UPDATE, DELETE & MERGE

DELETE - A Dangerous Operation

DELETE is a logged operation. DELETE may be slow from large table with indexes due to index reorganization. Warning: **DELETE is a dangerous operation since it removes data**. Protection: **regular database backup and/or creating a copy of the table prior to DELETE with SELECT INTO.**

```
USE [AdventureWorks2012]
GO
-- Create test table with SELECT INTO
SELECT [SalesOrderID]
    ,CONVERT(INT,[SalesOrderDetailID]) AS SalesOrderDetailID
    ,[CarrierTrackingNumber]
    ,[OrderQty]
    ,[ProductID]
    ,[SpecialOfferID]
    ,[UnitPrice]
    ,[UnitPriceDiscount]
    ,[LineTotal]
    ,[rowguid]
    ,[ModifiedDate]
INTO tempdb.dbo.SOD
FROM [Sales].[SalesOrderDetail];
GO -- (121317 row(s) affected)
```

```
-- Increase table population 64 fold
INSERT  tempdb.dbo.SOD  SELECT * FROM tempdb.dbo.SOD;
GO 6
/* Beginning execution loop
(121317 row(s) affected)
(242634 row(s) affected)
(485268 row(s) affected)
(970536 row(s) affected)
(1941072 row(s) affected)
(3882144 row(s) affected)
Batch execution completed 6 times.
Execution time - 00:01.27 */
```

```
CREATE INDEX idxSOD on tempdb.dbo.SOD (SalesOrderID, ProductID);
-- Command(s) completed successfully. Time: 00:00:06
```

```
SELECT COUNT(*) FROM tempdb.dbo.SOD;  -- 7764288
```

```
-- Delete even SalesOrderID records
DELETE FROM tempdb.dbo.SOD WHERE SalesOrderID % 2 = 0;
-- (3925184 row(s) affected) - Execution time - 00:01:30
```

CHAPTER 8: Modify Data - INSERT, UPDATE, DELETE & MERGE

TRUNCATE TABLE & DBCC CHECKIDENT

TRUNCATE TABLE command is very fast since it is minimally logged. It also resets IDENTITY column to (1,1). Warning: **TRUNCATE is a dangerous operation since it removes all the data in a table**. Protection: regular database backup and/or creating a copy of the table prior to TRUNCATE with SELECT INTO.

```
SELECT COUNT(*) FROM tempdb.dbo.SOD;  -- 3839104

TRUNCATE TABLE tempdb.dbo.SOD;
-- Command(s) completed successfully.  Execution time: 00:00:00

SELECT COUNT(*) FROM tempdb.dbo.SOD;   -- 0
GO

DROP TABLE tempdb.dbo.SOD;
GO
-- Command(s) completed successfully

-- Create new test table with SELECT INTO
USE tempdb;

SELECT * INTO SOD FROM AdventureWorks2012.Sales.SalesOrderDetail;
GO -- (121317 row(s) affected)

-- Next IDENTITY value will be 121318.
DBCC CHECKIDENT ("dbo.SOD");
/* Checking identity information: current identity value '121317', current column value '121317'.
DBCC execution completed. If DBCC printed error messages, contact your system administrator.  */

TRUNCATE TABLE SOD;
GO
-- Command(s) completed successfully.

-- IDENTITY is reset
DBCC CHECKIDENT ("dbo.SOD");
/* Checking identity information: current identity value 'NULL', current column value 'NULL'.
DBCC execution completed. If DBCC printed error messages, contact your system administrator. */

EXEC sp_help SOD;
GO
-- Partial results.
```

Identity	Seed	Increment	Not For Replication
SalesOrderDetailID	1	1	0

CHAPTER 8: Modify Data - INSERT, UPDATE, DELETE & MERGE

Reseeding IDENTITY

```
-- Without this command, it may not start at 1
DBCC CHECKIDENT ("SOD", RESEED, 1);


-- Populate the table with 5 rows
INSERT INTO SOD
      ([SalesOrderID]
      ,[CarrierTrackingNumber]
      ,[OrderQty]
      ,[ProductID]
      ,[SpecialOfferID]
      ,[UnitPrice]
      ,[UnitPriceDiscount]
      ,[LineTotal]
      ,[rowguid]
      ,[ModifiedDate])
SELECT  TOP (5)
      [SalesOrderID]
      ,[CarrierTrackingNumber]
      ,[OrderQty]
      ,[ProductID]
      ,[SpecialOfferID]
      ,[UnitPrice]
      ,[UnitPriceDiscount]
      ,[LineTotal]
      ,[rowguid]
      ,[ModifiedDate]
FROM AdventureWorks2012.Sales.SalesOrderDetail;
GO
-- (5 row(s) affected)
```

```
-- Next value assigned is 6
DBCC CHECKIDENT ("dbo.SOD");
/*Checking identity information: current identity value '5', current column value '5'.
DBCC execution completed. If DBCC printed error messages, contact your system administrator. */
```

```
SELECT * FROM SOD;
-- (5 row(s) affected) - Partial results.
```

SalesOrderID	SalesOrderDetailID	CarrierTrackingNumber	OrderQty	ProductID	SpecialOfferID	UnitPrice	UnitPriceDiscount	LineTotal
43659	1	4911-403C-98	1	776	1	2024.994	0.00	2024.994000
43659	2	4911-403C-98	3	777	1	2024.994	0.00	6074.982000
43659	3	4911-403C-98	1	778	1	2024.994	0.00	2024.994000
43659	4	4911-403C-98	1	771	1	2039.994	0.00	2039.994000
43659	5	4911-403C-98	1	772	1	2039.994	0.00	2039.994000

UPDATE - A Complex Operation

UPDATE changes data content at a row and column level (cell). It is a logged operation: deleted row contains previous data, inserted row contains new data. Warning: UPDATE is a dangerous operation since it changes the data in a table. Protection: regular database backup and/or creating a copy of the table prior to UPDATE with SELECT INTO.

Some UPDATEs are reversible, such as some calculated UPDATE, others may be irreversible.

Checking Cardinality & Changes by UPDATE Prior to Execution

Since UPDATE is replaces previous data, it is very important to check prior to execution that is works correctly. It is quite simple to convert UPDATE into a checking SELECT. We intend to UPDATE the SalesYTD column with the last day sales for each salesperson.

```
USE AdventureWorks2012;
SELECT   sp.BusinessEntityID, SalesYTD,
              [NewSalesYTD]=SalesYTD
        + (SELECT SUM(SODa.SubTotal)
          FROM   Sales.SalesOrderHeader AS SODa
          WHERE  CONVERT(date,SODa.OrderDate) = CONVERT(date,(SELECT MAX(OrderDate)
            FROM   Sales.SalesOrderHeader AS SODb
            WHERE
              SODb.SalesPersonID = SODa.SalesPersonID))
              AND sp.BusinessEntityID =  SODa.SalesPersonID
          GROUP  BY SODa.SalesPersonID)
FROM Sales.SalesPerson sp  ORDER BY sp.BusinessEntityID;
GO
```

BusinessEntityID	SalesYTD	NewSalesYTD
274	559697.5639	597350.4859
275	3763178.1787	4133185.161
276	4251368.5497	4534079.5941
277	3189418.3662	3527404.588
278	1453719.4653	1599132.4735
279	2315185.611	2548077.4756
280	1352577.1325	1503691.0098
281	2458535.6169	2678660.7921
282	2604540.7172	3030519.8258
283	1573012.9383	1714964.9067
284	1576562.1966	1719945.1917
285	172524.4512	176721.5652
286	1421810.9242	1649155.9058
287	519905.932	520578.226
288	1827066.7118	1962768.1658
289	4116871.2277	4556655.2802
290	3121616.3202	3240852.6195

ANSI Style UPDATE

T-SQL supports ANSI UPDATE, in addition T-SQL supports the FROM clause in UPDATE.

```
USE AdventureWorks2012;
UPDATE Sales.SalesPerson
SET   SalesYTD = SalesYTD
        + (SELECT SUM(SODa.SubTotal)
          FROM   Sales.SalesOrderHeader AS SODa
          WHERE  CONVERT(date,SODa.OrderDate) =
                  CONVERT(date,(SELECT MAX(OrderDate)
          FROM   Sales.SalesOrderHeader AS SODb
          WHERE
             SODb.SalesPersonID = SODa.SalesPersonID))
             AND Sales.SalesPerson.BusinessEntityID =   SODa.SalesPersonID
          GROUP  BY SODa.SalesPersonID);
GO
-- (17 row(s) affected)
```

```
SELECT BusinessEntityID, SalesQuota, SalesYTD, SalesLastYear
FROM Sales.SalesPerson
ORDER BY BusinessEntityID;
GO
```

BusinessEntityID	SalesQuota	SalesYTD	SalesLastYear
274	NULL	597350.4859	0.00
275	300000.00	4133185.161	1750406.4785
276	250000.00	4534079.5941	1439156.0291
277	250000.00	3527404.588	1997186.2037
278	250000.00	1599132.4735	1620276.8966
279	300000.00	2548077.4756	1849640.9418
280	250000.00	1503691.0098	1927059.178
281	250000.00	2678660.7921	2073505.9999
282	250000.00	3030519.8258	2038234.6549
283	250000.00	1714964.9067	1371635.3158
284	300000.00	1719945.1917	0.00
285	NULL	176721.5652	0.00
286	250000.00	1649155.9058	2278548.9776
287	NULL	520578.226	0.00
288	250000.00	1962768.1658	1307949.7917
289	250000.00	4556655.2802	1635823.3967
290	250000.00	3240852.6195	2396539.7601

UPDATE from Table in Another Database

UPDATE can be performed with data from a second database. ZorigAdventureWorks2012 is an original read-only copy of the AdventureWorks2012 database. The "Z" prefix is to force it to the end of alphabetical database list in SSMS Object Explorer.

```
UPDATE Sales.SalesPerson
     SET SalesYTD = (
                         SELECT SalesYTD
                         FROM ZorigAdventureWorks2012.Sales.SalesPerson sp
                         WHERE sp.BusinessEntityID =
Sales.SalesPerson.BusinessEntityID
                    );
GO


SELECT  BusinessEntityID,
        SalesQuota,
        SalesYTD,
        SalesLastYear
FROM Sales.SalesPerson
ORDER BY BusinessEntityID;
GO
```

BusinessEntityID	SalesQuota	SalesYTD	SalesLastYear
274	NULL	559697.5639	0.00
275	300000.00	3763178.1787	1750406.4785
276	250000.00	4251368.5497	1439156.0291
277	250000.00	3189418.3662	1997186.2037
278	250000.00	1453719.4653	1620276.8966
279	300000.00	2315185.611	1849640.9418
280	250000.00	1352577.1325	1927059.178
281	250000.00	2458535.6169	2073505.9999
282	250000.00	2604540.7172	2038234.6549
283	250000.00	1573012.9383	1371635.3158
284	300000.00	1576562.1966	0.00
285	NULL	172524.4512	0.00
286	250000.00	1421810.9242	2278548.9776
287	NULL	519905.932	0.00
288	250000.00	1827066.7118	1307949.7917
289	250000.00	4116871.2277	1635823.3967
290	250000.00	3121616.3202	2396539.7601

UPDATE Syntax Challenges

The UPDATE statement in SQL has perplexing and potentially confusing syntax. Typically mastered by expert DBA-s and SQL developers, and the rest of the database community uses it in an insecure manner: never sure if it works as intended. Simple T-SQL examples demonstrate some of the issues with the UPDATE syntax and offer solutions.

First we create a new table for experimentation from the AdventureWorks2012 database and perform a demo inner join UPDATE on the new table.

```
USE tempdb;

SELECT ProductID,
    ProductName = Name,
    StandardCost AS Cost,
    ListPrice,
    Color,
    CONVERT(date, ModifiedDate) AS ModifiedDate
INTO   Product
FROM   AdventureWorks2012.Production.Product
WHERE  ListPrice > 0.0
        AND Color IS NOT NULL;
GO
-- (245 row(s) affected)
```

```
SELECT TOP 5 * FROM Product
ORDER BY ProductID DESC;
GO
```

ProductID	ProductName	Cost	ListPrice	Color	ModifiedDate
999	Road-750 Black, 52	343.6496	539.99	Black	2008-03-11
998	Road-750 Black, 48	343.6496	539.99	Black	2008-03-11
997	Road-750 Black, 44	343.6496	539.99	Black	2008-03-11
993	Mountain-500 Black, 52	294.5797	539.99	Black	2008-03-11
992	Mountain-500 Black, 48	294.5797	539.99	Black	2008-03-11

We shall proceed and update ALL (no WHERE clause) the rows in the Product table. We increase the ListPrice by 5%.

```
UPDATE Product     SET ListPrice = ListPrice * 1.05;  -- (245 row(s) affected)
```

In this instance a reversible UPDATE. But not always.

```
UPDATE Product     SET ListPrice = ListPrice / 1.05;
-- (245 row(s) affected)
```

CHAPTER 8: Modify Data - INSERT, UPDATE, DELETE & MERGE

UPDATE with INNER JOIN

The UPDATE uses a table alias from the FROM clause.

SELECT TOP 2 * FROM Product WHERE Color = 'Yellow' ORDER BY ProductID DESC;

ProductID	ProductName	Cost	ListPrice	Color	ModifiedDate
976	Road-350-W Yellow, 48	1082.51	1700.99	Yellow	2008-03-11
975	Road-350-W Yellow, 44	1082.51	1700.99	Yellow	2008-03-11

```
UPDATE p  SET   p.ModifiedDate = DATEADD(HH,1,awp.ModifiedDate)
FROM   Product p   INNER JOIN AdventureWorks2012.Production.Product awp
                  ON p.ProductID = awp.ProductID  AND  p.Size LIKE '4%' ;
-- (91 row(s) affected)
```

Capturing Affected Rows with @@ROWCOUNT

When we have to know the number of updated rows, it is best to capture it into local variable and use it from there in the program logic.

```
DECLARE @UpdatedRows int;   -- capture @@ROWCOUNT for subsequent  use in the program

UPDATE p  SET   p.ModifiedDate = DATEADD(mm,1,awp.ModifiedDate)
FROM   Product p
    INNER JOIN AdventureWorks2012.Production.Product awp     ON p.ProductID = awp.ProductID
WHERE  p.Color = 'Yellow' ;
-- (36 row(s) affected)

SET @UpdatedRows = @@ROWCOUNT;

SELECT @@ROWCOUNT;             -- @@ROWCOUNT already changed
-- 1
SELECT TOP 5 * FROM Product  WHERE Color = 'Yellow' ORDER BY ProductID DESC;

SELECT @@ROWCOUNT;             -- @@ROWCOUNT changed again
-- 5
SELECT @UpdatedRows;           -- local variable kept the UPDATE count
-- 36
```

ProductID	ProductName	Cost	ListPrice	Color	ModifiedDate
976	Road-350-W Yellow, 48	1082.51	1700.99	Yellow	2008-04-11
975	Road-350-W Yellow, 44	1082.51	1700.99	Yellow	2008-04-11
974	Road-350-W Yellow, 42	1082.51	1700.99	Yellow	2008-04-11
973	Road-350-W Yellow, 40	1082.51	1700.99	Yellow	2008-04-11
965	Touring-3000 Yellow, 62	461.4448	742.35	Yellow	2008-04-11

CHAPTER 8: Modify Data - INSERT, UPDATE, DELETE & MERGE

UPDATE with Common Table Expression

UPDATE can be issued through a CTE to UPDATE the underlying table, Product in this case. Prices are increased 5% for products with over $1,000.00 list price.

```
SELECT TOP 5 * FROM Product  WHERE ListPrice > 1000.0 ORDER BY ProductID DESC;
GO
```

ProductID	ProductName	Cost	ListPrice	Color	ModifiedDate
976	Road-350-W Yellow, 48	1082.51	1700.99	Yellow	2008-04-11
975	Road-350-W Yellow, 44	1082.51	1700.99	Yellow	2008-04-11
974	Road-350-W Yellow, 42	1082.51	1700.99	Yellow	2008-04-11
973	Road-350-W Yellow, 40	1082.51	1700.99	Yellow	2008-04-11
972	Touring-2000 Blue, 54	755.1508	1214.85	Blue	2008-03-11

```
;WITH CTE
   AS (SELECT Price = ListPrice
     FROM   Product
     WHERE  ListPrice > 1000.0)
UPDATE CTE
SET   Price = Price * 1.05
GO
-- (86 row(s) affected)
```

```
SELECT TOP 5 * FROM Product  WHERE ListPrice > 1000.0 ORDER BY ProductID DESC;
```

ProductID	ProductName	Cost	ListPrice	Color	ModifiedDate
976	Road-350-W Yellow, 48	1082.51	1786.0395	Yellow	2008-04-11
975	Road-350-W Yellow, 44	1082.51	1786.0395	Yellow	2008-04-11
974	Road-350-W Yellow, 42	1082.51	1786.0395	Yellow	2008-04-11
973	Road-350-W Yellow, 40	1082.51	1786.0395	Yellow	2008-04-11
972	Touring-2000 Blue, 54	755.1508	1275.5925	Blue	2008-03-11

Similar data modification with ANSI SQL UPDATE.

```
UPDATE Product
SET   ListPrice = (SELECT p8.ListPrice * 1.05
         FROM   AdventureWorks2012.Production.Product p8   WHERE  Product.ProductID =
p8.ProductID)
WHERE  EXISTS (SELECT * FROM  AdventureWorks2012.Production.Product p8
       WHERE  Product.ProductID = p8.ProductID   AND Product.ListPrice > 1000.0);
```

Four Methods of UPDATE with GROUP BY Query

UPDATE can be done a few ways with GROUP BY aggregates.

```
USE tempdb;
SELECT Color=ISNULL(Color,'N/A'), ItemCount=0 INTO ProductColor
FROM AdventureWorks2008.Production.Product
GROUP BY Color
GO
-- (10 row(s) affected)
```

```
SELECT * FROM ProductColor
GO
```

Color	ItemCount
N/A	0
Black	0
Blue	0
Grey	0
Multi	0
Red	0
Silver	0
Silver/Black	0
White	0
Yellow	0

ANSI UPDATE

```
UPDATE ProductColor
SET ItemCount = (SELECT ProductColorCount FROM  (SELECT Color=ISNULL(Color, 'N/A'),
             ProductColorCount=COUNT(*)
              FROM AdventureWorks2008.Production.Product
              GROUP BY Color) cg WHERE  ProductColor.Color = cg.Color)
GO -- (10 row(s) affected)
```

FROM Clause UPDATE with Derived Table

```
UPDATE pc   SET pc.ItemCount = cg.ProductColorCount
FROM ProductColor pc
INNER JOIN (SELECT Color=ISNULL(Color, 'N/A'), ProductColorCount=COUNT(*)
      FROM AdventureWorks2008.Production.Product GROUP BY Color) cg
ON pc.Color = cg.Color;
-- (10 row(s) affected)
```

CHAPTER 8: Modify Data - INSERT, UPDATE, DELETE & MERGE

FROM Clause UPDATE with CTE

```
;WITH CTE AS (SELECT Color=ISNULL(Color, 'N/A'), ProductColorCount=COUNT(*)
      FROM AdventureWorks2008.Production.Product
      GROUP BY Color)
UPDATE pc
SET pc.ItemCount = CTE.ProductColorCount
FROM ProductColor pc
INNER JOIN CTE
ON pc.Color = CTE.Color;
GO
-- (10 row(s) affected)
```

CTE UPDATE

```
;WITH CTE AS (SELECT * FROM ProductColor pc
      INNER JOIN (SELECT ColorPrd=ISNULL(Color, 'N/A'), ProductColorCount=COUNT(*)
      FROM AdventureWorks2008.Production.Product
      GROUP BY Color) cg
                    ON pc.Color = cg.ColorPrd)
UPDATE CTE SET CTE.ItemCount = CTE.ProductColorCount;
GO
-- (10 row(s) affected)
```

```
SELECT * FROM ProductColor;
GO
```

Color	ItemCount
N/A	248
Black	93
Blue	26
Grey	1
Multi	8
Red	38
Silver	43
Silver/Black	7
White	4
Yellow	36

```
DROP TABLE tempdb.dbo.ProductColor;
```

MERGE for Combination INSERT, UPDATE or DELETE

The MERGE statement can be used to INSERT, UPDATE and/or DELETE all in one statement.

```
USE tempdb;
go


-- Setup 2 test tables
SELECT TOP (5000) ResellerKey,
        OrderDateKey,
        ProductKey,
        OrderQuantity,
        SalesAmount
INTO  FactResellerSales
FROM  AdventureWorksDW2012.dbo.FactResellerSales
ORDER BY OrderDateKey ;
go
-- (5000 row(s) affected)


SELECT TOP (8000) ResellerKey,
        OrderDateKey,
        ProductKey,
        OrderQuantity,
        SalesAmount
INTO  ResellerSalesTransaction
FROM  AdventureWorksDW2012.dbo.FactResellerSales ;
go
-- (8000 row(s) affected)


DELETE rsc
FROM  ResellerSalesTransaction rsc
    JOIN (SELECT TOP 1000 *
      FROM  ResellerSalesTransaction
      ORDER  BY ResellerKey DESC) x
    ON x.ResellerKey = rsc.ResellerKey ;
go
-- (1010 row(s) affected)

UPDATE TOP (6000) ResellerSalesTransaction
SET   SalesAmount = SalesAmount * 1.1 ;
go
-- (6000 row(s) affected)
```

MERGE is a very powerful statement

```
SELECT TOP (10) *
FROM   FactResellerSales
ORDER  BY ResellerKey,        OrderDateKey,        ProductKey ;
go
```

ResellerKey	OrderDateKey	ProductKey	OrderQuantity	SalesAmount
1	20050801	270	1	183.9382
1	20050801	275	1	356.898
1	20050801	285	1	178.5808
1	20050801	314	2	4293.924
1	20050801	317	1	874.794
1	20050801	319	2	1749.588
1	20050801	324	2	838.9178
1	20050801	326	1	419.4589
1	20050801	328	1	419.4589
1	20050801	332	2	838.9178

```
SELECT BeforeFactCount=COUNT(*)
FROM   FactResellerSales ;
-- 5000
```

```
-- Ready for the MERGE (update if exists,  insert otherwise)
MERGE FactResellerSales AS fact
USING (SELECT *
    FROM   ResellerSalesTransaction) AS feed
ON ( fact.ProductKey = feed.ProductKey
   AND fact.ResellerKey = feed.ResellerKey
   AND fact.OrderDateKey = feed.OrderDateKey )
WHEN MATCHED THEN
 UPDATE SET fact.OrderQuantity += feed.OrderQuantity,
       fact.SalesAmount += feed.SalesAmount
WHEN NOT MATCHED THEN
 INSERT (ResellerKey,
     OrderDateKey,
     ProductKey,
     OrderQuantity,
     SalesAmount)
 VALUES (feed.ResellerKey,
     feed.OrderDateKey,
     feed.ProductKey,
     feed.OrderQuantity,
     feed.SalesAmount);
go   -- (6990 row(s) affected)
```

Checking results after MERGE

```
SELECT TOP (10) *
FROM  FactResellerSales ORDER  BY        ResellerKey,   OrderDateKey,   ProductKey;
```

ResellerKey	OrderDateKey	ProductKey	OrderQuantity	SalesAmount
1	20050801	270	2	386.2702
1	20050801	275	2	749.4858
1	20050801	285	2	375.0197
1	20050801	314	4	9017.2404
1	20050801	317	2	1837.0674
1	20050801	319	4	3674.1348
1	20050801	324	4	1761.7274
1	20050801	326	2	880.8637
1	20050801	328	2	880.8637
1	20050801	332	4	1761.7274

```
SELECT AfterFactCount=COUNT(*)  FROM  FactResellerSales ;
go
-- 7658

DROP TABLE ResellerSalesTransaction;  DROP TABLE FactResellerSales;
go
```

CHAPTER 8: Modify Data - INSERT, UPDATE, DELETE & MERGE

Using MERGE Instead of UPDATE

MERGE statement can be used in the UPDATE only mode to replace UPDATE.

```
-- Prepare 2 test tables
USE tempdb;
SELECT TOP (5000) ResellerKey,  OrderDateKey, ProductKey, OrderQuantity, SalesAmount
INTO  FactResellerSales FROM  AdventureWorksDW2012.dbo.FactResellerSales;
GO -- (5000 row(s) affected)
SELECT TOP (8000) ResellerKey,  OrderDateKey, ProductKey, OrderQuantity, SalesAmount
INTO  ResellerSalesTransaction FROM  AdventureWorksDW2012.dbo.FactResellerSales;
GO -- (8000 row(s) affected)
```

```
-- Alter the test data
DELETE rsc
FROM   ResellerSalesTransaction rsc
    INNER JOIN (SELECT TOP 1000 * FROM   ResellerSalesTransaction
        ORDER  BY ResellerKey DESC) x  -- subquery inner join
    ON x.ResellerKey = rsc.ResellerKey;
GO --(1010 row(s) affected)
UPDATE TOP (6000) ResellerSalesTransaction SET SalesAmount = SalesAmount * 1.1;
GO -- (6000 row(s) affected)
```

```
SELECT BeforeFactCount=COUNT(*) FROM   FactResellerSales;
GO -- 5000
```

```
-- Ready for the MERGE UPDATE only mode
MERGE FactResellerSales AS fact
USING (SELECT * FROM   ResellerSalesTransaction) AS feed
ON ( fact.ProductKey = feed.ProductKey
   AND fact.ResellerKey = feed.ResellerKey
   AND fact.OrderDateKey = feed.OrderDateKey )
WHEN MATCHED THEN
 UPDATE SET fact.OrderQuantity = fact.OrderQuantity + feed.OrderQuantity,
        fact.SalesAmount = fact.SalesAmount + feed.SalesAmount;
GO -- 4332 row(s) affected)
```

```
SELECT AfterFactCount=COUNT(*) FROM   FactResellerSales;
GO -- 5000
```

```
DROP TABLE ResellerSalesTransaction;  DROP TABLE FactResellerSales;
```

APPENDIX A: Job Interview Questions

Selected Database Design Questions

D1. What is your approach to database design?

D2. Some of our legacy databases are far from 3NF. Can you work in such an environment?

D3. Can UNIQUE KEY be used instead of PRIMARY KEY?

D4. Can a FOREIGN KEY be NULL?

D5. Can a PRIMARY KEY be NULL?

D6. Can a PRIMARY KEY be based on non-clustered unique index?

D7. Do you implement OrderQty > 0 condition as a CHECK constraint or in the application software?

D8. What is a heap?

D9. Can a table have 2 IDENTITY columns, 2 FOREIGN KEYs, 2 PRIMARY KEYs and 2 clustered indexes?

D10. Should each table have a NATURAL KEY or is INT IDENTITY PK sufficient?

D11. How can you prevent entry of "U.S", "USA", etc. instead of "United States" into Country column?

D12. How would you implement ManagerID in an Employee table with EmployeeID as PRIMARY KEY?

D13. How would you implement the relationship between OrderMaster and OrderDetail tables?

D14. Product table has the Color column. Would you create a Color table & change column to ColorID FK?

D15. Can you insert directly into an IDENTITY column?

D16. Which one is better? Composite PRIMARY KEY on NATURAL KEY, or INT IDENTITY PRIMARY KEY & UNIQUE KEY on NATURAL KEY?

D17. What is the lifetime of a regular table created in tempdb?

D18. How many different ways can you connect tables in a database?

D19. How would you connect the Vehicle and Owner tables?

D20. Can you have the same table names in different schemas?

Selected Database Programming Questions

P1. Write a query to list all departments with employee count based on the Department column of Employee table.

P2. Same as above but the Employee table has the DepartmentID column.

P3. Write an INSERT statement for a new "Social Technology" department with GroupName "Sales & Marketing".

P4. Same query es in P2, but the new department should be included even though no employees yet.

P5. Write a query to generate 1000 sequential numbers without a table.

P6. Write a query with SARGable predicate to list all orders from OrderMaster received on 2016-10-23. OrderDate is datetime.

P7. Write a query to add a header record DEPARTMENTNAME to the departments listing from the Department table. If there are 20 departments, the result set should have 21 records.

P8. Make the previous query a derived table in an outer SELECT * query

P9. Write an ORDER BY clause for the previous query with CASE expression to sort DEPARTMENTNAME as first record and alphabetically descending from there on.

P10. Same as above with the IIF conditional.

P11. The table-valued dbo.ufnSplitCSV splits a comma delimited string (input parameter). The Product table has some ProductName-s with comma(s). Write a CROSS APPLY query to return ProductName-s with comma and each split string value from the UDF as separate line. ProductName should repeat for each split part.

ProductName	SplitPart
Full-Finger Gloves, L	Full-Finger Gloves
Full-Finger Gloves, L	L

P12. You need the inserted lines count 10 lines down following the INSERT statement. What should be the statement immediately following the INSERT statement?

P13. What is the result of the second query? What is it called?

SELECT COUNT_BIG(*) FROM Sales.SalesOrderDetail;   -- 121317

SELECT COUNT_BIG(*) FROM Sales.SalesOrderDetail x, Sales.SalesOrderDetail y;

P14. Declare & Assign the string variable @Text varchar(32) the literal '2016/10/23 10:20:12' without the "/" and ":".

P15. You want to add a parameter to a frequently used view. What is the workaround?

P16. When converting up to 40 characters string, can you use varchar instead of varchar(40)?

P17. Can you roll back IDENTITY seeds and table variables with ROLLBACK TRANSACTION?

P18. How do you decide where to place the clustered index?

P19. What is the simplest solution for the collation error: "Cannot resolve collation conflict..."?

P20. Which system table can be used for integer sequence up to 2^12 values?

APPENDIX B: Job Interview Answers

Selected Database Design Answers

D1. I prefer 3NF design due to high database developer productivity and low maintenance cost.

D2. I did have such projects in the past. I can handle them. Hopefully, introduce some improvements.

D3. Partially yes since UNIQUE KEYs can be FK referenced, fully no. Every table should a PRIMARY KEY.

D4. Yes.

D5. No.

D6. Yes. The default is clustered unique index. Only unique index is required.

D7. CHECK constraint. A server-side object solution is more reliable than code in application software.

D8. A table without clustered index. Database engine generally works better if a table has clustered index.

D9. No, yes, no, no.

D10. A table should be designed with NATURAL KEY(s). INT IDENTITY PK is not a replacement for NK.

D11. Lookup table with UDF CHECK Constraint. UDF checks the Lookup table for valid entries.

D12. ManagerID as a FOREIGN KEY referencing the PRIMARY KEY of the same table; self-referencing.

D13. OrderID PRIMARY KEY of OrderMaster. OrderID & LineItemID composition PK of OrderDetail. OrderID of OrderDetail FK to OrderID of OderMaster.

D14. Yes. It makes sense for color to be in its own table.

D15. No. Only if you SET IDENTITY_INSERT tablename ON.

D16. Meaningless INT IDENTITY PRIMARY KEY with UNIQUE KEY ON NATURAL KEY is better.

D17. Until SQL Server restarted. tempdb starts empty as copy of model database.

D18. There is only one way: FOREIGN KEY constraint.

D19. With the OwnerVehicleXref junction table reflecting many-to-many relationship.

D20. Yes. A table is identified by SchemaName.TableName . dbo is the default schema.

Selected Database Programming Answers

P1. SELECT Department, Employees=COUNT(*) FROM Employee
    GROUP BY Department ORDER BY Department;

P2. SELECT d.Department, Employees = COUNT(EmployeeID) FROM Employee e
    INNER JOIN Department d ON e.DepartmentID = d.DepartmentID
    GROUP BY d.Department ORDER BY Department;

P3. INSERT Department (Name, GroupName) VALUES ('Social Technology', 'Sales & Marketing');

P4. SELECT d.Department, Employees = COUNT(EmployeeID) FROM Employee e
    RIGHT JOIN Department d ON e.DepartmentID = d.DepartmentID
    GROUP BY d.Department ORDER BY Department;

P5. ;WITH Seq AS (SELECT SeqNo = 1 UNION ALL SELECT SeqNo+1 FROM Seq WHERE SeqNo < 100)
    SELECT * FROM Seq;

P6. SELECT * FROM OrderMaster WHERE OrderDate >='20161023'
    AND OrderDate < DATEADD(DD,1,'20161023');

P7. SELECT AllDepartments = 'DEPARTMENTNAME' UNION SELECT Department FROM Department;

P8. SELECT * FROM (SELECT AllDepartments = 'DEPARTMENTNAME' UNION SELECT Name
    FROM HumanResources.Department) x

P9. ORDER BY CASE WHEN AllDepartments = 'DEPARTMENTNAME' THEN 1 ELSE 2 END,
    AllDepartments DESC;

P10. ORDER BY IIF(AllDepartments = 'DEPARTMENTNAME', 1 , 2), AllDepartments DESC;

P11. SELECT ProductName, S.SplitPart FROM Product P CROSS APPLY dbo.ufnSplitCSV (Name) S
    WHERE ProductName like '%,%';

P12. DECLARE @InsertedCount INT = @@ROWCOUNT;

P13. 121317*121317; Cartesian product.

P14. DECLARE @Text varchar(32) =
    REPLACE(REPLACE ('2016/10/23 10:20:12', '/', SPACE(0)), ':', SPACE(0));

P15. Table-valued INLINE user-defined function.

P16. varchar(40). It is a good idea to specify the length always. The default is 30.

P17. No. ROLLBACK has no effect on IDENTITY seeds or table variables. If an INSERT advanced the
IDENTITY seed by 5 during the rollbacked transaction, it will stay that way after the ROLLBACK. It means a
gap in the IDENTITY sequence.

P18. Business critical queries are the determining factor in placing the clustered index. Clustered index
speeds up range queries.

P19. Place "COLLATE DATABASE_DEFAULT" on the right side of the expression.

P20. spt_values table.
SELECT N = number FROM master.dbo.spt_values WHERE type='P' ORDER BY N;

INDEX of SQL Easy

Index of the Most Important Topics

D

E

T

U

V

W

X

This page is intentionally left blank.